THE GARDENERS'
AND
POULTRY KEEPERS'
GUIDE AND
ILLUSTRATED CATALOGUE
OF
GOODS MANUFACTURED
AND SUPPLIED
By

W. Cooper Ltd.

· OFFICES ·
AND
· SHOW · GROUNDS ·
761, OLD KENT ROAD, LONDON, S.E.
· STEAM · WORKS ·
COVERING SEVERAL ACRES
DEVONSHIRE GROVE & SYLVAN GROVE
ADJOINING

Copyright   Price 2/6

Telephone:
   Nº 1246 HOP

Telegrams:
   "CONSERVATORIES LONDON"

The Shelter Bookshelf

SHELTER PUBLICATIONS INC.
BOLINAS, CALIFORNIA

Published in 1901 and 1914 by William Cooper Ltd., London
This special edition copyright © 2010, Shelter Publications, Inc.

Distributed in the United States by Publishers Group West
and in Canada by Publishers Group Canada

The Shelter Bookshelf is dedicated to keeping worthy old books in print.

For out of olde feldes, as men seyth
Cometh al this newe corn from yer to yere,
And out of olde bokes, in good feyth,
Cometh al this newe science that men lere.

          –Geoffrey Chaucer, 1343–1400

Library of Congress Cataloging-in-Publication Data
William Cooper Ltd.
   The gardeners' and poultry keepers' guide and illustrated catalogue
of goods manufactured and supplied by William Cooper Ltd. /
[editor, Lloyd Kahn ; associate editor, Robert Lewandowski].
      p. cm.
   Abridged version of this title, first published in 1914 by
William Cooper Ltd., London.
   ISBN 978-0-936070-47-6
    1. Gardening—Equipment and supplies—Catalogs.
2. Poultry—Housing—Catalogs. 3. Buildings—Catalogs.
4. Ironwork—Catalogs. I. Kahn, Lloyd, 1945–
II. Lewandowski, Robert, 1948– III. Title.
   SB454.8.W52 2009
   635.028′4—dc22

                                 2009033319

Printed in China
5 4 3 2 1—14 13 12 11 10
(Lowest digits indicate number and year of latest printing)

Shelter Publications, Inc.
P. O. Box 279
Bolinas, California 94924
Orders, toll-free: 1-800-307-0131
Email: shelter@shelterpub.com

SHELTER ONLINE
www.shelterpub.com

Photo of William Cooper
courtesy of Sheila Campbell

This book is an abridged version of *The Gardeners' and Poultry Keepers' Guide and Illustrated Catalogue of Goods Manufactured and Supplied By William Cooper Ltd.* (circa 1914). The Cooper company manufactured a great variety of prefabricated greenhouses, sheds, shacks, stables, kiosks, and rustic furniture in London, England around the turn of the 20th century. These buildings were not only shipped all over the British Isles, but also to British colonies all over the world.

I found a smaller version of the Cooper catalogue (circa 1901) in a used bookstore in London in the early '70s, and fell in love with it. Not only was it a charming picture of turn-of-the-century country life in England, but the drawings—of greenhouses, chicken coops, barns and small buildings—were still relevant 100 years later. Here was a source of ideas for builders, architects, and homeowners. This seems even more relevant in these early years of the 21st century.

Two things are striking about this catalogue, relevant to present times:

1. The designs for greenhouses and cold frames (for starting seeds)—*(see pp. 1–50)* are instructive for gardeners and homeowners in these times when there is a renewed interest in producing food at home, and gardens are booming.

2. Perhaps even more interesting is the section on prefabricated buildings using corrugated steel panels *(pp. 213–272)* for walls and roofing. Coincidentally, many commercial as well as residential buildings these days utilize corrugated metal roofing and/or siding, and the Cooper designs can be instructive for designers and architects.

* * *

In 2007, one of the Cooper metal buildings was put up for sale in Dulnain in the Scottish Highlands. It was originally bought by a farmer for £425 and assembled by hand, and was being offered for £175,000. An article on the sale, which was printed in the September 6, 2007 issue of *The Independent* newspaper in London, included the following:

"These days, most of us associate corrugated iron with those cheap, crudely assembled homes packed together in slums across the developing world but, in the 19th century, it was one of the inventions in which Britain took pride. It was exported all over the world to make buildings of every size. While others were putting up corrugated iron churches or civic centres, the staff of William Cooper Limited, based in London's Old Kent Road, cornered the market in cheap, prefabricated agricultural buildings, including the one now up for sale at Dulnain.

"Simon Holloway, who has co-written an illustrated history of corrugated iron, published this month, said yesterday: "William Cooper were at the poorer end of the market. They supplied small-time farmers with every sort of building, from chicken coops to farmhouses. Back then, £425 was quite expensive—their prices started at less than £100—but the buildings were customized and the price may have included optional extras, such as a fireplace."

* * *

In the course of researching this book, we came into contact with William Cooper's grandson, John Cooper, and his great-grandson, Paul Campbell.

John Cooper wrote us that the earliest Cooper catalogue he came across was dated 1880, 4th edition, and that "...if one allows 5 years per issue, this takes the first edition back to about 1860—well before any knowledge we have about the subject!"

Paul Campbell wrote us:

"William Cooper appears to have been a great entrepreneur because, as well as the huge range of buildings, conservatories and general garden buildings which are referred to in the catalogue, at some stage he was producing 1000 Cooper bicycles per week at the Old Kent Road site...He also had a department store (The Savoy Stores) somewhere in or near Regent Street in central London, and owned nine Turkish bath establishments dotted around London....

At some stage the company changed its name to T. Bath and Co. (named after the Turkish baths interest) and by 1925 it had a pretty extensive empire of factories (in England with over 20 acres of floor space).

Sadly, William Cooper's death in 1937 followed by the second world war, which led to timber being almost unobtainable, led to the company's decline and it was sold out of the family in, I believe, 1946...."

* * *

This is the third in our series of Shelter Bookshelf reprints, dedicated to keeping worthy old books in print. We hope you find it interesting, useful, and charming.

–Lloyd Kahn
December, 2009

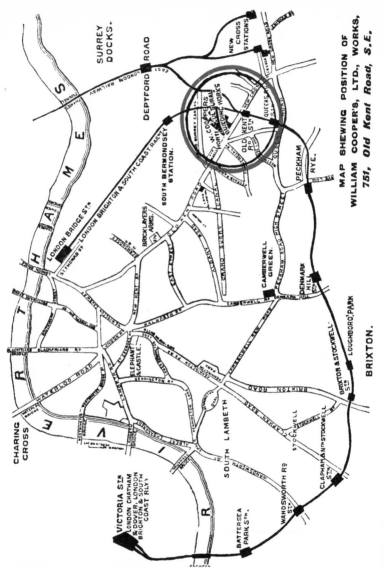

MAP SHEWING POSITION OF
WILLIAM COOPER'S, LTD., WORKS,
751, Old Kent Road, S.E.

Steam Works are situated in Devonshire Grove and adjoin the Office—751, Old Kent Road, two minutes' walk from Old Kent Road Station, to which trains run frequently from Victoria and London Bridge Stations (London, Brighton and South Coast Railway), and Shoreditch Station (East London Railway), and 10 minutes' walk from New Cross Stations (London, Brighton and South Coast, and South Eastern Railways). Greenwich Trams from Westminster, Waterloo and Blackfriars Bridges pass the door. White Trams from St. George's Church stop at the door. Brixton Trams pass St. George's Church, and stop at the Lord Wellington, five minutes' walk, and 'Buses from Islington stop at the Shard Arms, three minutes' walk from the Works.

CONTENTS OF SECTIONS

WILLIAM COOPER, Limited,

Horticultural Providers,

751, OLD KENT ROAD, LONDON, S.E.

SECTION I.

llustrated Catalogue

OF

CONSERVATORIES, GREENHOUSES, VINERIES,

Orchid Houses,
Plant and Forcing Houses,

MELON AND CUCUMBER FRAMES,

Garden Frames, Forcing Pits, Handlights, &c., &c.

EXTENSIONS AND REPAIRS.

We undertake these to any extent, and give Estimates for alterations of, or additions to, existing Houses and Heating Apparatus.

SURVEYS BY APPOINTMENT,

When any special designs are required we shall be pleased to let one of our Representatives wait upon Ladies or Gentlemen at their residences, in any part of the country, to take all necessary particulars, and we will then submit Designs and Estimates in accordance with his report.

1

The Amateur Forcing House.

Tenant's Fixture—Lean-to.

No. 1.

Wherever a Lean-to is required, this will be found an excellent House. It is offered at a very low rate, and as a tenant's fixture can be easily removed.

SPECIFICATION.—Framework substantially constructed of red deal; the whole of sides, and 2ft. 6in. of ends, boarded with well-seasoned tongued and grooved matchboards; half-glass door, complete with rim lock and brass fittings, in one end; glass 16oz. throughout; ventilators supplied, according to size of House, and stays necessary for opening same; stages for plants entire length of House. All woodwork painted one coat of good oil paint, and the whole structure securely packed on rail, being carefully marked in readiness for erection, or delivered, erected and glazed, with extra coat of paint at Works, within 50 miles of London Bridge (beyond this distance special prices will be quoted upon application) at the following respective prices:—

Length.	Width.	Height.	Packed on rail. £ s. d.	Erected within 50 miles. £ s. d.
7ft.	5ft.	7ft.	2 5 0	4 5 0
8ft.	5ft.	7ft.	2 15 0	4 15 0
9ft.	6ft.	7ft. 3in.	3 5 0	5 10 0
10ft.	7ft.	7ft. 6in.	3 15 0	6 5 0
12ft.	8ft.	8ft.	4 12 6	7 10 0
15ft.	9ft.	8ft. 6in.	6 10 0	9 15 0
20ft.	10ft.	9ft.	8 5 0	12 5 0
25ft.	10ft.	9ft.	10 0 0	15 0 0
50ft.	10ft.	9ft.	18 0 0	33 0 0
100ft.	10ft.	9ft.	35 0 0	65 0 0

In ordering, it should be stated at which end door is to be inserted when facing House from outside. 21oz. glass throughout 10 per cent. extra.

Tarred Sleepers to erect this house on, 3d. per foot run.

The Amateur Forcing House.

Tenant's Fixture—Span Roof.

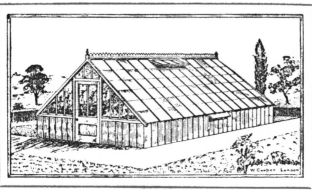

No. 2.

The constantly increasing demand for Forcing Houses has caused special attention to be given to this class of house, both with regard to construction and economy. As shown in the above illustration, brickwork is entirely dispensed with, thus effecting a considerable saving.

It is suitable for both professional and amateur gardeners, and good crops of cucumbers, tomatoes, melons, &c., can be grown.

SPECIFICATION.—Framework substantially constructed of red deal; the whole of sides and 2ft. 6in. of ends, boarded with well-seasoned tongued and grooved matchboards. Half-glass door, complete with rim lock and brass fittings in one end; glass 16oz. throughout; ventilators supplied according to size of house, and stays necessary for opening same; stages for plants each side of house. All woodwork painted one coat of good oil paint, and the whole structure securely packed on rail (being carefully marked in readiness for erection), or delivered erected and glazed, with extra coat of paint at Works, within 50 miles of London Bridge, at the following respective prices (beyond this distance, special prices will be quoted on application):

Length.	Width.	Height.	Packed on rail.	Erected within 50 miles.
ft.	ft.	ft. in.	£ s. d.	£ s. d.
7	5	7 0	2 10 0	4 10 0
8	5	7 0	3 0 0	5 0 0
9	6	7 0	3 10 0	5 15 0
10	7	7 6	4 0 0	6 10 0
12	8	8 0	5 0 0	7 17 6
15	9	8 0	7 0 0	10 5 0
20	10	9 0	9 0 0	13 0 0
25	10	9 0	11 0 0	16 0 0
50	10	9 0	20 0 0	35 0 0

21oz. Glass throughout, 10 per cent. extra.

Tarred Sleepers to erect this house on, 3d. per foot run.

Amateur Lean-to Greenhouse.

TENANT'S FIXTURES.

No. 3.

This Greenhouse is substantially constructed, and can be fixed to any wall. As a tenant's fixture it can be easily removed at will, and being made in separate parts, all of which are marked, it can readily be put together without skilled knowledge.

SPECIFICATION.—The framework is red deal, the lower part being filled in with good, sound, well-seasoned, tongued and grooved matchboards. The house is fitted with door, complete with rim lock and brass furniture, painted one coat of good oil colour, supplied with all necessary ironwork and stage for one side, and good 16oz. glass throughout. Securely packed on rail, or delivered, erected and glazed complete, with an extra coat of paint at Works, within 50 miles of London Bridge, at the following respective prices (beyond this distance special prices will be quoted on application) :

Length. ft.	Width. ft.	Height. ft. in.	To Eaves. ft. in.	Packed on on rail. £ s. d.	Erected within 50 miles. £ s. d.
7	5	7 0	4 0	2 12 6	4 12 6
8	5	7 0	4 0	3 0 0	5 0 0
9	6	7 0	4 0	3 10 0	5 15 0
10	7	7 6	4 6	4 5 0	6 15 0
12	8	8 0	5 0	5 10 0	8 7 6
15	9	8 6	5 6	7 10 0	11 0 0
20	10	8 6	5 6	9 10 0	13 10 0
25	10	9 0	5 6	12 0 0	17 0 0
50	12	9 0	5 6	25 0 0	33 0 0

21oz. Glass for roof 5 per cent., throughout 10 per cent. extra.
When ordering, please state which end the door is required (when facing front of house from outside).
Tarred Sleepers to erect this house on, 3d. per foot run.

Amateur Span-Roof Greenhouse.

TENANT'S FIXTURE.

No. 4.

This illustration shows a type of Greenhouse eminently adapted for amateurs, and at the exceedingly low prices at which it is offered, in various sizes, it is within the reach of every lover of flowers.

It is constructed in sections marked for putting together, and it can be easily fixed by any handy person in a short space of time.

SPECIFICATION.—The framework is substantially constructed of red deal, the lower part being filled in with good, sound, well-seasoned, tongued and grooved match-boards. The House is fitted with door, complete with rim lock and brass furniture, painted one coat of good oil colour, supplied with all necessary ironwork and stages for each side, and good 16oz. glass throughout. Securely packed on rail, or delivered, erected and glazed complete, with extra coat of paint at Works, within 50 miles of London Bridge, at the following prices (beyond this distance special prices will be quoted on application):

Length. ft.	Width. ft.	Height. ft. in.	To Eaves. ft. in.	Packed on rail. £ s. d.	Erected within 50 miles. £ s. d.
7	5	7 0	4 0	2 17 6	4 17 6
8	5	7 0	4 0	3 5 0	5 5 0
9	6	7 3	4 0	3 15 0	6 0 0
10	7	7 6	4 6	4 10 0	7 0 0
12	8	8 0	5 0	5 15 0	8 12 6
15	9	8 6	5 0	7 10 0	11 0 0
20	10	9 0	5 6	9 15 0	14 0 0
25	10	9 0	5 6	13 0 0	18 0 0
30	12	9 0	5 6	18 0 0	25 0 0
35	14	10 0	6 0	27 10 0	37 10 0
40	14	10 0	6 0	32 0 0	45 0 0

**21oz. Glass for roof 5 per cent., throughout 10 per cent. extra.
Tarred Sleepers to erect this house on, 3d. per foot run.**

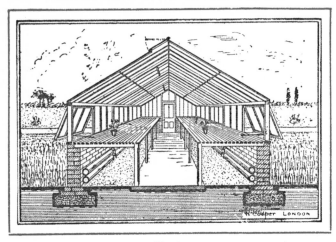
6

Amateur Three-quarter Span-Roof Greenhouse.

No. 6.

The advantages of this house will be apparent on a glance at the illustration, which shows a combination of the span-roof and lean-to principles.

SPECIFICATION.—The framework is substantially constructed of red deal, the lower part being filled in with good, sound, well-seasoned, tongued and grooved matchboards. The house is fitted with door, complete with rim lock and brass furniture, painted one coat of good oil colour, supplied with all necessary ironwork and staging along one side. Good 16oz. glass throughout. All parts are carefully marked, securely packed on rail, or delivered, erected, and glazed complete, with extra coat of paint at Works, within 50 miles of London Bridge, at the following respective prices (beyond this distance, special prices quoted on application):

Length. ft.	Width. ft.	Height. ft. in.	To Eaves. ft. in.	Packed on rail. £ s. d.	Erected within 50 miles. £ s. d.
7	5	7 0	4 0	2 15 0	4 15 0
8	5	7 0	4 0	3 0 0	5 0 0
9	6	7 3	4 0	3 15 0	6 10 0
10	7	7 6	4 6	4 10 0	7 0 0
12	8	8 0	5 0	5 15 0	8 10 0
15	9	8 6	5 0	7 10 0	10 10 0
20	10	9 0	5 6	9 15 0	14 0 0
25	10	9 0	5 6	12 10 0	17 10 0

21oz. Glass for roof, 5 per cent., throughout 10 per cent. extra.

When ordering kindly state height of wall, also at which end door is to be fitted.

Tarred Sleepers to erect this house on, 3d. per foot run.

Lean-to Villa Conservatory.
TENANT'S FIXTURE.

No. 7.

This Lean-to Conservatory is of superior construction; it is a necessary adjunct to all well-appointed walled-in gardens, and it will be found useful for a variety of purposes to which a conservatory can be applied.

SPECIFICATION.—The framework is substantially built of red deal, the lower part being enclosed with matchboards, tongued and grooved in diagonal panels, the wood being sound and thoroughly seasoned. The House is provided with half-glass door, complete with rim lock and brass fittings, lattice staging for plants, footpath the entire length of house; gutters and downpipes, glass 21oz. throughout, and all necessary fittings, and is painted one coat of good oil paint. Houses are securely packed on rail, all parts being carefully marked, or delivered, erected and glazed, with an extra coat of paint at Works, within 50 miles of London Bridge, at the following respective prices (state which end door is required when ordering) :

Length. ft.	Width. ft.	Height. ft. in.	To Eaves. ft. in.	Packed on rail. £ s. d.	Erected within 50 miles. £ s. d.
7	5	7 0	4 0	4 0 0	6 0 0
8	5	7 0	4 0	4 15 0	6 15 0
9	6	7 6	4 6	6 5 0	8 10 0
10	7	7 6	5 0	7 0 0	9 10 0
12	8	8 6	5 6	8 0 0	11 0 0
15	9	8 6	5 6	10 5 0	14 10 0
20	10	9 0	6 0	15 0 0	20 10 0
25	10	9 0	6 0	18 10 0	24 10 0
50	12	9 0	6 0	35 0 0	45 0 0
100	12	9 0	6 0	55 0 0	75 0 0

If required for brickwork, deduct 10 per cent.

Span-Roof Villa Conservatory.

No. 8.

This illustration shows a well-made Span-Roof Conservatory, placed in grounds away from the house; being exposed, not only to view, but to the elements, it is so proportioned, both in substance and design, as to render it durable and effective.

SPECIFICATION.—The framework is of red deal. The lower part is lined with tongued and grooved matchboards, in diagonal panels, giving artistic finish. The house is fitted with a half-glass door, complete with rim lock, brass fittings, and key, and is supplied with lattice staging for each side; footpath the entire length of house; gutters and downpipes; top and side ventilators, according to size, and necessary ironwork for opening same. All woodwork painted one coat of good oil paint; good 21oz. glass throughout, and all parts securely packed on rail (being properly marked), or delivered, erected and glazed (with an additional coat of paint at Works), within 50 miles of London Bridge, at the following respective prices (beyond this distance special prices will be quoted on application):

Length. ft.	Width. ft.	Height. ft. in.	To Eaves. ft. in.	Packed on rail. £ s. d.	Erected within 50 miles. £ s. d.
7	5	7 0	4 0	4 5 0	6 5 0
8	5	7 0	4 0	5 0 0	7 0 0
9	6	7 0	4 6	6 10 0	9 0 0
10	7	7 6	5 0	7 10 0	10 5 0
12	8	8 0	5 6	9 0 0	12 0 0
15	9	8 6	5 6	11 0 0	15 10 0
20	10	9 0	6 0	16 0 0	22 0 0
25	10	9 0	6 0	20 0 0	27 0 0
30	12	10 0	6 0	27 10 0	37 10 0
35	14	10 0	6 0	40 0 0	55 0 0
40	14	10 0	6 0	45 0 0	65 0 0

Deduct 10 per cent. if required for brickwork.

Tarred Sleepers to erect this house on, 3d. per foot run.

Three-Quarter Span-Roof Conservatory.

TENANT'S FIXTURE.

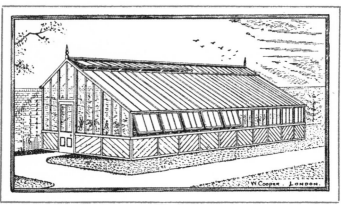

No. 9.

This is a very useful form for Plant-houses or Vineries, more especially where the back wall is not high enough for a Lean-to; as by adding extra cost for brickwork to the price of latter, it will then at once be perceived to be in favour of the Three-quarter Span; moreover, plants will grow much better, the House being thoroughly lighted.

This House is made of the best materials, well and substantially built, and so constructed that any handy man can put it together, and is artistically finished with diagonal panels. The whole of framework consists of good sound 3in. by 2in. and 3in. by 3in. red deal, the lower part doubly lined with tongued and grooved matchboards. The House is supplied with 21oz. glass throughout, half-glass door, rim lock, key, and brass fittings for same, two plant stages the length of both sides, and foot-path for centre. Continuous ventilators, the entire length of House, at ridge and in front, and necessary Ironwork for opening same, also gutters and downpipes. Woodwork is painted two coats good oil colour. Houses are securely packed on rail (all parts being carefully marked), or delivered, erected, and glazed (with an extra coat of good oil paint after glazing) within 50 miles of London Bridge at the following respective prices :—

Length.	Width.	Height.	To Eaves.	Packed on rail.	Erected within 50 miles.
ft.	ft.	ft. in.	ft. in.	£ s. d.	£ s. d.
7	5	7 0	4 0	4 10 0	7 0 0
8	5	7 0	4 0	5 10 0	8 15 0
9	6	7 6	4 6	6 10 0	10 10 0
10	7	8 0	5 0	7 10 0	11 15 0
12	8	8 6	5 6	9 0 0	14 10 0
15	9	9 0	6 0	11 0 0	18 0 0
20	10	9 0	6 0	16 0 0	25 0 0
25	10	9 0	6 0	21 0 0	32 0 0
50	12	9 0	6 0	40 0 0	60 0 0
100	12	9 0	6 0	70 0 0	100 0 0

Deduct 10 per cent. if for brickwork.

For Heating Apparatus suitable for above house, see Section VII.

Glazed Cover for Fruit Walls.

Invaluable to those who value their fruit, and are desirous of protecting it, thus securing a heavier crop.

No. 10.

This illustration shows a Cover, with sloping front, which allows for a narrow walk and for fruit trees in pots near the glass. It can be adapted to walls of different heights, and is also made in three widths.

SPECIFICATION.—Framework substantially constructed of red deal; the whole of sides, and 2ft. 6in. of ends, boarded with well-seasoned tongued and grooved matchboards. Half-glass door, complete with lock and brass fittings, in one end; glass 21oz. throughout; ventilators supplied, according to size, and necessary ironwork for opening same; stages for plants entire length of Cover. All woodwork painted one coat of good oil paint, and the whole structure securely packed on rail (being carefully marked in readiness for erection), or delivered, erected and glazed, with extra coat of paint at Works, within 50 miles of London Bridge, at the following respective prices:—

Length.		Width.		On rail.		Erected within 50 miles complete.
ft.		ft.		£ s. d.		£ s. d
20	......	6	......	15 0 0	......	19 10 0
40	......	6	......	27 10 0	......	36 0 0
60	......	7	......	42 10 0	......	55 0 0
100	......	8	......	70 0 0	......	90 0 0

Please state height of back wall when ordering, also which end door is required when facing house.

Other sizes and for erecting in any part of the country at proportionate prices.

For Heating Apparatus suitable for above cover, see Section VII.

Tarred Sleepers to erect this cover on, 3d. per foot run.

Lean-to Conservatory with Pit.

No. 11.

This Lean-to Conservatory, with Pit, is of superior construction. It is a necessary adjunct to all well-appointed walled-in gardens, and it will be found useful for a variety of purposes to which a Conservatory can be applied.

SPECIFICATION. —The framework is substantially built of red deal, the lower part being enclosed with matchboards tongued and grooved, the wood being sound and thoroughly seasoned, and the front finished with diagonal panels, as illustrated. The house is provided with half-glass door, complete with rim-lock and brass fittings, lattice staging for plants; footpath entire length of house; gutters and downpipes; glass 21oz. throughout, all necessary fittings, and is painted two coats of good oil paint. Houses are securely packed on rail (all parts being carefully marked), or delivered, erected and glazed (with an extra coat of paint after erecting), within 100 miles of London Bridge, at the following respective prices (beyond this distance special prices will be quoted on application):

Length.	Width of House.	Height.	To Eaves.	Width of Pit.	Packed on rail.	Erected within 100 miles.
ft.	ft.	ft. in.	ft. in.	ft. in.	£ s. d.	£ s. d.
7	5	7 0	4 0	2 0	6 0 0	8 10 0
8	5	7 0	4 0	2 0	6 10 0	9 15 0
9	6	7 6	4 6	2 0	8 0 0	11 10 0
10	7	7 6	5 0	2 6	9 0 0	13 0 0
12	8	8 6	5 6	3 0	10 10 0	15 10 0
15	9	8 6	5 6	3 0	13 15 0	19 0 0
20	10	9 0	6 0	3 0	17 10 0	24 0 0
25	10	9 0	6 0	3 0	22 0 0	31 0 0

When ordering, it should be stated at which end the door is required, when facing front of house from outside.

For Heating Apparatus suitable for above house, see Section VII.

Span-Roof Conservatory
with Pits.

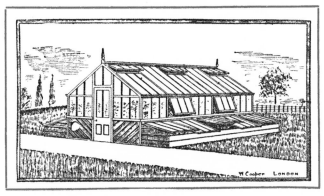

No. 12.

This illustration shows a well-made Span-roof Conservatory, with Pits each side, placed in grounds away from the House; being exposed not only to view, but to the elements, it is so proportioned, both in substance and design, as to render it durable and effective.

SPECIFICATION.—The framework is of red deal, the lower part lined with tongued and grooved matchboards, as illustration.

The house is fitted with a half-glass door, complete with rim-lock, brass fittings, and key, and is supplied with lattice staging for each side; footpath the entire length; and side and roof ventilators, according to size, and necessary ironwork for opening same; gutters and downpipes. All woodwork painted two coats of good oil paint, good 21oz. glass throughout, and all parts securely packed on rail, being properly marked, or delivered, erected. and glazed, with an additional coat of paint after erecting, within 100 miles of London Bridge, at the following respective prices (beyond this distance special prices will be quoted on application):

Length.	Width of House.	Height.	To Eaves.	Width of Pits.	Packed on Rail.	Erected within 100 miles.
ft.	ft.	ft. in.	ft. in.	ft. in.	£ s. d.	£ s. d.
7	5	7 0	4 0	2 0	6 10 0	9 0 0
8	5	7 0	4 0	2 0	7 0 0	10 5 0
9	6	7 0	4 6	2 0	8 10 0	12 0 0
10	7	7 6	5 0	2 6	9 10 0	13 10 0
12	8	8 0	5 6	3 0	11 5 0	16 5 0
15	9	8 6	5 6	3 0	14 0 0	20 0 0
20	10	9 0	6 0	3 0	18 0 0	25 0 0
25	10	9 0	6 0	3 0	22 0 0	32 0 0

Zinc Gutters, 6d., iron 9d. per foot run.

For Heating Apparatus suitable for above house, see Section VII.

Tarred Sleepers to erect this house on, 3d. per foot run.

Span-Roof Circular Light Conservatory.

TENANT'S FIXTURE.

No. 13.

This Conservatory is of ornamental design and artistic finish, and the materials employed in its construction are selected with the greatest regard for substantiality.

SPECIFICATION.—The framework is made of thoroughly seasoned red deal, and the lower part is enclosed with diagonal panels, with tongued and grooved matchboards, lattice staging for plants on each side of the house; footpath the entire length. Gutters and downpipes. Ample ventilation on the most approved plan is given, according to the size of the house; rim-lock, with brass fittings and key for door; and all necessary ironwork and fittings provided, including 21oz. glass throughout, and carefully packed. Each house is made in sections; each part is carefully numbered, so that any handy person can fit it in a few hours. The whole of the woodwork is painted one coat good oil paint. Securely packed on rail, or delivered erected and glazed (with extra coat of good oil paint at works) within 50 miles of London Bridge, at the following respective prices (beyond this distance, special prices quoted on application):·

Length. ft.	Width. ft.	Height. ft. in.	To Eaves. ft. in.	Packed on rail. £ s. d.	Erected within 50 miles. £ s. d.
7	5	7 0	4 0	5 10 0	7 10 0
8	5	7 0	4 0	6 0 0	8 0 0
9	6	7 0	4 6	7 0 0	9 10 0
10	7	7 6	4 6	8 10 0	11 0 0
12	8	8 0	5 0	10 0 0	13 0 0
15	9	8 6	5 3	14 0 0	18 10 0
18	12	9 6	5 6	19 0 0	25 10 0

Lantern-Roof Conservatory.

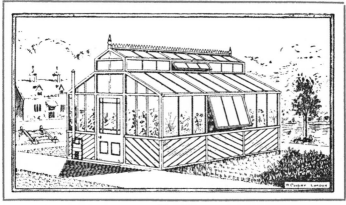

No. 14.

This handsome elevation is recommended for a prominent position in the grounds of a villa residence. Artistic in design, and finished with the utmost care, it will prove ornamental and durable wherever established.

SPECIFICATION.—All timbers employed are of thoroughly seasoned and carefully selected red deal; the lower part enclosed with diagonal panels of tongued and grooved matchboard, half glass door in one end, 21oz. glass throughout; staging along each side; footpath the entire length; gutters and downpipes; ample provision for ventilation made, and necessary ironwork for ventilators; painted one coat of good oil colour. Carefully packed on rail, and marked ready for fixing, or delivered, erected and glazed complete (with additional coat of paint at works), within 50 miles of London Bridge at the following respective prices (beyond this distance special prices quoted on application):—

Length. ft.		Width. ft.		Height. ft. in.		Packed on rail. £ s. d.		Erected within 50 miles. £ s. d.
10	....	7	....	10 6	....	9 0 0	....	11 10 0
12	....	7	....	10 6	....	11 10 0	....	14 10 0
15	....	9	....	10 6	....	14 15 0	....	19 10 0
20	....	10	....	10 6	....	18 10 0	....	25 0 0
25	....	12	....	10 6	....	24 0 0	....	32 0 0

Proportionate prices for other sizes.

Deduct 12½ per cent. if required for Brickwork.

For Heating Apparatus suitable for above house, see Section VII.

Tarred Sleepers to erect this house on, 3d. per foot run.

Lean-to Forcing House.

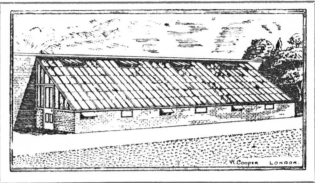

No. 15.

The value of this House for forcing purposes will be at once apparent by the illustration; inexpensive in design and economical in space are its characteristics. It is indispensable to the private gentleman or professional grower of cucumbers, melons, tomatoes, &c., and one cropping should repay its cost of construction.

SPECIFICATION.—Built for brickwork, 3ft. high; framework throughout 3in. by 2in. well-seasoned red deal; door complete, with lock, and brass furniture at one end; roof ventilation according to size, necessary ironwork for opening same, and good 21oz. glass throughout. House painted one coat good oil colour, carefully marked, packed, on rail at the following prices:—

Length.		9ft. wide.		12ft. wide.		14ft. wide.
ft.		£ s. d.		£ s. d.		£ s. d.
20	......	7 10 0	......	9 10 0	......	12 10 0
30	......	10 5 0	......	13 5 0	......	17 15 0
40	......	14 0 0	......	18 0 0	......	21 10 0
60	......	20 10 0	......	25 10 0	......	30 10 0
100	......	33 0 0	......	40 0 0	......	47 0 0

Ventilating Boxes for Side Walls, 3s. 9d. each extra.

If made with strong wood base instead of for brickwork, add 15 per cent.

Estimates for Stages, Footpath, Heating Apparatus, also for erecting Forcing Houses in any part of the country, free on application.

For Heating Apparatus suitable for above house, see Section VII.

We undertake all Brickwork (in 9in. work) with necessary footings at 1s. 6d. per foot super, measuring from concrete, also door space.

Span-Roof Forcing House.

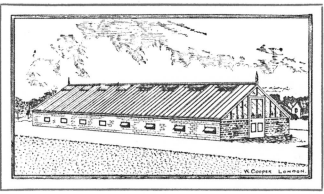

No. 16.

This illustration shows a Span-Roof Forcing House, the advantages of which are apparent where space will admit of its erection. It is indispensable to every grower of cucumbers, tomatoes, melons, &c., where a succession of crops are required in all seasons. Though cheap in construction, it is soundly built, and will repay its cost in a season.

SPECIFICATION.—Built for brickwork, 3ft. high; framework throughout 3in. by 2in. well-seasoned red deal; door complete, with lock, and brass furniture at one end; roof ventilation according to size, necessary ironwork for opening same, and good 21oz. glass throughout. House painted one coat good oil colour, carefully marked, and packed on rail at the following prices:—

Length.	9ft. wide.	12ft. wide.	14ft. wide.
ft.	£ s. d.	£ s. d	£ s. d.
20	8 0 0	10 0 0	13 0 0
30	11 0 0	14 0 0	18 10 0
40	15 0 0	19 0 0	22 10 0
60	22 0 0	27 0 0	32 0 0
100	35 0 0	42 0 0	50 0 0

Partitions, with extra door, 9ft., £1 10s. ; 12ft., £1 15s. ; 14ft., £2 each.

Ventilating boxes for side walls, 3s. 9d. each extra.

If made with strong wood base instead of for Brickwork, add 20 per cent.

Estimates for stages, footpaths, heating apparatus, also for erecting forcing houses in any part of the country, free on application.

We have erected several hundreds of these houses, complete with Brickwork, Heating Apparatus, etc., in all parts of the Kingdom. Satisfaction guaranteed; good sound materials and workmanship. Competition defied.

For Heating Apparatus suitable for above house, see Section VII.

17

Lean-to Greenhouse or Vinery.

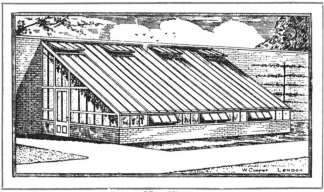

No. 17.

A well-made Lean-to House, suitable for Greenhouse or Vinery, built to fit against existing wall, and for 2ft. 6in. of brickwork at base.

SPECIFICATION.—Constructed of the very best materials, well and substantially built, all woodwork consisting of good, well-seasoned red deal; 21oz. glass throughout; alternate ventilation as shown in illustration, with necessary ironwork for opening same; gutters and downpipe; door in one end fitted with lock, brass furniture, and key; woodwork painted two coats of good oil colour, all carefully packed on rail, marked ready for erection, or delivered or erected by us at the following respective prices (with extra coat of paint after glazing, within 100 miles London Bridge), exclusive of brick-work, or made with wood base instead of for brickwork as illustration, 10 per cent. extra:

Length.	Width.	Height.	To Eaves.		Packed on rail.		Erected within 100 miles.
ft.	ft.	ft. in.	ft. in.		£ s. d.		£ s. d.
15	9	8 0	4 0	..	13 10 0	..	17 10 0
20	10	8 6	4 6	..	15 15 0	..	21 0 0
30	12	9 0	4 9	..	27 10 0	..	40 0 0
40	12	9 6	5 0	..	37 10 0	..	55 0 0
50	14	10 0	5 3	..	50 0 0	..	70 0 0
100	14	10 6	5 6	..	90 0 0	..	130 0 0

Proportionate prices for otLer sizes and erecting in any part of the Kingdom.

For Heating Apparatus suitable for above house, see Section VII.

We undertake all Brickwork (in 9in. work) with necessary footings at 1s. 6d. per foot super, measuring from concrete, also door space.

Span-Roof Plant House or Vinery.

No. 18.

A well-made Span-roofed House, suitable for Plant House or Vinery, built to fit on 2ft. 6in. of brickwork at base.

SPECIFICATION. — Constructed of the very best materials, well and substantially built, all woodwork consisting of good, well-seasoned red deal; 21oz. glass throughout; alternate ventilation as shown in illustration, with necessary ironwork for opening same, gutters and downpipes; door in one end, fitted with lock, brass furniture, and key; woodwork painted two coats of good oil colour, all carefully packed on rail, marked ready for erection, or delivered and erected by us at the following respective prices (with extra coat of paint after erecting within 100 miles London Bridge) exclusive of brickwork:

Length.	Width.	Height.		To Eaves.		Packed on rail.			Erected within 100 miles.		
ft.	ft.	ft.	in.	ft.	in.	£	s.	d.	£	s.	d.
15	9	8	0	4	0	15	10	0	20	0	0
20	10	8	6	4	9	17	15	0	23	0	0
30	12	9	0	4	9	32	10	0	45	0	0
40	12	9	6	5	0	42	10	0	60	0	0
50	14	10	0	5	3	57	10	0	77	10	0
100	14	10	6	5	6	105	0	0	145	0	0

If supplied with wood base, 10 per cent. extra.
Proportionate prices for other sizes.

For Heating Apparatus suitable for above house, see Section VII.
We undertake all Brickwork (in 9in. work) with necessary footings at 1s. 6d. per foot super, measuring from concrete, also door space.

Three-Quarter Span-Roof Conservatory.

No. 19.

This House is constructed of the very best materials, and is well, substantially, and handsomely built, all woodwork consisting of good, well-seasoned red deal; ventilators at top and in front, with necessary ironwork for opening same; 21oz. glass throughout; half-glass door, complete with lock, brass fittings, and key, lattice stages, footpath the entire length, gutters and downpipes, &c. All woodwork painted two coats of good oil colour. Carefully packed on rail, with every part marked ready for fixing, or delivered erected and glazed, with extra coat after erecting, within 100 miles of London Bridge, at the following respective prices (exclusive of Brickwork) :—

Length.	Width.	Ridge.	Eaves.		Packed on Rail.			Erected within 100 miles.		
ft.	ft.	ft.	ft.	in.	£	s.	d.	£	s.	d.
20 ..	9 ..	9 ..	5	0	25	0	0	33	0	0
24 ..	10 ..	9 ..	5	6	30	0	0	40	0	0
36 ..	12 ..	10 ..	6	0	40	0	0	55	0	0
60 ..	12 ..	10 ..	6	6	70	0	0	100	0	0
100 ..	14 ..	12 ..	7	0	130	0	0	175	0	0

Proportionate prices for other sizes, and for erecting in any part of the country, free on application.

Plan for Brickwork supplied free on receipt of order.

In ordering, it should be stated at which end the door is required; also height of back wall.

For Heating Apparatus suitable for above house, see Section VII.

We undertake all Brickwork (in 9in. work) with necessary footings at 1s. 6d. per foot super, measuring from concrete, also door space.

Span-Roof Conservatory

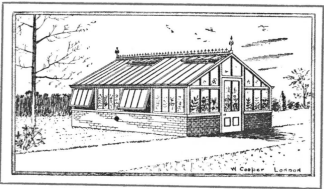

No. 20.

This well-proportioned design represents a commodious and substantial structure, suitable either for the garden, or annexed to a house.

SPECIFICATION.—Constructed of the very best materials, all woodwork consisting of well-seasoned red deal; ample ventilation is given at ridge and sides according to size, with necessary ironwork for opening same; 21oz. glass throughout; stages each side, footpath the entire length; half-glass door, complete with lock, brass fittings, and key, and handsome ornamental iron cresting at ridge, giving an artistic finish, gutters and downpipe. All woodwork painted two coats of good oil colour. Carefully packed on rail, marked ready for fixing, or delivered, erected, and glazed, with extra coat after erecting, within 100 miles of London Bridge, at the following prices, exclusive of brickwork, or made with wood base instead of for brickwork, as illustration :

Length.	Width.	Height.		To Eaves.		Packed on rail.			Erected within 100 miles.		
ft.	ft.	ft.	in.	ft.	in.	£	s.	d.	£	s.	d.
15	9	9	0	6	0	15	0	0	21	10	0
20	12	10	0	6	6	22	0	0	30	0	0
25	14	10	6	7	0	27	10	0	40	0	0
30	15	11	0	7	0	43	0	0	62	0	0
40	16	11	6	7	0	70	0	0	90	0	0

If supplied with wood base, in double lined panels, 15 per cent. extra. Proportionate prices for other sizes.

For Heating Apparatus suitable for above house, see Section VII· We undertake all Brickwork (in 9in. work) with necessary footings at 1s. 6d. per foot super, measuring from concrete, also door space.

Span-Roof Conservatory.

No. 21.

This Conservatory, as designed, makes a handsome addition to any garden, and will harmonise with, or can be adapted to, many gentlemen's residences in town or country.

SPECIFICATION.—Constructed of the very best materials, and is well, substantially, and handsomely built, all woodwork consisting of good, well-seasoned red deal; ventilators at top and front, according to size, with necessary ironwork for opening same; 21oz. glass throughout; half-glass door, complete with lock, brass fittings, and key; stages each side, footpath the entire length; ornamental iron cresting along ridge; iron O.G. gutters and downpipes, etc. All woodwork painted two coats of good oil colour. Carefully packed on rail, with every part marked ready for fixing, or delivered, erected and glazed complete, with extra coat oil paint after erecting, within 100 miles London Bridge, at the following prices (exclusive of Brickwork:

Length.	Width.	Height.	To Eaves.	Packed on Rail. £ s. d.	Erected within 100 miles. £ s. d.
15ft.	9ft.	9ft.	6ft.	17 10 0	24 0 0
20ft.	12ft.	10ft.	6ft. 6in.	25 0 0	33 0 0
25ft.	14ft.	10ft. 6in.	7ft.	30 0 0	43 0 0
30ft.	15ft.	11ft.	7ft.	47 10 0	66 0 0
40ft.	16ft.	11ft. 6in.	7ft.	80 0 0	100 0 0

Proportionate prices for other sizes. Estimates for erecting in any part of the country, also for Heating Apparatus (see Section VII.), free on application.

Plan for Brickwork supplied on receipt of order.

We undertake all Brickwork (in 9in. work) with necessary footings at 1s. 6d. per foot super, measuring from concrete, also door space.

Span-Roof Conservatory.

No. 22.

The Illustration represents a House 30ft. by 15ft.

This Conservatory, as designed, makes a handsome addition to any Garden, and will harmonise with or can be adapted to many gentlemen's residences in town or country, all the materials—wood, glass, and paints—being of the very best.

SPECIFICATION.—Constructed of the very best materials, and is well, substantially, and handsomely built, all woodwork consisting of good, well-seasoned red deal; ample ventilation according to size of house, at top and front, with necessary ironwork for opening same; 21oz. glass throughout; half-glass door, complete with lock, brass fittings, and key; lattice stages each side, footpath the entire length; iron O.G. gutters and downpipes, &c. All woodwork painted two coats of good oil colour. Carefully packed on rail, with every part marked ready for fixing, or delivered, erected and glazed complete, with extra coat oil paint after erecting, within 100 miles of London Bridge, at the following prices (exclusive of brickwork):

Length.	Width.	Height.	To Eaves.	Packed on rail. £ s. d.	Erected within 100 miles. £ s. d.
15ft.	9ft.	9ft.	6ft.	20 0 0	26 10 0
20ft.	12ft.	10ft.	6ft. 6in.	27 10 0	35 10 0
25ft.	14ft.	10ft. 6in.	7ft.	34 0 0	47 0 0
30ft.	15ft.	11ft.	7ft.	52 10 0	72 10 0
40ft.	16ft.	11ft. 6in.	7ft.	80 0 0	105 0 0

Proportionate prices for other sizes.

Estimates for erecting in any part of the country free on application.

For Heating Apparatus suitable for above house, see Section VII.

We undertake all Brickwork (in 9in. work) with necessary footings at 1s. 6d. per foot super, measuring from concrete, also door space.

Ornamental Span-Roof Conservatory.

No. 23.

Illustration shows a building, neat in design, which may be used for either a greenhouse or conservatory, and can be well recommended for a prominent position in the grounds of a villa residence. The upper side lights are filled in with tinted glass.

SPECIFICATION. — All timbers composed of good, well-seasoned red deal; 21oz. glass throughout; staging each side for plants; footpath entire length; ample ventilation, according to size; with necessary ironwork for opening same; iron O.G. gutters and downpipe; ornamental iron cresting along ridge; woodwork painted two coats of good oil colour. Carefully packed on rail, marked ready for erection, or delivered and erected by us (and painted an extra coat after erecting), at the following respective prices, exclusive of brickwork, or made with wood base instead of (as illustration) for brickwork at 10 per cent. extra.

Length.	Width.	Height.	To eaves.	Packed on rail.	Erected within 100 miles.
ft.	ft.	ft. in.	ft. in.	£ s. d.	£ s. d.
15	9	9 0	6 0	19 0 0	25 0 0
20	12	10 0	6 6	26 0 0	34 0 0
25	14	10 6	7 0	32 0 0	45 0 0
30	15	11 0	7 0	50 0 0	70 0 0
40	16	11 6	7 0	75 0 0	95 0 0

Proportionate prices for other sizes.

For Heating Apparatus suitable for above house, see Section VII.

We undertake all Brickwork (in 9in. work) with necessary footings at 1s. 6d. per foot super, measuring from concrete, also door space.

Ornamental Lean-to Conservatory.

No. 24.

This is a light, but strong and ornamental design, well adapted for communication with an inner room. It is ventilated at top and front, and forms a cheerful addition to a residence.

SPECIFICATION.—Constructed of the best materials, and substantially built, all woodwork of well-seasoned red deal; necessary ironwork for opening ventilators; gutters and down-pipes; 21oz. glass throughout; half-glass door, complete with lock, brass fittings, and key; lattice stage along front; footpath entire length. All woodwork painted two coats of good oil colour. Carefully packed on rail, marked ready for fixing, or delivered, erected, and glazed within 100 miles of London Bridge, with an extra coat after erecting, at the following prices, exclusive of brickwork, or made with wood base instead of for brickwork (as illustration), 10 per cent. extra.

Length.	Width.	Height.	To Eaves.	Packed on rail.	Erected within 100 miles.
ft.	ft.	ft. in.	ft. in.	£ s. d.	£ s. d.
15	9	9 6	6 6	17 10 0	24 0 0
20	12	10 0	6 6	25 0 0	32 10 0
25	14	10 6	6 6	30 0 0	42 10 0
30	15	11 0	6 6	47 10 0	67 10 0
40	16	11 0	6 6	77 10 0	97 10 0

In ordering it should be stated at which end door is required when facing house; if required, it can be fixed in front at the same price.

Lean-to Conservatory.

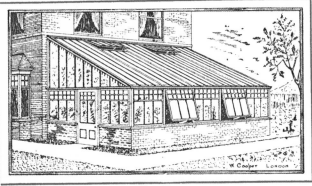

No. 25.

This chaste design is eminently suitable for addition to most residences, and a delightful entrance may be had from an inner room if desired. The upper side lights, as shown in the illustration, represent tinted glass, which affords an agreeable and subdued shade of light.

SPECIFICATION.—Constructed of the very best materials, all woodwork consisting of well-seasoned red deal; ventilators at top and front, with necessary ironwork for opening same; gutters and downpipes; 21oz. glass throughout; half-glass door, complete with lock, brass fittings, and key; lattice stages, footpath entire length. All woodwork painted two coats of good oil colour. Carefully packed on rail, marked ready for fixing, or delivered erected and glazed, within 100 miles of London Bridge, with extra coat of paint after erecting, at the following prices (exclusive of Brickwork), or made with wood base instead of for Brickwork (as illustration) 10 per cent. extra:

Length.	Width.	Height.	To Eaves.	Packed on rail.	Erected within 100 miles.
ft.	ft.	ft. in.	ft. in.	£ s. d.	£ s. d.
15	9	10 0	6 6	20 0 0	26 10 0
20	12	10 6	7 0	27 10 0	35 10 0
25	14	11 0	7 0	34 0 0	47 0 0
30	15	11 6	7 0	52 10 0	72 0 0
40	16	12 0	7 0	85 0 0	105 0 0

Proportionate prices for other sizes.

In ordering, it should be stated at which end door is required, when facing house; if required, it can be fixed in front at same price.

Plan for Brickwork supplied free on receipt of order.

For Heating Apparatus suitable for above house, see Section VII.

We undertake all Brickwork (in 9in. work) with necessary footings at 1s. 6d. per foot super, measuring from concrete, also door space.

Range of Houses.

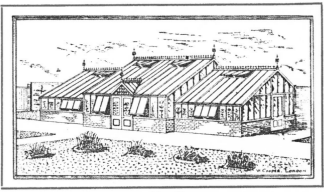

No. 26.

This is a very useful range of three-quarter span houses, divided into three parts, the centre part projecting 2ft. more than the ends. This is about the most economical in form that can be devised. It can be varied in form to almost any extent.

Designs and Estimates for Ranges of Houses, including Conservatory, Peach Houses, Vineries, &c., prepared and furnished free.

SPECIFICATION.—Constructed of the very best materials, and are well, substantially, and handsomely built, all woodwork consisting of good, well-seasoned red deal; ventilators at top and front, with necessary ironwork for opening same; 21oz. glass throughout; half-glass doors, complete with lock, brass fittings, and key; lattice stages for plants; footpath the entire length; iron O.G. gutters and downpipes, &c. All woodwork painted two coats of good oil colour. Carefully packed on rail, with every part marked ready for fixing, or delivered, erected and glazed, with extra coat after erecting, within 100 miles London Bridge, exclusive of brickwork, at the following respective prices:

Length.	Width.	Width of Centre.	On rail. £ s. d.	Erected within 100 miles. £ s. d.
36ft.	10ft.	12ft.	45 0 0	60 0 0
48ft.	11ft.	13ft.	50 0 0	67 10 0
60ft.	12ft.	14ft.	65 0 0	90 0 0
72ft.	13ft.	15ft.	80 0 0	100 0 0
84ft.	14ft.	16ft.	105 0 0	130 0 0
96ft.	15ft.	18ft.	130 0 0	160 0 0

Proportionate prices for other sizes, Estimates for erecting in any part of the country free on application.

For Heating Apparatus suitable for above house, see Section VII.

We undertake all Brickwork (in 9in. work) with necessary footings at 1s. 6d. per foot super, measuring from concrete, also door space.

Lantern-Roof Conservatory.

No. 27.

This design can be made detached if desired. Prices on application. The upper side lights are filled in with tinted glass.

SPECIFICATION.—Constructed of the very best materials, and is well, substantially, and handsomely built, all woodwork consisting of good well-seasoned red deal; ventilators at top and front, with necessary ironwork for opening same; 21oz. glass throughout; half-glass doors, complete with lock, brass fittings, and keys; lattice stages each side; footpath the entire length; iron O.G. gutters and downpipes, &c. All woodwork painted two coats of good oil colour. Carefully packed on rail with every part marked ready for fixing, or delivered erected and glazed complete, with extra coat after erecting within 100 miles of London Bridge at the following prices (exclusive of brickwork):

Length.		Width.		Height.			To Eaves.			Packed on rail.				Erected within 100 miles.		
ft.		ft.		ft.	in.		ft.	in.		£	s.	d.		£	s.	d.
15	....	9	....	10	6	....	6	0	....	25	0	0	....	32	10	0
20	...	12	....	11	0	....	6	6	....	42	0	0	....	52	10	0
25	....	14	....	11	6	....	7	0	....	65	0	0	....	80	0	0
30	...	15	....	12	0	....	7	0	....	80	0	0	....	100	0	0
40	...	16	....	12	6	....	7	6	100		0	0	....	125	0	0

Proportionate prices for other sizes.

Estimates for erecting in any part of the country, free on application.

We undertake all Brickwork (in 9in. work) with necessary footings at 1s. 6d. per foot super, measuring from concrete, also door space.

Stoke Courey, Eastville.
"SIR,—Greenhouse arrived safe, and I think it will give great satisfaction.—Yours respectfully, (Signed) W. J. MILLAIA."

Hipped-Roof Conservatory with Lantern.

No. 28.

An ornamental Conservatory of a design adapted to secure the maximum of light with thorough ventilation.

SPECIFICATION.—Constructed of the very best materials, and are well, substantially, and handsomely built, all woodwork consisting of good, well-seasoned red deal; ventilators at top and sides, with necessary ironwork for opening same; 21oz. glass throughout, half-glass door, complete with lock, brass fittings, and key; lattice stages each side; footpath the entire length; iron O.G. gutters, and downpipes, &c. All woodwork painted two coats of good oil colour. Carefully packed on rail, with every part marked ready for fixing, or delivered, erected, and glazed complete, with extra coat after erecting, within 100 miles London Bridge, exclusive of brickwork, at the following respective prices:

Length.	Width.	Height.	To Eaves.	Packed on rail. £ s. d.	Erected within 100 miles. £ s. d.
15ft.	10ft.	10ft. 6in.	6ft.	25 0 0	32 10 0
20ft.	12ft.	11ft.	6ft. 6in.	35 0 0	52 10 0
25ft.	14ft.	11ft. 6in.	7ft.	50 0 0	62 0 0
30ft.	16ft.	12ft.	7ft.	65 0 0	77 10 0
35ft.	18ft.	12ft. 6in.	7ft.	85 0 0	105 0 0
40ft.	20ft.	13ft.	7ft. 6in.	110 0 0	130 0 0

Proportionate prices for other sizes. Estimates for erecting in any part of the country free on application.

For Heating Apparatus suitable for above house, see Section VII.

We undertake all Brickwork (in 9in. work) with necessary footings at 1s. 6d. per foot super, measuring from concrete, also door space.

Hipped-Roof Conservatory.

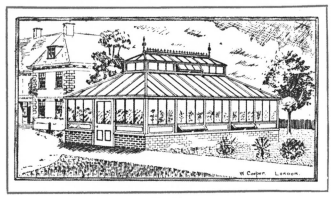

No. 29.

SPECIFICATION.—Constructed of the very best materials, and is well, substantially, and handsomely built, all woodwork consisting of good well-seasoned red deal; ventilators at top and front, with necessary ironwork for opening same; 21oz. glass throughout; half-glass door, complete with lock, brass fittings, and key; lattice stages each side; footpath the entire length; iron O.G. gutters and downpipes, &c. All woodwork painted two coats of good oil colour. Carefully packed on rail with every part marked ready for fixing, or delivered, erected, and glazed complete, with extra coat after erecting, within 100 miles of London Bridge, at the following prices :

Length.	Width.	Height.	To Eaves.	Packed on rail.	Erected complete within 100 miles.
ft.	ft.	ft. in.	ft. in.	£ s. d.	£ s. d.
15	9	10 6	6 0	22 10 0	30 0 0
20	12	11 0	6 6	37 10 0	55 0 0
25	14	11 6	7 0	60 0 0	72 10 0
30	15	12 0	7 0	72 10 0	87 10 0
40	16	12 6	7 6	85 0 0	105 0 0

Proportionate prices for other sizes.

Estimates for erecting in any part of the country, free on application.

For Heating Apparatus suitable for above house, see Section VII·

We undertake all Brickwork (in 9in. work) with necessary footings at 1s. 6d. per foot super, measuring from concrete, also door space.

Hipped-Roof Conservatory.

No. 30.

This is a very striking and attractive structure of a new design.

SPECIFICATION.—Constructed of the very best materials, and is well, substantially, and handsomely built, all woodwork consisting of good well-seasoned red deal; ventilators at top and sides, with necessary ironwork for opening same; 21oz. glass throughout; half-glass door, complete with lock, brass fittings, and key; lattice stages each sides, with footpath the entire length, iron O.G. gutters and downpipes, &c. All woodwork painted two coats of good oil colour. Carefully packed on rail with every part marked ready for fixing, or delivered erected and glazed complete, with extra coat after erecting within 100 miles of London Bridge at the following respective prices (exclusive of brickwork) :

Length.	Width.	Height.	To Eaves.	Packed on rail.			Erected within 100 miles.		
ft.	ft.	ft. in.	ft. in.	£	s.	d.	£	s.	d.
15	9	10 0	6 6	25	0	0	32	0	0
20	12	10 6	7 0	32	10	0	40	0	0
25	14	11 0	7 6	40	0	0	54	0	0
30	15	11 6	7 6	60	0	0	80	0	0
40	16	12 0	7 6	95	0	0	115	0	0

Proportionate prices for other sizes. Estimates for erecting in any part of the country free on application.

For Heating Apparatus suitable for above house, see Section VII.

We undertake all Brickwork (in 9in. work) with necessary footings at 1s. 6d. per foot super, measuring from concrete, also door space.

Lean-to Conservatory.

No. 31.

This elegant Lean-to Conservatory is designed for the side of a modern residence. It is made in various sizes, according to requirements, and entrance can be had either from the garden or the house.

The upper lights over the door, as shown in the illustration, represent tinted glass.

SPECIFICATION.—Constructed of the very best materials, all woodwork consisting of well-seasoned red deal; ventilators at top and front, with necessary ironwork for opening same; gutters and downpipes; 21oz. glass throughout; half-glass door, complete with lock, brass fittings, and key; lattice stages along front and ends; footpath entire length. All woodwork painted two coats of good oil colour. Carefully packed on rail, every part marked ready for fixing, or delivered, erected, and glazed (with extra coat after erecting), at the following respective prices (exclusive of brickwork), or made with wood base instead of for brickwork, 10 per cent. extra :

Length.	Width.	Height.		To Eaves.		Packed on rail.				Erected within 100 miles.		
ft.	ft.	ft.	in.	ft.		£	s.	d.		£	s.	d.
15	9	10	0	7	..	25	0	0	..	37	10	0
20	12	11	6	7	..	40	0	0	..	52	10	0
25	14	12	0	8	..	60	0	0	..	75	0	0
30	15	12	6	8	..	80	0	0	..	100	0	0
40	16	13	0	8	..	100	0	0	..	130	0	0

Proportionate prices for other sizes.

Estimates for erection in any part of the country free on application.

For Heating Apparatus suitable for above house, see Section VII.

We undertake all Brickwork (in 9in. work) with necessary footings at 1s. 6d. per foot super, measuring from concrete, also door space.

Lean-to Conservatory.

No. 32.

This elegant Lean-to Conservatory, with projecting gable front, is designed for the side of a modern residence. It is made in various sizes, according to requirements, and entrance can be had either from the garden or the house.

The front of Gable over door, as shown in illustration, represents tinted glass.

SPECIFICATION.—Constructed of the very best materials, all woodwork consisting of well-seasoned red deal. Ventilators as shown, with necessary ironwork for opening same; O.G. gutters and downpipes; 21oz. glass throughout; one pair of doors complete with lock, brass furniture, key, and bolts; stages along front and ends; footpath entire length; all woodwork painted two coats of good oil colour. Carefully packed on rail, every part marked ready for erection, or delivered and erected by us (painted an extra coat after erection), within 100 miles of London Bridge, at the following respective prices, exclusive of brickwork, or made with wood base instead of for brickwork (as illustration) 15 per cent. **extra .**

Length.	Width.	Project in centre.	Packed on rail.	Erected within 100 miles.
ft.	ft.	ft. in.	£ s. d.	£ s. d.
20	9	2 0	40 0 0	55 0 0
20	12	2 0	50 0 0	67 10 0
25	14	2 6	70 0 0	90 0 0
30	15	2 6	100 0 0	122 10 0
40	16	2 6	125 0 0	150 0 0

Proportionate prices for other sizes. Plan of brickwork Free on receipt of Order.

For Heating Apparatus suitable for above house, see Section **VII.**

We undertake all Brickwork (in 9in. work) with necessary footings at 1s. 6d. per foot super, measuring from concrete, also door **space.**

Improved Wall Fruit Protector.

This form of Wall Fruit Protector will be found most convenient, it being easily detached or attached at will. It is also the cheapest form introduced, and it is strongly recommended. The price includes the wall fittings, 21oz. glass, and the necessary lights; painted one coat.

PRICE

1s. 9d. per foot run.

If less than 25 feet is ordered, 2s. per foot.

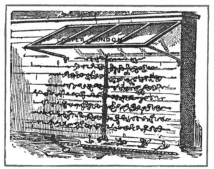

No. 33.

Wall Cover.

No. 34.

This Cover is made in sashes in lengths of 10ft. of good sound, well-seasoned red deal; the stiles, which are 2in. by 3in., being well mortised and pinned to tenoned rails, properly rabbeted for the glass, and fitted with 2in. sash-bars. Complete with 21oz. glass; and strong cast iron brackets necessary for fixing same. All woodwork painted one coat of good oil paint.

The whole securely packed on rail (being marked in readiness for erection) at the following respective prices :—

Lengths.	Width.	£	s.	d.	Lengths.	Width.		£	s.	d.
ft.	ft.				ft.	ft.	in.			
10	2	1	0	0	10	2	6	1	5	0
20	2	1	15	0	20	2	6	2	0	0
30	2	2	10	0	30	2	6	2	15	0
40	2	3	5	0	40	2	6	3	10	0
50	2	4	0	0	50	2	6	4	15	0
60	2	4	15	0	60	2	6	5	10	0

From the eaves of the glass coping, tiffany or other protecting materials may be suspended.

35

Window Conservatories.

No. 36.   No. 37.

Either of these designs will make an elegant addition to the windows of gentlemen's Mansions and Villa Residences, and also exclude all draught from the windows, keeping the rooms warm and comfortable.

PRICES :

No. 36.—Made whole and sent ready glazed with 21oz. glass, and painted three coats of best oil colour. Any size to order at 1s. 6d. per inch run.

No. 37.—Made in sections, all fitted ready for erection on arrival. Glazed part 21oz. glass, and part tinted cathedral glass, and painted three coats of best oil colour. One casement in front hung and fitted with fastener (as illustrated). Any size to order at 3s. 6d. per inch run.

H. W. THOMPSON, Patent B. K. Works, Alreschurch, Worcester.
"I am very pleased with the forcing-house you supplied me with last year."

Skeld, Sandsting, Shetland.

DEAR SIR,—I have now received the Greenhouse and two boxes of glass. I am astonished to see how safe it has arrived here. The wood-work is not damaged in the least, and the glass is so little broken that I may say it has come here safe and sound. Whoever has packed the glass deserves credit, if you only knew the rough handling it had to get after it landed in Shetland ere it arrived here. I am well pleased with it all ; it is a novelty here, as there is no other greenhouse in the locality. I wish to thank you for your prompt attention to my order. I and others are astonished to see such a good house for the money.—I remain, dear Sir, yours most faithfully,   PETER PETERSON."
WILLIAM COOPER, Esq.

Window Conservatory.

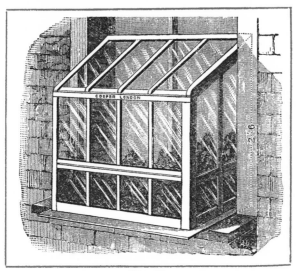

No. 38.

It is well and strongly made of best red deal, glazed with 21oz. glass, painted three coats, and is fitted with a set-open for opening the ventilating light provided at top.

PRICE.—Any size made to order at 1s. 3d. per inch run.

Elstow Lodge, Bromley Hill, Kent.
"Sir,—The Greenhouse we bought of you last September we have found to be quite satisfactory in every way, and consider it really good value for the money.—Yours faithfully, A. M. DUMAS."

Willesbury, Brading, I.W.
"Sir,—Kennel and Bench received yesterday. I am quite satisfied with them. G. F. DAVENPORT."

Greenhead, Low Bentham, Lancaster.
"Dear Sir,—The Lights arrived at the station to-day, and give every satisfaction.—I remain, yours, &c., JNO. CARR."

Radnoor, Holmbury St. Mary, Dorking.
"Sir,—Major-General Kincaid was well pleased with Greenhouse you sent him.—Yours, &c., H. GOODYER (Gardener)."

Leuton House, Leuton Street, Alton, Hants.
"Dear Sir,—Lights to hand with satisfaction.—Yours, S. CHIEM."

The "Rapid" Propagator.

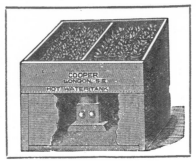

No. 39.

The only perfect Propagator for Raising Plants from Seeds, Slips, or Cuttings.

This Propagator is the best and cheapest now before the public, and will be found especially serviceable to amateurs and gardeners who require to strike cuttings and raise seeds in a short space of time.

One of these Propagators will raise large quantities of plants in the spring, thus—to a great extent—dispensing with the necessity of striking cuttings in the autumn, it being well known that many cuttings fall victims to the frost and damp atmosphere so prevalent in this country. This method of propagating saves the trouble and annoyance resulting from the loss of so many plants in the winter time, and also makes it unnecessary to occupy so much space in storing a large quantity of autumn cuttings.

The Propagators are composed of an outside casing with hinged glazed sash on top. The bed or bottom is formed of a tank, in which a constant circulation of hot water is kept up by the heater (see illustration), the pots being plunged in a bed of cocoanut fibre refuse, which should be kept moist. It is heated by oil, one pint of which will last 30 hours. Packed and put on rail complete at the following respective prices:—

		£	s.	d.
Lean to shape	1ft. 8in. by 1ft. 6in.	1	1	0
,, ,,	2ft. 6in. by 1ft. 10in.	1	10	0
,, ,,	4ft. by 2ft.	2	10	0
Span-Roof Shape	4ft. by 4ft.	4	10	0

Estimates for larger sizes free on application.

Garden Lights.

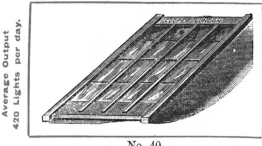

Average Output 420 Lights per day.

Several Thousands always in Stock.

No. 40.

SPECIFICATION.—These lights are substantially constructed of good, sound, well-seasoned red deal; the stiles, which are 2in. by 2in., being well mortised and pinned to tenoned rails properly rabbeted for the glass, and fitted with 2in. sash bars. The glazed lights are painted one coat good oil paint, and the glass in same nailed and bedded in superior oil putty. Packed on rail at the following respective prices:—

	ft.	ft.	in.	Each. s.	d.	Per Doz. £	s.	d.	Per 100. £	s.	d.
Unglazed Lights.	6 by 4		0	2	9	1	11	0	11	10	0
	5 by 3		6	2	6	1	8	0	10	10	0
	4 by 3		0	2	3	1	5	0	9	7	6
	3 by 2		0	1	6	0	16	6	6	5	0
Lights glazed with 21oz. glass.	6 by 4		0	9	0	5	0	0	37	10	0
	5 by 3		6	7	6	4	5	0	32	0	0
	4 by 3		0	6	0	3	7	6	25	15	0
	3 by 2		0	4	0	2	5	0	17	0	0
Unglazed Lights with sufficient 21oz. glass to glaze same.	6 by 4		0	6	0	3	7	6	25	15	0
	5 by 3		6	5	0	2	16	0	21	0	0
	4 by 3		0	4	0	2	5	0	17	0	0
	3 by 2		0	2	6	1	8	0	10	0	0

Iron Strengthening Bar, 1s. extra.

Prices given by return of post for all kinds of Sashes and Doors, glazed and painted.

Special Quotations for larger quantities and other sizes by return of post.

We have a number of specially constructed machines always making these lights from one year's end to the other, planing all four sides and rabbeting at one operation, and for making sashbars at the rate of 25ft. per minute.

Special strong Market Gardeners' Light for rough use, 3in. by 2in. stiles with iron bar, 6ft. by 4ft., 4s. 6d. each, unglazed.

The "Amateur" Plant Frame.

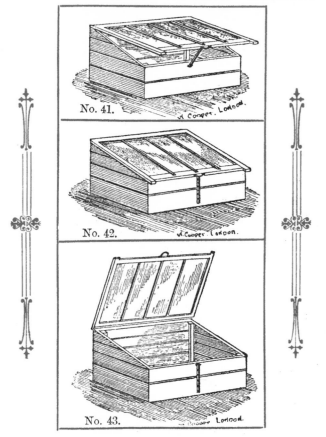

No. 41.

No. 42.

No. 43.

Made of 1in. thoroughly well-seasoned red deal boards. Lights are 2in. thick, hinged at back, and are glazed with good 21oz. glass, nailed and bedded in oil putty, and fitted with iron set to open for ventilation, &c. Painted two coats best oil paint, and securely packed on rail.

	£	s.	d.			£	s.	d.
4ft. by 3ft. ...	1	1	0	|	5ft. by 3ft. ...	1	5	0

Inside of all frames painted with our Patent ROT PROOF Composition,

Melon and Cucumber Frames.

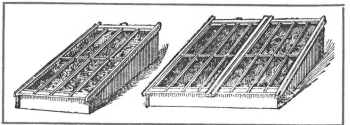

No. 44.	No. 47.
SINGLE LIGHT AND FRAME.	TWO LIGHTS AND FRAME.

These are very useful Frames, being suitable for the storage of plants in winter, and well adapted for the cultivation of melons, cucumbers, &c., in summer. The illustrations show One-, Two-, and Three-Light Frames. Height at front 11in., and at back 22in.

They are composed of 1¼in. thoroughly well-seasoned red deal boards, have necessary parting pieces, and runners for the lights,

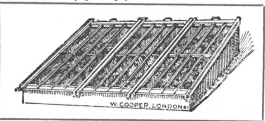

NO. 46.—THREE LIGHTS AND FRAME.

which are 2in. thick, and which are glazed with good 21oz. glass, nailed and bedded in oil putty, and fitted with an iron handle. All parts painted two coats of good oil paint, and securely packed on rail, at the following prices :—

			ft. in.	ft.			£	s.	d.
One-Light Frames	..	..	3 6 by	3	..	..	0	15	0
,, ,,	..	..	4 0 ,,	3	..	..	0	18	0
,, ,,	..	..	4 0 ,,	4	..	..	1	1	0
,, ,,	..	..	5 0 ,,	4	..	..	1	3	0
,, ,,	..	..	6 0 ,,	4	..	..	1	8	0
Two-Light ,,	..	..	6 0 ,,	4	..	..	1	10	0
,, ,,	..	..	8 0 ,,	4	..	..	1	16	0
,, ,,	..	..	8 0 ,,	6	..	..	2	10	0
Three-Light ,,	..	..	10 0 ,,	6	..	..	3	0	0
,, ,,	..	..	12 0 ,,	6	..	..	3	10	0
Four-Light ,,	..	..	16 0 ,,	6	..	..	4	10	0
Five-Light ,,	..	..	20 0 ,,	6	..	..	5	15	0
Six-Light ,,	...	..	24 0 ,,	6	..	..	6	10	0

Estimates submitted for special sizes free.

Inside of all frames painted with our Patent ROT PROOF Composition.

Three-Quarter Span Garden Frame.

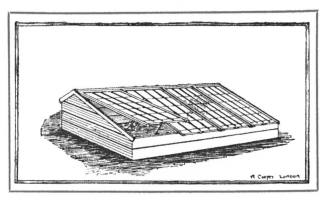

No. 47.

This frame was introduced a short time ago from a suggestion made by a celebrated grower of picotees and carnations. Its advantages are in height and light; the part span diffusing the sun's rays, while economy in space is effected. It is generally admitted to be without a rival in the trade.

SPECIFICATION.—It is made of 1¼in. sound red deal. The lights are 2in., and are glazed with good 21oz. glass, hung with iron hinges, and painted two coats of the best white lead paint. With set-opes complete. Securely packed on rail at the following prices:

Size. ft. ft.			Price. £ s. d.	Size. ft. ft.			Price. £ s. d.
4 by 4	..	..	1 8 0	16 by 6	..	..	5 10 0
4 by 6	..	..	2 0 0	20 by 6	..	..	7 0 0
8 by 6	..	..	3 5 0	24 by 6	..	..	8 10 0
12 by 6	..	..	4 10 0				

Roofing Felt.

Patent Asphaltic Rolls, 25yds. long by 32in. wide, 3s. 6d. per Roll. Better quality, 4s. 6d.

Nails for fixing Felt, in boxes of 250, 6d.; 500, 1s.

Span-Roof Garden Frame.

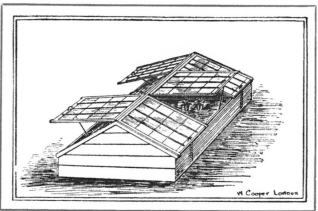

No. 48.

The Span-Roof Garden Frame claims the highest advantages in the matter of light and air, and is more convenient to work than the Lean-to. Cucumbers, Melons, &c., thrive well in it, and it is handy for storing plants in the winter.

SPECIFICATION.—The illustration shows a six-light frame 12ft. by 6ft., height at sides 11in., and ridge 24in. These frames are composed of 1¼in. thoroughly well-seasoned red deal boards. Painted two coats of best oil colour. The lights are glazed with good 21oz. glass, bedded in superior oil putty; and are fitted with iron stays, which safely support them for ventilation. Securely packed on rail at the following prices :—

ft. ft.	£	s.	d.	ft. ft.	£	s.	d.
4 by 4	1	8	0	16 by 6	5	10	0
4 „ 6	2	0	0	20 „ 6	7	0	0
8 „ 6	3	5	0	24 „ 6	8	10	0
12 „ 6	4	10	0				

Estimates given for larger sizes Free on application.

Wood Propagating Trays,

For sowing Seeds, Sticking Cuttings, &c., in Bundles, ready for nailing together.

Length. in.	Depth. in.	Width. in.	100 s. d.
12	9	2	8 0
15	10	2¼	10 0
18	12	3	15 0

Outside measure. Other sizes to order.

The Market Gardener's Violet Frame.

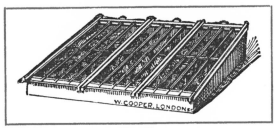

No. 49.

These frames are used very largely for Violet growing by Nurserymen, &c., but are suitable for a number of purposes, Very strong. Composed of good sound well-seasoned timbers, 1¼in. thick, with necessary runners for lights, &c., and Painted inside and out with our Patent ROT PROOF Composition. The lights are 2in. thick. Glazed 21oz., and fitted with iron handle, and securely packed on rail at the following prices :—

Three-light frames, 10ft. 6in. long, 5ft. wide, 11in. high at back, 9in. in front, £2 5s. each. £25 per doz.

Woodmancote, Dursley.
"GENTLEMEN,—I beg to thank you for your promptness in sending my Lights off. They came to hand all right last night. I would esteem it a favour if you would send me one of your lists, and oblige.—I remain, yours faithfully, (Signed) E. DEAN."

Wimborne House, Bar Lane, Old Bradford, Nottingham.
"DEAR SIR,—Received the Lights. I am very pleased with them. If I want any more I shall not forget you.—I remain, yours faithfully, (Signed) J. BAKER."

High Street, Rowley Regis.
"DEAR SIR,—I received the Lights to-day, and I am well satisfied with them.—Yours truly, (Signed) T. BARNSLEY."

Streetly Road, Aldridge, Walsall.
"DEAR SIR,—The Garden Lights came safely to hand, and they are very satisfactory.—Yours, &c., A. ELSLEY."

Firewood.

2-bushel sacks new chumps, nothing over 6in. long. 6d. per sack; 12 for 5s. Sacks included.

44

Lean-to Frame or Forcing Pit.

No. 50.

For small gardens this Lean-to Plant Preserver is entirely without precedent, especially where only a limited space is obtainable. They can be either fixed against a wall or by the side of Greenhouse, to suit convenience. The Lights are 2in. thick, glazed with good 21oz. glass, each Light being fitted with strong hinges and casement stays, which support lights for ventilating. The Frame-work and Lights are of well-seasoned red deal, painted two coats good oil colour.

GLAZED DIVISION, 7s. each.

Lengths.				Width.				Height at Back above end wall.				Prices. £ s. d.		
8ft.	..	..	..	3ft.	..	..	..	1ft. 9in.	..	..	..	1	10	0
10ft.	..	..	..	3ft.	..	..	..	1ft. 9in.	..	..	..	1	17	6
12ft.	..	..	..	3ft.	..	..	..	1ft. 9in.	..	..	..	2	5	0
16ft.	..	..	..	3ft.	..	..	..	1ft 9in.	..	..	..	2	12	6
2. ft.	..	..	..	3ft.	..	..	..	1ft. 9in.	..	..	..	3	7	6
24ft.	..	..	..	3ft.	..	..	..	1ft. 9in.	..	..	..	4	2	6
28ft.	..	..	..	3ft.	..	..	..	1ft. 9in.	..	..	..	4	17	6
32ft.	..	..	..	3ft.	..	..	..	1ft. 9in.	..	..	..	5	5	0
36.ft.	..	..	..	3ft.	..	..	..	1ft. 9in.	..	..	..	5	12	6

GLAZED DIVISION, 9s. each.

12ft.	..	..	..	4ft.	..	..	..	2ft.	..	..	..	2	15	0
16ft.	..	..	..	4ft.	..	..	..	2ft.	..	..	..	3	7	6
20ft.	..	..	..	4ft.	..	..	..	2ft.	..	..	..	4	5	0
24ft.	..	..	..	4ft.	..	..	..	2ft.	..	..	..	5	0	0
28ft.	..	..	..	4ft.	..	..	..	2ft.	..	..	..	5	15	0
32ft.	..	..	..	4ft.	..	..	..	2ft.	..	..	..	6	0	0
36ft.	..	..	..	4ft.	..	..	..	2ft.	..	..	..	6	5	0

GLAZED DIVISION, 10s. each.

16ft.	..	..	..	5ft.	..	..	..	2ft. 3in.	..	..	..	4	0	0
20ft.	..	..	..	5ft.	..	..	..	2ft. 3in.	..	..	..	5	0	0
24ft.	..	..	..	5ft.	..	..	..	2ft. 3in.	..	..	..	6	0	0
28ft	..	..	..	5ft.	..	..	..	2ft. 3in.	..	..	..	7	5	0
32ft.	..	..	..	5ft.	..	..	..	2ft. 3in.	..	..	..	8	0	0
36ft.	..	..	..	5ft.	..	..	..	2ft. 3in.	..	..	..	8	5	0
40ft.	..	..	..	5ft.	..	..	..	2ft. 3in.	..	..	..	9	0	0

If made with Strong Wooden Base, 1ft. 3in. high, instead of as illustration, for brickwork ; 25 per cent. extra.

45

Forcing Pits with Sliding Lights.

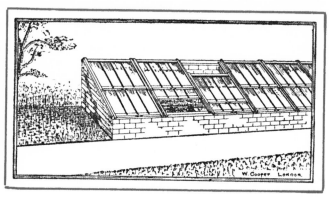

No. 51.

These Forcing Pits are usually constructed with long heavy lights running over into the path and monopolising double the width of the frame itself. In this design we have entirely done away with these difficulties, having arranged a double row of lights : the upper row slides down over the lower, and *vice versa*. Bearers are provided between each light, the latter being 2in. thick, and fitted with a handle. Sills are also provided for the wall. Painted two coats good oil colour, and glazed with 21oz. glass. All ready for fixing on brick-work on delivery.

PRICES :
FOR PITS WITH DOUBLE ROWS OF LIGHTS.

Length.	6ft. wide.			7ft. 6in. wide.			9ft. wide.		
	£	s.	d.	£	s.	d.	£	s.	d.
8ft.	2	8	0	2	18	0	3	2	6
12ft.	3	8	0	4	0	0	4	7	6
16ft.	4	8	0	5	1	0	5	15	0
20ft.	5	8	0	6	2	0	6	15	0
24ft.	6	8	0	7	3	0	8	5	0
32ft.	8	8	0	9	5	0	11	10	0
40ft.	10	8	0	11	7	0	13	15	0

If made with strong wooden base 2ft. high at back, 1ft. in front, instead of as illustration, 25 per cent. extra.

G. MYCROFT, Thornbank, Sheffield.
"The greenhouse arrived safely on Friday last, and I am very well satisfied with it."

J. COOPER, Coventry.
"I am pleased to say the greenhouse arrived this afternoon, and nothing broken. I am very much pleased with it."

H. IMBER PARSONS, Chemist, Axminster.
"Am very pleased with greenhouse which arrived this afternoon."

46

Span-Roof Pit or Forcing Frame

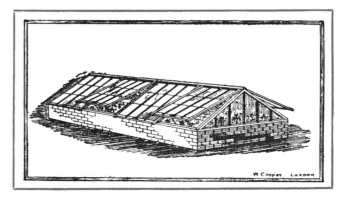

No. 52.

These are perhaps the most useful form of Frame before the public, as they are suitable for the storage of plants in winter, and well adapted for growing cucumbers or melons, &c., in summer. For these purposes they are largely used by nurserymen and gardeners. Constructed for building upon brickwork, and made of well-seasoned redwood deal; all the lights are fitted with set-opes, which afford ample ventilation; the framework and lights are fitted and numbered before leaving the works, so that any handy man can fix them. Lights 2in. thick, painted two coats of best oil colour, and glazed with 21oz. glass, including ends. Carefully packed on rail.

Length of Frame.	5ft. Wide.	6ft. Wide.	7ft. Wide.
ft.	£ s. d.	£ s. d.	£ s. d.
10	3 5 0	3 10 0	3 15 0
15	4 8 0	5 0 0	5 10 0
20	5 10 0	6 10 0	7 0 0
25	7 0 0	8 0 0	8 10 0
30	8 10 0	9 10 0	10 0 0
40	11 10 0	12 10 0	13 10 0
50	14 0 0	15 0 0	15 10 0
60	16 10 0	18 0 0	18 10 0

Any size made; Estimates free.

For Heating Apparatus suitable for above Frame, see Section VII.

We undertake all Brickwork (in 9in. work) with necessary footings at 1s. 6d. per foot super, measuring from concrete.

Three-Quarter Span Garden Frame.

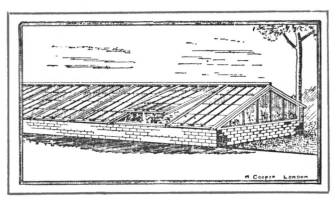

No. 53.

This illustration shows a Frame adapted for building on brick walls, making the most useful Frame that can be had for general purposes. Owing to plenty of light and air, plants grow quickly and healthy. The framework is made of good sound well-seasoned red deal, and a plate is formed to rest on the wall. The Lights are very strong. Two glazed ends are included. Set-opes to each light. Painted two coats and glazed with 21oz. glass. Carefully packed on rail.

Length of Frame.		5ft. Wide.				6ft. Wide.				7ft. Wide.		
ft.		£	s.	d.		£	s.	d.		£	s.	d.
10	...	3	5	0	...	3	10	0	...	3	15	0
15	...	4	8	0	...	5	0	0	...	5	10	0
20	...	5	10	0	...	6	10	0	...	7	0	0
25	...	7	0	0	...	8	0	0	...	8	10	0
30	...	8	10	0	...	9	10	0	...	10	0	0
40	..	11	10	0	...	12	10	0	...	13	10	0
50	...	14	0	0	...	15	0	0	...	15	10	0
60	...	16	10	0	...	18	0	0	...	18	10	0

Any size made. Estimates free.

For Heating Apparatus suitable for above frame, see Section VII.

We undertake all Brickwork (in 9in. work) with necessary footings at 1s. 6d. per foot super, measuring from concrete.

Square Zinc Hand Frames.

WITH LOOSE TOPS.

These Frames will be found to be very useful for protecting plants, seeds, slips, or cuttings during the spring, which, if left uncovered, would probably fall victims to the extreme cold so prevalent in this country during that season.

The Frames are made of strong corrugated zinc, fitted with zinc clips for glazing same, no putty or solder being required; therefore the services of a glazier are not requisite for either fixing the glass or repairing, which can be accomplished by any inexperienced person. The glass can be removed instantly from one frame, and fixed to another of its size, without fear of breakage, glass being interchangeable.

No. 54.

With 21oz. Glass, cut to sizes: 12in., 5s. 6d.; 14in., 6s. 6d.; 16in., 7s.; 18in., 8s.; 20in., 9s.; 22in., 10s.; 24in., 11s. each.

Single frames charged 6d. extra for packing. If 3 or more ordered, packing free.

Cap Glasses.

20in., 3s. 3d. each.

36s. per doz.

Carefully packed on rail.

No. 55.

Single glasses charged 6d. extra for packing. If 3 or more ordered, packing free.

Potting Shed, Tool House, Workshop, etc.

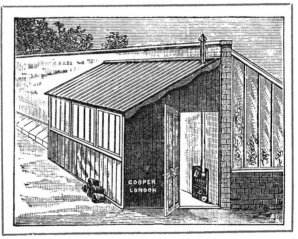

No. 62.

Constructed with strong wood framework, and covered with tongued and grooved boards, with roof of galvanised corrugated iron. Woodwork painted outside one coat. Made in sections. Door hung and fitted with lock and key. 21oz. glass. Carefully packed on rail.

Length.	Width.	To Ridge.	To Eaves.	Lean-to* as Illustration.			Span Roof.†		
ft.	ft.	ft. in.	ft. in.	£	s.	d.	£	s.	d.
7	5	7 0	5 0	2	10	0	3	0	0
9	6	7 3	5 3	3	10	0	4	5	0
10	7	7 6	5 6	4	10	0	5	10	0
12	8	8 0	6 0	5	10	0	6	15	0

* Door may be had in end or front as required.

† Both sides glass similar to side in Illustration, with door in centre one end.

Gardeners' Plant Barrow.

Well and strongly made, and painted two coats best oil colour.

	£	s.	d.
Size 3ft. by 2ft.	0	15	0
,, 4ft. by 2ft. 3in.	1	0	0
,, 5ft. by 2ft. 6in.	1	7	6

WILLIAM COOPER, Limited,

Horticultural Providers,

751, OLD KENT ROAD, LONDON, S.E.

SECTION II.

Illustrated Catalogue

OF

Incubators,

⊱FOSTER MOTHERS,⊱

Poultry Houses and Runs,

COOPS, DUCK HOUSES,

PIGEON COTES AND HOUSES,

FENCING, AVIARIES,

❊ RABBIT HUTCHES, ❊

&c., &c.

"Peripage" Patent Hot-Water Rearer or Foster Mother.

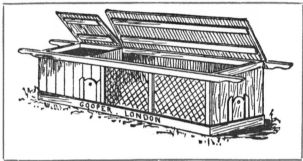

No. 90.

Do not confound this with similar Hot-Air Rearers sold, and do not buy a Rearer that will kill your Chicks, and will fall to pieces after a month or two's wear.

Carefully packed on rail at the following prices:—

Chick Size.		Length. ft.		Width. ft. in.			£ s. d.
15	...	4	...	2 0	...		1 0 0
60	...	6	...	2 6	...		1 10 0
120	...	8	...	2 6	...		2 10 0

This form of Hot-Water Rearer is very popular and convenient, and has been pronounced by Poultry Authorities the most perfect Rearer that has ever come under their notice.

The Sleeping Chamber, heated by a Hot-Water Tank (best Copper), is spacious and quite devoid of projections of any sort behind or under which the Chicks can be injured or left in the cold.

It is double cased, and has a double roof, the floor being raised a few inches from the ground.

The Dormitory obtains light from the lamp fixed in outer run, and is also fitted with a shutter, so that Chicks can have light or be in darkness as is desired.

The fumes from lamp are directly conducted outside the Rearer, so that the air in both Sleeping Chamber and Runs is always pure as well as warm.

The Run is fitted with wire netting of small mesh, and is also fitted for glass panes, so that in cold weather the Chicks can be protected from draughts, and the warm air can be kept in the Run.

Poultry-Keeping.

In presenting to fanciers, breeders, and all interested in the successful rearing of poultry, our List of Houses, Runs, and Appliances, a few general remarks will not be out of place.

Situation of the Poultry-Yard.—It is difficult to lay down any hard-and-fast rules as to the site for a poultry-yard, as this must depend on what land is available for the purpose. A south or south-west aspect is desirable; at any rate, the place should be sheltered from keen winds. Poultry thrive apace, and pick up a good proportion of their own food, where a grass run is available, and this can be readily enclosed with wire netting in order to prevent the birds from roaming.

Houses, Runs, and Coops.—Whether kept for exhibition, for egg-production, or for the table, it is imperative that fowls be properly housed; and the structure devoted to the purpose must be well ventilated without being draughty. Portable houses are strongly recommended by experts, especially where they can be kept in a dry field and moved from place to place where there are few or no trees, such as might entice the birds to roost in their branches. Some good types of houses and runs, and an assortment of coops of the most approved patterns, are shown in the following pages.

Varieties.—Dorkings, Plymouth Rocks, Scotch Greys, Silkies, Brahmas, and Cochins are considered by Prof. James Long to be the best sitters and mothers. The best layers are Hamburghs, Minorcas, Leghorns, Andalusians, Plymouth Rocks, and Houdans; while Spanish, La Flèche, Crèvecœurs, Minorcas, Andalusians, Houdans, and Langshans produce the largest eggs. Among the hardiest fowls are Plymouth Rocks, Langshans, Brahmas, Indian Game, Andalusians, Scotch Greys, Cochins, and Houdans. For size and weight, Dorkings, Cochins, Brahmas, and Langshans are recommended, and the Indian Game and Dorking cross is acknowledged to produce the best quality table-fowl.

Food and Feeding.—The morning meal should consist of grain, such as crushed oats, or barley meal and sharps, mixed to a tough or crumbly consistency with hot water. It must not be sloppy; if it has been made too wet, dry it with pollard or bran. A second meal may be supplied at midday if thought desirable; but it should be sparse, varied, and well scattered abroad, so that the birds may find occupation in searching for it. Where a large grass run is available, no midday meal is necessary. The third and last feed, consisting of sound corn, should be given before the fowls retire to roost. Food should not be given in such abundance that it is left lying about. The birds require more hand-food in winter than in summer; and although they do not then lay so freely (taking a flock together)

Movable Poultry Houses.

(Span-Roof.)

No. 91.

No waiting, hundreds in stock.

Thousands sold every season.

These Houses are made of thoroughly seasoned match-boards, in sections, so that they may be easily put together. They have ventilator, sliding shutter, and the doors are fitted with locks.

(Lean-to.)

The outsides are oil-painted with one good coat. They are well constructed throughout, and have a neat appearance when fixed.

Packed on rail at the following prices :—

No. 92.

Length. ft.	Width. ft. in.	Height. ft. in.	To Eaves. ft. in.	Span-Roof. £ s. d.	Lean-to. £ s. d.
3	2 6	4 6	2 9	0 15 0	0 12 6
4	3 0	5 0	3 0	1 0 0	0 17 6
5	4 0	6 0	3 6	1 5 0	1 0 0
6	4 0	6 0	3 9	1 10 0	1 5 0
7	5 0	6 6	4 0	1 16 0	1 10 0
9	6 0	7 0	4 3	2 2 0	1 15 0

The following are extra:—Nest-boxes, 6d. each, 5s. per doz. Perches, 1d. per foot.

These Houses are exceedingly adaptable for Potting, Tricycle, Coal, and Wood Sheds.

Folding Doors for Tricycle Houses, 3s. extra.

If Outside Woodwork painted with our Patent Rot-Proof Composition, 10 per cent. extra.

yet the older pullets and the strongest of the young hens may generally be induced to lay with great regularity if fed from day to day with the object of encouraging them to do so. Table scraps and sheep's paunches are useful stimulating foods for winter. Fowls will not thrive unless provided with plenty of coarse grit or crushed oyster-shells to aid digestion (sand is useless for this purpose), and they must have a dust bath.

Prevention of Diseases.—The extreme importance of cleanliness cannot be too earnestly impressed upon all who keep birds. By means of the frequent use of our Disinfectas, which is cheap and clean, two bushels only costing 2s. 6d., many of the scourges of our poultry-yards may be kept at bay. In the case of disease manifesting itself, the patients should be promptly removed to a hospital (for which purpose a cheap lean-to house, such as that shown on page 110, is well adapted), so that other healthy birds may not be infected.

Hatching and Rearing Chickens.—Birds intended for early breeding should be selected in December. Some breeders make a point of hatching their chickens for exhibition purposes as early as 1st January. In any case, early hatching is as valuable to the breeder for the table and the egg-producer as to the fancier: it enables them to obtain the high prices which rule in the early months of the season, and to rear a much larger number of birds than they would otherwise be able to do. The strongest of the two-year-old hens should be mated with an early-bred cockerel of the year. Plenty of hard corn must be provided for them, and a swede or mangold to peck at is desirable. The number of eggs given to a broody hen must be regulated by her size. She should be removed from the other fowls, and her nest made of straw. upon the ground, in a properly-constructed nest-box (see p. 137), if it is prepared in any other position, it should have a freshly-cut turf at the bottom. Feed the hen once a day with barley or barley-meal; give also clean water and a few blades of grass. Hatching commences on the evening of the twenty-first day. When, a few hours after hatching, the chicks are removed to a coop (see p. 139) give them finely-chopped egg (shell included) and skimmed milk. As they grow, this food may be varied considerably, and may include new milk, rice boiled in skim milk, boiled and chopped macaroni, and a little cooked meat, adding gradually to the dietary boiled and raw groats, broken wheat, and buckwheat. Barley-meal and ground oats, stiffly mixed, form a staple food throughout the bird's career. When the chicks are old enough to leave the hen, they should be provided with a suitable lodging, such as my Portable Chicken Coop and Run (see pp. 142 and 145). With suitable houses, well-bred birds, energy, and scrupulous cleanliness, poultry-keeping is not only a pleasing occupation, but also a source of considerable profit.

POULTRY.

The keeping of poultry, which has greatly increased of recent years, continues to make steady progress in all parts of the kingdom. There are still numbers of people with room for a few hens in a back garden, or with plenty of space at their disposal, who would find it advantageous to take to poultry culture. It is such a luxury to have really new-laid eggs, or a chicken for the table, of one's own growing. A good deal of attention, too, is being devoted to poultry farming, and to keeping fowls in sufficient numbers to add considerably to the means of livelihood.

HOUSES.—One of the first essentials to profitable poultry-keeping is a suitable house. Excellent houses are made at most moderate prices for large or small quantities of all breeds of fowl. The amateur who is going to have half a dozen hens in his back yard will find our lean-to houses just the thing for him. Placed against a wall facing south or south-east, the house, No. 70, makes a most snug and comfortable abode. If the ground inside is rammed tight, raised a couple of inches above the surrounding soil, and a few sifted ashes thrown on the top, it will always be dry and easily cleaned.

Another most useful lean-to house, especially where space is very limited, is No. 73. It is fitted with sliding shutter, and has a raised floor, under which the fowls can shelter in wet or windy weather. Wire runs of various sizes are made to go with this house. A house which is in great request, and of which we sell thousands, is the "Favourite Poultry House," No. 71. It is made in sections that screw together. There is a window at one end, and a raised floor 2ft. from the ground.

Our improved span-roof poultry house, No. 110, is strongly recommended where a lean-to house is not required. For keeping the fowls dry in all weathers our house, No. 111, is invaluable. The whole run is covered with a weather-board roof, and the bottom part of the front and sides is boarded up. This allows of some loose straw, or chaff, being thrown in the run, affording exercise for the birds in scratching for any grain that is scattered about. A specially convenient house is "The Gem." It is a double house, enabling two breeds to be kept apart, yet under the same roof. There are many other houses to meet all possible requirements, including lean-to poultry houses with corn room and run, portable houses, and span-roof houses on wheels.

THE STOCK.—When the house has been decided upon, and purchased, the fowls must be obtained. Although there is still a prejudice in some rural districts in favour of mongrels, there are so many useful and free-laying pure breeds that a beginner should make a start with some recognised variety.

Span-Roof Improved Poultry House.

No. 94.

These Houses are very roomy and well ventilated, and specially constructed so that they may easily be taken to pieces or erected. They have a door and windows at the ends, a flap at back for easy access to the nest-boxes, are raised from the ground 2ft. so as to form a dry run underneath, made of good sound materials, painted one coat outside, and roofed with weatherboarding. Carefully packed on rail at the following prices:—

Length. ft.	Width. ft.	Height to Ridge. ft. in.	Height to Eaves. ft. in.	£ s. d.
4	3	5 9	4 0	1 10 0
5	4	6 0	4 0	2 0 0
6	4	6 3	4 3	2 10 0
7	5	6 6	4 6	3 5 0
9	6	7 0	4 9	4 0 0

If Outside Woodwork painted with our Patent Rot-Proof Composition, 10 per cent. extra.

To keep your Poultry healthy, make their Nests of **Cooper's Disinfectas,** and sprinkle same about House and Run daily. Per Sack (2-bushel), 2s. 6d.; 10 for 22s. 6d.

"IT IS CHARMING."

Westover, Teddington.

GENTLEMEN,—I am much obliged by your sending the little house so quickly. It is charming, and looks so nice now it is up.

Faithfully yours,

(Signed)   R. G. FERGUSON (Mrs.)

POULTRY—*continued.*

If he selects mongrels he cannot know beforehand whether the hens will lay large or small eggs, whether the eggs will be white or brown, or whether the birds will be prolific or poor layers. He cannot tell if the mongrels will stand confinement well, or the class of chickens that will be produced. The eggs, moreover, will only be of value for eating, and the cockerels will sell solely for killing prices, being of no use for stock purposes.

If pure breeds are kept, the characteristics are at once known. One can be chosen suited for a confined run, or for a free and exposed situation; to lay either white or brown eggs, to be a non-sitter or broody, and to produce free-laying pullets or good table chickens. And the eggs of pure breeds can be disposed of in the spring for hatching, if desired, at from 3s. 6d. to 10s. 6d. a sitting, according to the quality of the birds. Our egg boxes, No. 174, with separate compartments for each egg and movable partitions, enable sittings of eggs to be sent safely all over the kingdom. There are no mongrels that will lay as well as the White Wyandotte, the Black Leghorn, the White Leghorn, or the Minorca. And there are no mongrels to equal the Dorking, the Buff and Black Orpington, or the Indian Game for the table.

AGE OF STOCK.—To attain success it is necessary that the fowls should be young. Old hens lay but few eggs, and those only at a time of year when eggs are plentiful, and of least value. Pullets in their first season are most prolific. In their second season hens ought to lay enough eggs to be profitable. But when they cease laying as they are about to moult—that is, when they are two and a half years old—they should be killed, or got rid of for whatever they will fetch. If valuable for her good looks, or for having produced high-class chickens, a hen should, of course, be kept longer.

If eggs are required only for eating, and not for hatching, no cock bird is necessary. But if it is wished to rear chickens, the male bird should be either a two-year-old running with pullets, or a cockerel mated with second-season hens. If it can be avoided, it is better not to mate a cockerel with pullets. The progeny seldom fledge well, and there are usually a large percentage of cockerels among the chicks.

EGG AVERAGE.—From a few of the statistics that are recorded of the laying powers of hens, the novice will be able to know if his hens are producing as many eggs as they ought, and whether he is treating them satisfactorily. During a twelve months' laying competition, promoted by the Utility Poultry Club, the first-prize pen of White Wyandottes laid 904 eggs, or an average for the six pullets in the pen of 166 eggs each. The second-prize pen averaged 165 eggs, and the third-prize

Cheap Lean-to Fowl House.

For placing against a wall.

This House will be found useful where space is limited. Made in sections it can be easily fixed against wall, fence, &c. It has a raised floor and ladder, is fitted with perches, nest-boxes, sliding shutter, and lock and key to door. Complete, and oil-painted outside. Carefully packed on rail at the prices given below.

No. 95.

THE ABOVE HOUSE WITH RUN.

No. 96.

Length.	Width.	Height to Ridge.	House only.	Portable Run, Length.	Run only.
ft.	ft. in.	ft. in.	£ s. d.	ft.	£ s. d.
3	2 6	5 0	1 5 0	4	0 7 6
4	4 0	5 9	1 12 6	6	0 10 0
5	5 0	6 3	2 0 0	7	0 15 0
6	6 0	7 3	2 5 0	8	1 2 6

Use **Cooper's Disinfectas** for Nests. Per Sack (2-bush.), 2s. 6d

POULTRY—*continued.*

pen 158 eggs. The Irish Board of Agriculture obtained records for the year 1908 from 125 flocks, representing over 5,000 hens. The general average of all these was 120 eggs per hen per annum. The averages at the Utility Poultry Club competition were from selected hens, and can hardly be expected to be realised by the ordinary amateur. But an average of 130 eggs per hen is frequently attained, and ought to be within the reach of all.

FERTILISING THE EGGS.—When eggs are required for incubation it is sometimes important to be able to know how soon after mating the eggs can be used. In the United States some experiments were made with Leghorns to ascertain this. After the male was introduced to the hens it was found that on the second day two eggs out of eighteen were fertile; on the third day twelve out of twenty-four; and on the sixth day nineteen out of twenty-four. On the eighth day eighteen were fertile out of twenty. This proves that eggs may safely be used for hatching within a week of mating.

FOOD.—One of the first maxims to be strictly followed in poultry keeping is never to overfeed the fowls. They should always leave off after a meal slightly hungry. Directly they begin to pick and choose, that particular feed should be brought to an end. When fowls are kept in confinement they should have one meal of soft food at least three times a week. This is better if given for breakfast, as it is sooner digested than hard grain. The soft food can consist either of pea-meal and middlings, biscuit meal and middlings, or maize meal and middlings, mixed crumbly, and not wet, with hot water. One of these mixtures one day, and another the next. Only a small feed must be given—as much as they can eat eagerly and no more. If they eat a full meal at this time they will sit about afterwards and take no exercise.

About eleven o'clock a handful or two of grain—such as oats or wheat—should be thrown about the run. If there is some loose straw, or dead leaves, in the run, the grain must be well scattered, so that the fowls can find employment in scratching for it. About one o'clock, if the fowls are in a small run, they must have some cut grass or cabbage. If the latter is given, the cabbage should be tied up to hang a couple of feet from the ground, so that the fowls have to jump for it. If green food cannot easily be obtained, a swede or a turnip or two cut in half will answer the purpose.

It is important that poultry in a confined run should be supplied with some animal food. They should, therefore, have some meat scraps from the house, or some fresh cut bone, at least three times a week. This can be given at midday—not more than half an ounce of the cut bone to each hen. At

Improved Span-Roof Poultry House.

No. 97.

This style of House is recommended for profitable fowl-keeping. It has a raised floor, sliding shutter, and ladder, as shown in illustration, and is fitted inside with Nest-boxes, with

THE ABOVE HOUSE WITH RUN.

No. 98.

flap at back for access to Nest-boxes and Perches. Lock and key are supplied to both flap and side door. Oil-painted outside, and carefully packed on rail complete at the prices below:—

Length.		Width.		Height to Ridge.		House only.		Portable Run. Length.		Run.	
ft.		ft. in.		ft. in.		£ s. d.		ft.		£ s. d.	
3	....	2 6	....	5 0	....	1 10 0	....	4	....	0 7 6	
4	....	4 0	....	5 9	....	2 0 0	....	6	....	0 12 6	
5	....	5 0	....	6 3	....	2 15 0	....	7	....	0 17 6	
6	....	6 0	....	7 3	...	3 0 0	....	8	....	1 5 0	

Fitted with Wheels, 10s. extra.

If Outside Woodwork Painted with our Patent Rot-Proof Composition, 10 per cent. extra.

Sprinkle **Cooper's Disinfectas** in all Houses and Runs daily. Cheap, Clean, and Healthy. Per Sack (2-bushel), 2s. 6d.

Poultry—*continued.*

roosting time some grain must be given; white oats, or wheat, or maize. Only one kind of grain at a time, not a mixture. On the mornings when the fowls do not have soft food they can have oats, wheat, or peas. Grit must always be within reach.

Fresh, clean water must be given at least once a day, placed out of reach of the sun's rays, and where snow cannot fall into it. In the summer the soft food need only be given about twice a week. Maize had better be discontinued then. During warm weather many hens will take a rest from laying. To start them again, also to bring them on to lay after moulting, and to induce pullets to commence, as well as to keep the stock in grand condition, our egg producer should be used. A well-known tonic for occasional use is the "Douglas Mixture," made by dissolving a quarter of a pound of sulphate of iron and half an ounce of sulphuric acid in a gallon of water. A teaspoonful of the solution can be added to each pint of the fowls' drinking water four or five days running, and then stopped for a time. This tonic must be given in earthenware and not in metal vessels.

HATCHING.—Eggs that are intended for hatching must be of normal size and shape. Specially large ones should be avoided, as well as those that are palpably thin shelled and misshapen in any way. If the eggs are to be hatched by a hen, they can be kept for a fortnight or three weeks without fertility being impaired. There are many instances of eggs having hatched freely when they have been laid a month before incubation commenced. None the less, the fresher the eggs the better. If an incubator is to be used, the eggs must not have been laid for more than a week.

In some country places it is thought that the sex of eggs can be foretold before incubation. The shape of the egg is believed to show whether a cockerel or pullet will be produced. Pointed eggs are credited with containing cockerels, and rounder eggs pullets. No reliance is to be placed on this theory. Most pullets when they commence to lay produce slightly pointed eggs. Early in the season more cockerels are hatched than later on. Hence the pointed-egg idea. The position of the air cell at the larger end of the egg is also supposed to indicate the sex. This, however, is fallacious.

THE SITTING HEN.—A hen can be known to be broody, or ready to incubate, when she remains in the nest day and night, coming off only for a few minutes to feed, and clucking and screaming when touched. Before the eggs that she is to hatch are entrusted to her, she must be placed in the nest-box for two or three days, to accustom her to her surroundings. Our hatching boxes are made specially for sitting hens. For several hens sitting at the same time our hatching boxes,

Portable Lean-to Poultry House and Run.

No. 99.

This House can be readily moved for change of ground. It is easily fixed, being made in sections. The floor is raised above the run, and the roof weather-boarded, rendering it rain-proof. It is fitted with nest-boxes, perches, sliding shutter, and door with lock and key. The wire-netted run is 4ft. high, and is made with door at the end, oil-painted outside with one good coat. Carefully packed on rail at the following prices :—

House.	Run.	£	s.	d.
4ft. by 3ft.	4ft. long	2	2	0
5ft. by 4ft.	6ft. ,, ...	2	15	0
6ft. by 5ft.	7ft. ,, ...	3	10	0
8ft. by 7ft.	8ft. ,, ...	5	0	0

These Poultry Houses are portable and complete in themselves, requiring no wall to lean against.

Cooper's Egg Producer.

Keep your stock in perfect condition, and have abundance of eggs all the year round. YOUNG CHICKS thrive well on it, and become strong and good layers. LAYING HENS—improves condition, increases number of eggs, and promotes fertility. A WONDERFUL BONE AND SIZE PRODUCER. Keeps the plumage bright, gives protection against climatic changes.

PRICE 1s. 6d., post free. Full directions with each tin.

POULTRY—*continued*.

Nos. 117 and 118 are unsurpassed. For small runs, or where only one or two broods of chickens are required, our sitting-box, No. 121, is constructed. The bottom is hollowed in order that the natural shape of the nest may be preserved. It is made of fine meshed galvanised wire netting, proof against rats.

Our range of hatching-boxes and runs, No. 126, is most useful in preventing the hens straying when off the nest for feeding. The tops of the runs are hinged to open, enabling food to be put in, or the hen easily caught. A little fine hay should be put in the nest, and patted down with the hand. The best time to sit a hen is at dusk. She is less likely to be wild, or dash off the nest then. The number of eggs must depend on the size of the hen and the time of year. In cold weather it is as well not to give more eggs than the hen can comfortably cover. The number can be varied from nine to fifteen.

Before the eggs are given to the hen the nest must be well dusted with an insect powder. This helps to keep her free from insect vermin. The eggs can be placed one or two at a time in the nest, just in front of the hen, so that she can see them. She will then tuck them underneath her, one by one, with her beak. The hen need not be taken off the eggs on the first day. If she does not come off to feed on the second day, when the lid of the hatching-box is dropped, she must be gently lifted out, care being taken not to remove any of the eggs with her. From ten to twenty minutes is the time she should be absent, according to the weather. If the hen has not gone on the eggs again of her own accord, she must quietly be induced to do so.

The period of incubation is twenty-one days. The best food for sitting hens is either maize, wheat, or barley, and fresh, clean water. Some dry ashes or sand must be provided near the nest-box, in which the hen can have a dust-bath after feeding. The ashes should have some of our Disinfectas mixed with them.

TESTING THE EGGS.—If several hens commence to sit on the same day, it is advantageous to test the eggs, so that any unfertiles can be removed. To test the eggs, each egg should be taken from under the hen and placed in one of our egg-testers. An unfertile egg will appear clear, as if just laid. One containing a chicken will show a circular spot floating at the top of the egg when held sideways, the top being surrounded by a clouded substance, showing blood vessels. And an addled egg looks turgid and darkish, with no sign of blood vessels. Some experienced poultry-keepers can correctly test the eggs when they have been incubated four days; but a beginner had better not attempt testing before eight days. The unfertile eggs can be removed and used for cooking pur-

Poultry House with Covered Run.

No. 100.

A strongly-built serviceable structure, constructed of good sound tongued and grooved matching, weatherboard roof. The Run is covered at sides and front with galvanised wirenetting, the bottom part being boarded up, thus excluding draughts. Constructed in sections in readiness for erection. All outside woodwork painted in good oil-colour. Carefully packed on rail at the following respective prices :—

	£	s.	d.
12ft. by 4ft. by 6ft. high	3	5	0
12ft. by 6ft. by 7ft. high	4	0	0

Poultry House and Covered Run.

This is a compact House for a few birds; thoroughly well made. It has a raised floor and ladder, a door at back, and hinged flap at side for collecting eggs; weather-boarded roof over House and Run, painted one coat outside.

No. 101.

Fitted complete with Nest-boxes and Perches. Carefully packed on rail at the following prices :—

Long. ft.		Wide. ft. in.		Height to Eaves. ft. in.		£	s.	d.
7	......	3 0	......	4 0	......	2	10	0
9	......	3 6	......	4 6	......	3	0	0
12	......	4 0	......	5 0	......	3	10	0

Sprinkle the Sleeping Chamber and Run daily with **Cooper's Disinfectas.**

66

POULTRY—*continued.*

poses. When they have been taken away there will probably not be enough eggs remaining to employ all the hens. The surplus hens can then be put in a coop, and broken of their desire to sit.

THE CHICKENS.—On the nineteenth or twentieth day after sitting commenced, the eggs, if all has gone well, will begin to chip, and the young birds can be heard. After they are out of the shell the chicks will not require food for twenty-four hours. The hand can be put gently under the hen to investigate. If some of the eggs are still unhatched, yet are chipped and contain live chicks, and if the hen is restless, the young birds should be taken away in a basket containing some warm flannel, and placed near a fire. These can be returned to the hen when the remaining chicks are hatched out. The hen should have a feed of grain while she is on the nest. The next step is to put her in a coop facing south, and when she has settled down the chicks can be given her. We make a variety of excellent coops suitable for all breeds of chickens. There is the Safety Chicken Coop, made in two patterns, of which we sell many thousands, No. 120, very strong and serviceable, with fitted shutter to be used as a shelter from rain, wind, and hot sun; and No. 122, fitted with sliding shutter, with handles to the shutter, enabling it to be used from either right or left side.

A most useful form of coop, where there is plenty of space, is our coop and run on wheels, No. 134. This can be moved from place to place, and, having a floor, is vermin-proof. We make chicken coops of many descriptions with fitted runs; some with boarded roofs to the runs, with the tops hinged to lift up; others with wire netting that is sparrow- and rat-proof.

Many different ways of feeding young chickens are advocated. The old method, and one by which millions of chicks have been reared, is to give chopped-up hard-boiled egg and breadcrumbs for the first three days at least five times a day, followed by some chicken groats in the evening. At the end of three days the egg food is discontinued. The chicks then have equal parts of ground oats and middlings, mixed crumbly with warm water, with a feed of bruised wheat in the evening. If there is no access to grass they must have some finely-chopped lettuce, dandelion, or onions.

The method followed by some people is to give egg and breadcrumbs only for one day; then to give nothing but dry food for a month. Various mixtures of grain are used for the dry food. The Board of Agriculture has issued a leaflet suggesting that for the first eight days a combination of canary seed, millet, finely-cracked green peas, and hemp seed is the correct thing. This is to be followed by a mixture composed of eight different

Double Improved Fowl House and Run.

No. 102.

This is a Span-Roof Poultry House, with partition through centre, thus forming two complete Houses; each House has raised floor, which forms a dry run underneath; fitted with nests, perches, ladders, and flap for access to eggs. The runs are composed of wood framing covered with galvanised wire-netting at sides, ends, and top; each being fitted complete with gate. Constructed in sections in readiness for erection, and securely packed on rail at the following respective prices:—

Total Size		Height at Ridge.	Height at Eaves.			
Length. ft.	Width. ft.	ft. in.	ft. in.	£	s.	d.
6	6	6 0	4 0	2	10	0
6	8	7 0	4 6	3	15	0
7	10	7 6	4 6	4	5	0
8	12	9 0	5 0	5	0	0

If outside woodwork painted with our Patent Rot-Proof Composition, 10 per cent. extra.

Cooper's Disinfectas.

Cheap, clean, and healthy. Sprinkle a little in Poultry House daily. Nothing to equal it for keeping Poultry in good health. Try it. Per sack (2-bushel), 2s. 6d., sack included; 10 for 22s. 6d.

Maltby, near Rotherham.

W. COOPER, ESQ.

"DEAR SIR,—I was advised this morning that the Poultry House was at the station. This is the third Poultry House I have had from you, and I beg leave to say I am very much pleased with them. Should I require anything for the future, I shall be very pleased to give you the order.—Yours faithfully,   THOS. INNOCENT."

POULTRY—*continued*.

items. When the chicks are a month old they are gradually to be taught to eat soft food.

There is little doubt that the dry food method prevents diarrhœa, often a trouble with chicks. The dry food can be bought ready for use at most corn dealers. A good supply of grit must be within reach of the chicks, such as road scrapings or fine gravel, or coal ashes. The food for the chickens should not be thrown on the ground to be trampled on and made dirty. It should be given in our feeding troughs. These are made of zinc, with a guard to prevent the little birds standing on the food. The guard is removable for cleaning. The advisability of supplying water for the young chickens to drink has been questioned. It has been stated that water induces gapes, diarrhœa, and other ailments. But the chicks love it, and if dry food is used it is essential that water be given. Our drinking fountains for chicks always maintain a fresh supply of water, and can be easily filled and cleaned.

ARTIFICIAL INCUBATION.—Where there are a fair number of fowls, and chicken rearing is carried on, artificial incubation is of great assistance. The advantages of this form of hatching are many. The difficulty in obtaining broody hens early in the season; the trouble of taking the hens off the nest daily, and seeing that they go on again; the risk of broken eggs, and of trampled on chickens; these, and many other annoyances, are avoided by using incubators.

Our Peripage patent incubator has been before the public for years. It continues to make friends wherever used. It is absolutely reliable, is simple to work, will hatch every possible egg, and is absurdly cheap. It has received the highest awards in incubator competitions, it is economical in use, and will last for years. Full and easily understood instructions are sent with each machine. It is important that the incubator be set quite level. A suitable place to locate it is a cellar, if fairly dry and ventilated; or any ordinary room will do, if in a quiet place, where there will be no jars or banging of doors, no draught, and if the floor is firm.

The eggs to be incubated must not be more than a week old. The machine must be started two or three days before the eggs are put in, in order that it may be seen how to maintain the desired temperature. And if the first batch of eggs does not hatch as well as could be wished, the fault will not be in the machine, but in the operator, who has probably not followed the directions correctly.

ARTIFICIAL REARING.—When the chicks have been hatched in an incubator they are usually reared in a foster-mother. Our Peripage patent hot-water rearer, or foster-mother, is very popular. It is constructed for indoor or outdoor

The "Gem" Poultry House.

No. 103

This is a double House, constructed to economise space, and admit of two varieties being kept apart. Each division is 6ft. by 4ft., and the floor is raised 2ft. from the ground, with ladders connecting, as represented in the illustration. It is well lighted and fitted. The eggs are collected from outside by raising a hinged flap provided for the purpose. The house is made of well-seasoned red deal boards, each being tongued and grooved, and put together in sections for screwing together; oil painted outside. Carefully packed on rail.

8ft. long, 6ft. wide, 6ft. high to eaves, 7ft. 6in. to ridge, £3 5s. Runs 6ft. long, complete for this house, 30s. extra. Making two Houses and Runs. Complete for £4 15s.

Cooper's Disinfectas.

Cheap, clean and healthy. There is nothing better to keep Poultry Houses sweet, and Stock in good condition. Per Sack, (2-bushel), 2s. 6d.

Drinking Fountains.

FOR YOUNG CHICKS.

Strong, well made of Zinc. Last a lifetime.

Always maintains a fresh supply of clean water, and can be easily filled.

PRICE, 1s. 6d.

use all the year round. It is airy in summer, yet will keep the chicks warm in the coldest weather. It is weather-proof, and well and strongly made, and there are no corners for the chicks to be crushed in.

As soon as the chickens are settled in the rearer some egg food should be given them. They can be fed in all respects in the same manner as the chicks reared under a hen. Dry food is more useful in the rearer than when a hen is bringing up the chicks. It can be sprinkled in the dry earth, or other litter, to encourage the youngsters to scratch; and this can be done without the grain being consumed at once by the hen. Green food is even more necessary to artificially hatched chicks than to others. The meals must be given at regular intervals. An important matter is not to overcrowd the foster-mother, or to attempt to use a smaller size than will hold the chickens comfortably as they grow.

The usual temperature to begin with in rearers is 90deg. By the end of a week this is reduced to 80deg, and gradually to 70deg. But these temperatures will depend a good deal on the time of the year and the outside atmosphere. The best way to tell if the temperature is as it should be is to notice the behaviour of the chickens. If they are quiet and scattered over the floor of the sleeping chamber, things are going well. But if they are crowding towards the hottest part and are restless and make a noise, more heat is required. If the temperature is too high some of the little birds will be panting and looking exhausted.

After the chickens have left their mother, or have done with the rearer, they must not be allowed to perch too soon. Crooked breast-bones are considered to be caused by the young birds perching when young. Our cockerel houses are very useful as sleeping places for chickens until they are old enough to roost with the older birds.

TABLE POULTRY.—When the chickens are between three and four months old is a good age to commence to prepare them for the table. There are many breeds suitable for the table and for fattening. The Dorking is unequalled; the Orpingtons are good, and so also are Houdans, Plymouth Rocks, Faverolles, Game, Indian Game, and Wyandottes. All these fowls, and their crosses, are worth fattening when they are intended for killing. The term "fatted" does not mean loaded with fat; only that the quality of the flesh is to be improved and made tender, and the quantity of the meat increased.

The usual method adopted is to place the fowls in a fattening pen. For this purpose we make a most convenient pen, No. 147, to hold either four or six fowls. The floor is of bars, under which is a drawer into which the droppings fall.

Chicken House and Run.

Suitable also for Bantams, Rabbits, &c.

No. 104.

This House and Run is well adapted for chickens, bantams, rabbits, &c., and is vermin and cat proof. It is soundly constructed of good sound timbers, and has raised floor about 12in. from the ground. The roof of house is hinged, thus affording easy access inside.

The Run is constructed in sections, the upper part being covered with galvanised wire netting, and is supplied complete.

Woodwork of House and Run painted outside.

All complete in sections in readiness for erection at the following respective prices :—

House Length. ft.	Back to Front. ft.	Height of Front. ft.	Length of Run. ft.	£ s. d.
2	2	3	4	1 5 0
3	2	3	6	1 10 0
4	2	3	6	1 15 0

Cooper's Disinfectas.

For Poultry Houses and Runs, Kennels, Rabbit Hutches, Stables, &c. Clean, cheap, and healthy. Per sack (2-bushel), 2s. 6d.; 10 for 22s. 6d. Sacks included.

Hoolewood Cottage, Hind Head, Haslemere.
"Messrs. Cooper,—I have had one of your Chicken Houses for eight years, and I am most thoroughly satisfied with the wear of it.—Yours, &c.,
G. J. Williams."

New Park, Messing Heath, Kelvedon, Essex.
"Sir,—The Coops and Runs duly came to hand forthwith, and I am obliged. We find them satisfactory and useful.—Yours faithfully,
H. B. Looker."

POULTRY—*continued*.

The drawer can be taken out for cleaning as often as required. The birds are put in and taken out at the top, which is hinged. A feeding trough runs along the front of the pen.

The food consists of ground oats, barley meal, or maize meal. Ground oats mixed with skim milk give the best results. The meal is given in a semi-fluid state for the first week, placed in the trough. At the end of a week the meal is made thicker, and some beef or mutton fat is added. Fat helps to finish the birds off, and gives tenderness to the flesh. No whole grain is necessary, though some fatteners give boiled barley as the last feed of the day. Three meals a day are generally given. Some grit is placed in a separate vessel. Boiled nettles, or other green food, are allowed three times a week.

The process does not take so long in the spring as later in the year; but in three weeks the chickens ought to be ready for eating. Some chickens will not fatten at all. If a bird declines to feed at first, it is turned out of the pen for a day, and then tried again.

KILLING.—Fowls should be left for twenty-four hours without food before they are killed. If any food remains undigested in the crop, the whole body quickly decomposes. The most humane way to kill a fowl is to wring the neck. This is the method employed by poulterers. If possible it is advisable to have a practical illustration, although it is not difficult. The operation is performed by placing the bird across the knees, breast downwards, with the head and neck hanging over. The head of the fowl is taken in the right hand, the legs in the left. The neck is then quickly extended, and the head jerked back with some force. By this means the neck should be dislocated just below the junction with the head. If it is found impossible to dislocate the neck, a painless way of killing the fowl is to tie the legs, and stick it with a small and sharp knife in the jugular vein behind the ear.

The feathers come out more easily if the plucking is done while the bird is warm. When this is finished—the short quills as well as the feathers having been removed—the fowl is ready for "shaping." There are several methods of shaping. That adopted with the celebrated Surrey fowls is to tie the legs loosely together, and place the birds in the shaping trough, breast downwards, with the head and neck hanging over the front. The shaping troughs are made like shelves, about 15in. apart. The shelves are sloped so as to be 1in. lower at the back; they are 6in. wide. The fowls are placed tightly together in the shelves, the sterns pressed well back. At the end of six hours they look more compact and meaty.

PRIZE STOCK.—Many amateurs who keep pure bred fowls are anxious to breed some chickens that are fit for prize com-

Portable Bantam House and Run.

Suitable also for Chickens, Rabbits, Dogs, &c.

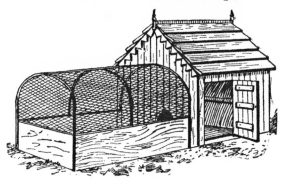

No. 105.

This is a neat design, and the quantity of purposes it can be utilised for commends it as a most useful article. It is constructed of good sound tongued and grooved matching, and is fitted with ornamental barge boards, loose floor, door in one side, complete with lock.

The Run is covered with galvanised wire netting. Perches and nests are included if for bantams or chickens; a partition included if for dogs, thus excluding draught; a spline floor and wire netting bottom for Run, if for rabbits. Complete in sections, in perfect readiness for erection, and packed on rail, at the following respective prices :—

Length. ft.	Width. ft. in.	Length of Run. ft.	£ s. d.
2	2 6	4	1 10 0
3	3 6	6	2 0 0
4	4 6	8	3 0 0

Sprinkle a little **Disinfectas** in your house Daily.

2s. 6d. per Sack (2-bushel).

Roofing Felt.

Patent Asphaltic Rolls, 25yd. long by 32in. wide.,
3s. 6d. per Roll. Better quality, 4s. 6d.

Nails for fixing Felt, in boxes of 250, 6d. ; 500, 1s.

POULTRY—*continued*.

petition. Not only is it a most interesting and pleasing pursuit, but if the birds are successful a greater value is attached to their eggs and to their progeny. When commencing the novice must first learn thoroughly the points of the breed he selects. Then he must make himself acquainted with a few of the general principles of breeding, which the experience of fanciers has proved to be correct.

A fact to be specially noted is that while the quality of a hen only affects her own chickens, the quality of the male bird affects the chickens from every hen in the same pen with him. In breeding for size it is necessary that the hen should be large, as in this respect the influence of the mother predominates. The hen also has most influence over the general structure and shape, though this does not affect the cockerels as much as the pullets. The chickens of each sex have a tendency to inherit the properties of the ancestors of that sex. It is therefore important to know how the stock birds have been bred.

With regard to external points, such as colour or comb, the male parent has usually the greatest influence. It would be of little use to breed from a cock bird having an imperfect comb, as many of his progeny would probably be defective in that point.

If the stock is sound and healthy it will be found advantageous, and, indeed, necessary, to inbreed to some extent. However good the stock birds may be, unless they are related in some measure, the probability is that their chickens will not be as handsome as their parents. So there need be no hesitation in mating the father with his own daughters, or cockerels to their mother. Fertility in the offspring will not be affected, yet good looks will be improved. As the beginner gains experience he will find other rules and principles to guide him in producing exhibition birds.

EXHIBITING.—It is a good thing for a beginner, when he thinks he has bred a high-class bird, to send it to a show where he can have the opinion of a judge, and be able to compare his fowl with others. He must not send a bird that has any prominent fault. However good it may be in other respects, it is not likely to win. About three weeks before a show the fowl should be specially attended to. Hens or pullets must be kept apart from the male, or the plumage will be damaged. A cock or cockerel should be separated from the hens for at least a fortnight. If he is allowed a couple of hens with him for two or three days before the show, it will brighten him up and make him look lively and vigorous.

Be careful to give the bird shelter from cold winds and rain. The diet can be altered somewhat. The morning feed can be cooked meal and bran, with which some linseed is occasionally

76

POULTRY—*continued.*

mixed. At noon some cooked meat and chopped onions, cabbage, or other vegetables; and at night whole grain—either good wheat, oats, or maize. Now and then a little chopped-up raw meat will do good. Some of the sulphate of iron tonic will help to redden the comb and face. Grit must be within reach. Game and other hard-feathered birds are better for a handful or two of maple peas daily.

Some practice is required to wash a fowl well; but this is only necessary with light or white plumaged birds. The head, face, feet, and legs want attention. The feet and legs must be cleaned with a damp cloth or sponge. The scales on the legs must be scrubbed with a small nailbrush, the head and face gently brushed with a soft toothbrush that is first rubbed on a piece of soap. When this has been done, the lather is removed with a sponge damped with warm water. The face and head are then rubbed with the sponge, moistened with a mixture of oil and glycerine. Any superfluous oil must be carefully removed. Broken or bent small feathers should be taken away. The whole body must afterwards be rubbed over with a silk handkerchief.

GENERAL HINTS.—When the hens are laying freely in the spring and summer, and prices are at their lowest, it is sometimes advisable to preserve eggs for use in the following winter. The most successful method is to preserve them in water-glass. This can be bought from many chemists and grocers. The mode of using is first to boil the water so as to destroy all germs, and then allow it to cool. Next, add by measure one part of water-glass to ten parts of water, and partly fill the vessels in which the eggs are to be preserved. Put the eggs into the liquid the day after they are collected, washing clean any that are dirty. The topmost layer of eggs in the jar, or other vessel that is used, must be well covered by the liquid. The water must be cooled to the temperature of the air before the water-glass is mixed with it.

The oldest method used, and one that is largely in vogue all over the kingdom, is treating the eggs with lime-water. A pint of unslaked lime is added to a gallon of water. This is boiled, then well stirred, and when cold the clear water is poured into earthenware jars, into which the eggs are packed in layers. The jars are covered over and put in a cool place. A little fresh water is added from time to time, so that all the eggs are under water.

Brown eggs are as common nowadays as white eggs, yet the supposed superiority of the former is still believed in; so much so, that in some neighbourhoods brown eggs sell more readily and realise slightly higher prices than the others. It is difficult to conceive how the colour of the shell can possibly affect

Portable Poultry House.

WITH CURVED ROOF.

No. 107.

A very neat design, and well made. The House is constructed of good, sound, tongued and grooved matching; the roof of curved galvanised corrugated iron sheets; complete with nests, perches, ladder, and flap for access to eggs. It has a raised floor, thus affording a dry shelter underneath. The run is covered with galvanised wire netting, and is fitted complete with gate; all outside woodwork painted one good coat of oil-colour, and inside whitewashed. Constructed in sections in readiness for erection, and securely packed on rail at the following prices :—

Size. Sizes over all of Houses and Runs.				£	s.	d.
1. 10ft. by 4ft., 6ft. high to ridge	..	..	..	3	15	0
2. 12ft. by 4ft., 6ft. ,, .,	..	..	..	4	5	0
3, 16ft. by 4ft., 6ft. ,, ,,	..	...	..	5	0	0

Make your Nests with Cooper's Disinfectas.

Better than Hay or Straw. Cheap, Clean, Healthy. Try it. Per Sack, 2s. 6d. (2-bushel), sack included; 10 for 22s. 6d.

Poultry—*continued*.

the quality of the contents. This is governed by the nature of the food eaten by the hen, and by the way the hen is managed. It is not unusual for artificial means to be employed to turn white eggs brown. The colouring of eggs artificially is not a recent discovery. The shells, after all, are not eaten by human beings. The poultry-keeper, therefore, if he prefers brown shells, can satisfy his taste by keeping a breed such as the Minorca, which lays large white eggs, and staining some of the eggs any shade of brown that he wishes, by dipping them in tea or coffee, or a little permanganate of potash.

One of the most important matters in successful poultry keeping is never to overfeed the fowls; always to stop giving food directly they begin to hesitate and cease eating eagerly. And another most important detail is never to overcrowd. These are the two chief stumbling-blocks of amateurs. More eggs will be laid by six hens with space enough, than by two dozen crowded and cramped.

Regular feeding is of much importance. Fowls will not thrive if they have no food for a number of hours, and then a double quantity to make it up. Grain should never be left lying about on the ground. That is a sure sign that the fowls are overfed, besides the fact that profit is diminished by the waste of food. The feed of warm meal in the morning in cold weather is one of the greatest incentives to winter laying, though it is often neglected, and cold, hard grain given instead.

Broody hens, valuable as they are in the beginning of the year, are a great nuisance in the summer. When they are not wanted for hatching purposes, they should be taken off the nest directly they are seen there after the fowls have gone to roost, and put in a coop in a light place. If kept in this, and given a moderate supply of grain, some green food, and water, they will get over their broodiness in four or five days, and shortly commence to lay again.

While the hen is sitting it sometimes happens that she remains off the nest until the eggs are cold. It does not follow as a matter of course that in such circumstances the eggs will not hatch. There have been many accounts of satisfactory hatches when the hen has been allowed to continue sitting on the chilled eggs. Another matter of importance is that of assisting the chick when it cannot make its way out of the shell. If the egg is chipped and the beak can be seen, help can be given by gently picking away the shell at the chipped end with the finger-nail. Care must be taken to avoid drawing blood. After a small quantity of the shell has been removed the egg must be put back under the hen. In three or four hours' time, if it has not hatched out, the process can be repeated. After that the bird will generally be found free from the shell—or dead.

Span-Roof Poultry House on Wheels.

This House is substantially constructed of good, sound tongued and grooved matching; complete with floor, nests, perches, and ladder. It is mounted on four strong wheels. All outside woodwork painted with our Patent Rot-Proof Composition.

No. 108.

PRICES, 6ft. by 4ft., £3; 6ft. by 5ft., £3 10s.

Lean-to Poultry House with Covered Run.

This is a neat structure, and made of the best tongued, grooved, and beaded boards; with shelter underneath. Roof, feather-edge boards. Door complete, with lock. The run is covered with netting, and is complete with gate and lock to same. Carefully packed on rail at the following prices:—

No. 109.

Length of House. ft.	Width of House and Run. ft.	Length of House and Run. ft.	Height in Front. ft. in.	£ s. d.
4	6	12	4 6	3 0 0
6	6	18	4 6	4 5 0
8	6	24	4 6	5 10 0

80

POULTRY—*continued.*

THE VARIOUS BREEDS.

ANCONAS.—Free layers of white eggs, of not large size. There are both single and rosecombed Anconas, black in plumage, with each feather tipped with white. They mature quickly, are rather wild, and are non-sitters.

ANDALUSIANS.—Very handsome, slaty-blue plumaged fowls, laying very large white eggs. Are suitable for the small poultry-keeper, or for a free range. The chickens do not come very true to colour. Non-sitters.

ASEELS.—An old breed, celebrated for its indomitable courage. It is heavier for its apparent size than any other fowl. The hen is a poor layer, and very quarrelsome. Aseels are not generally kept. Sitters.

BANTAMS.—The attractiveness of these little fowls consists more in their beauty than in any economic value. Most of the large breeds of fowl are reproduced in miniature amongst the Bantams. The Sebright is one of the most beautiful. It is bred

SEBRIGHT BANTAM.   **BRAHMA.**   COCHIN.

in two varieties, Gold and Silver. The plumage of the Gold is of a golden bay throughout, each feather evenly laced all round its edge with glossy green-black. That of the Silver is silvery-white, laced as in the Gold. The comb is rose, the tail, in both sexes, hen-shaped.

The Japanese Bantam is a most quaint little bird, with large head and immense tail, containing feathers sticking out in all directions. Most of the other Bantams are diminutive counterparts of the large fowls. The weight of the majority of the Bantams should be from 16oz. to 22oz.

Bantams are mostly hardy. They can be kept in health and comfort in very small runs, requiring but little food. Grain, such as wheat, buckwheat, dari, and now and then a little canary seed, and a few scraps from the house, cut up very small, so as not to soil the plumage, are all that is necessary. A little cut grass or green food must be given daily, and fresh water and grit supplied. Our Span-roof Bantam House and Run, No. 104, is unsurpassed for these birds.

Lean-to Poultry House, with Corn-Room and Run.

No. 112.

This House is substantially constructed of good, sound, tongued and grooved matchboard. It is provided with raised floor, and fitted complete with nests, perches, ladder, and ventilator; 2ft. partitioned off to form corn-room, which has door and lock complete to same. The roof is of feather-edge boards. The run is formed of wood framework covered with galvanised wire-netting, and is fitted complete with gate. All outside woodwork painted one coat of good oil-colour. In sections in readiness for erection. Securely packed on rail at the following respective prices:—

Length.	Back to Front.	Height at Back.	Height in Front.	Length of Run.			
ft.	ft. in.	ft. in.	ft. in.	ft.	£	s.	d.
6	3 6	5 6	4 6	6	3	15	0
9	5 0	7 0	6 0	8	4	10	0
12	5 6	8 0	7 0	12	6	0	0

Cooper's Disinfectas.

Make your Nests with **Cooper's Disinfectas,** and sprinkle some in House and Run daily to keep your Stock healthy. 2s. 6d. per Sack.

POULTRY—*continued.*

BRAHMAS.—Large, handsome, useful fowls, holding their own well in public esteem, notwithstanding the strong competition with more modern breeds. The Light and the Dark Brahmas should both weigh upwards of 12lb. for cock birds, and not less than 9lb. for hens. They are excellent winter layers of rich brown eggs. In the summer they are apt to often become broody. Their weight prevents flying, so that a low fence will confine them. They cross well with many other breeds, especially for table purposes.

COCHINS.—Unequalled for massive beauty. They, like the Brahmas, can be kept without any fear of their flying over a low fence. They are wonderfully placid and tame. The eggs are deep brown, and not very large. Cochins are good winter layers and energetic sitters.

CREVECŒURS.—Large black French fowls, with two horned, V-shaped comb, large crest, and face muffled. Large and square in body, breast-bone long and straight, and legs black or slate. The Crève lays a large white egg, and is a non-sitter. It stands high in estimation as a table fowl in France. It is considered rather delicate in our climate.

CREVECŒUR.   CAMPINE.   DORKING.

CAMPINES.—Non-sitting fowls, resembling single-combed Pencilled Hamburghs. They are bred in two colours, Gold and Silver. They are good layers of white eggs, and are tame and hardy.

DORKINGS.—These grand fowls, pre-eminently of English breed, are always general favourites. There are four varieties, the Coloured, the Silver-grey, the White, and the Cuckoo. No fowl is superior to the Dorking for the table, and it is used with the best results in crossing with almost every other breed for the production of chickens for eating purposes. The Coloured variety is the largest. Cocks have been exhibited over 14lb. in weight. Dorking hens lay good-sized white eggs, but there are many fowls that are better layers. The hens are first-rate sitters and mothers. Dorkings do not thrive in damp situations, nor in small runs.

New Improved Span-Roof Poultry House, with Extended Sides.

No. 113.

As will be seen by the illustration, this House is constructed to facilitate both cleanliness of the Nests and collecting the eggs without disturbing the Birds inside. It has a raised Floor with ladder; under this the Birds can find shade from sun and shelter from rain. The elevation of this House renders it suitable, with the addition of an Extended Top, for keeping Pigeons as well as Fowls. Strongly made, painted, and fitted with Nest-boxes and Perches. Carefully packed on rail at the following prices:

	£	s.	d.
House, 5ft. long, 5ft. wide	2	10	0
Run, 6ft. long	0	12	6
House, 6ft. long, 5ft. wide	3	0	0
Run, 7ft. long	0	17	6
House, 8ft. long, 6ft. wide	4	0	0
Run, 8ft. long	1	5	0

The above can be supplied with the top extended as a Pigeon House for which it is very suited, at an extra cost of 12s. 6d., 15s., and £1 respectively.

Cooper's Cramp Cure.

FOR YOUNG CHICKENS, FOWLS, &c.

Sold in Bottles. Price, 1s. 6d., post free. Full directions with each bottle.

POULTRY—*continued.*

FAVEROLLES.—One of the most useful fowls we have. Like most of the poultry that have come to us from France, the Faverolle is a fine table bird. It is very hardy, is a free layer of eggs that are mostly light brown, will stand confinement well, and is eminently suited both for the small poultry-keeper and for the man who has a large flock. The Faverolle has a single comb, a swollen throat, slight feathering on the leg, and five toes. It is a good sitter, but quickly broken of the desire.

GAME.—A celebrated race of fowls, bred for centuries for fighting. There are now two separate classes of Game, the Old English Game and the Modern Game. The principal colours are Black-breasted Reds, Brown-breasted Reds, Duckwings, and Piles. The Modern Game is bred with very long legs and thighs. They are splendid table birds, but not very prolific layers. They require a good range, and are not suited for small confined runs. They are good sitters.

HAMBURGHS.—An old and extremely beautiful breed. Free layers of white eggs, but the eggs being small the Hamburghs have receded in public favour. Of the several varieties —the Silver and Golden Spangled, the Silver and Golden Pencilled, and the Black—the Black is the hardiest, and lays the largest eggs. They are non-sitters.

GAME.   HOUDAN.   LA FLECHE.

HOUDANS.—Large birds, black and white in plumage, evenly mottled, with pinky-white legs and feet, and five toes. Houdans have a large crest, and whiskers and beard. The eggs are white and of good size; for table purposes this fowl has few superiors; it is hardy, matures quickly, stands confinement well, and can strongly be recommended to all poultry-keepers. The hens do not sit.

INDIAN GAME.—Valuable for table purposes owing to the large size and wide and deep breast. Crossed with the Dorking, it produces chickens that are the perfection of table poultry. The Indian Game is a poor layer, and the hens are good sitters and mothers, but very pugnacious.

LA FLECHE.—Another large black French fowl, excellent for the table, and a layer of large white eggs. It does not thrive in any but a dry situation.

85

Lean-to Fowl House with Covered Run.

No. 114.

This House is strongly constructed of good sound matching; the roof of both House and Run is of matchboarding covered with felt; the House is fitted complete with glazed window, nests, and perches, but no floor; the Run is formed of wood framing covered with galvanised wirenetting. All outside woodwork painted one coat of good oilcolour. In sections in readiness for erection, and securely packed on rail at the following respective prices :—

Length. ft.	Width. ft.	Height at Back. ft.	Height at Front. ft.	£ s. d.	Boarded Back extra. £ s. d.
8	4	6	4	2 10 0	0 5 0
10	5	7	5	3 10 0	0 7 6
12	5	7	5	4 0 0	0 7 6
12	6	8	5	5 0 0	0 10 0

To keep your Stock healthy, sprinkle a little of **Cooper's Disinfectas** daily in House and Run. 2s. 6d. per Sack.

Feeding Troughs.

FOR YOUNG CHICKS.

Strong, well made of zinc. Last a lifetime.
With removable guard for cleansing.
Price, 1s. 6d.

POULTRY—*continued.*

LANGSHANS.—Of the large breeds the Langshans are among the most valuable. There are two types, exhibited as Croad Langshans and Langshans. The Croad Langshan is much the stamp of the Langshan as originally imported by Major Croad in 1871. The Langshan is taller and more leggy. Both these breeds are black in plumage, with white skin. They are first-rate table birds, very hardy, splendid winter layers of good-sized eggs of various shades of brown, and they make a fine cross with the Minorca and many other breeds. The hens become broody, but are easily broken of their desire to sit. There is a Blue Langshan, which is increasing in popularity, and also a White variety, which at present is not in much request.

LANGSHAN. LEGHORN. MALAY. JUNGLE FOWL.

LEGHORNS.—There are six varieties of this particularly useful breed—the Brown, White, Pile, Duckwing, Buff, and Black. The White is a wonderful layer. In America it is largely kept. Instances are recorded of flocks of White Leghorns that have averaged 196 eggs per hen in the year. The Black Leghorn is a more recent variety, but is, if possible, more hardy and prolific than the White. The eggs are white and of medium size. Leghorns are non-sitters.

LINCOLNSHIRE BUFFS.—Made by crossing the Buff Cochin with the Dorking. It is hardy, much like a mongrel Cochin in appearance, lays brown eggs, and often becomes broody.

MALAYS.—The tallest member of the poultry-yard, some specimens standing 2ft. 6in. high. It is a good table bird, and a poor layer of brown eggs. The hens become broody.

MINORCAS.—One of the very best and most valuable of fowls. Black in colour, handsome, a layer of large white eggs, a small eater, adaptable either to a free range or a small run, it is no wonder that the Minorca is to be seen in all parts of the kingdom. They are most profitable fowls. Non-sitters.

ORPINGTONS.—There are several varieties of Orpington—the Black, Buff, White, Jubilee, and Spangled. The Black is in appearance much like a short, clean-legged Langshan. The Buff is a very popular fowl, good for the table, and a layer,

88

POULTRY—*continued.*

particularly in the winter, of good-sized brown eggs. It is rather too much inclined to become broody in warm weather. The White Orpington is an excellent fowl both for laying and the table. The Jubilee is of a mahogany colour, and the Spangled is black, speckled with white. All the Orpingtons are hardy, useful fowls.

PLYMOUTH ROCKS.—The Barred Plymouth Rock came from America, making its first public appearance at the Birmingham Show in 1873. It is a large cuckoo-coloured fowl, the cocks weighing from 9lb. to 12lb., is hardy, stands confinement well, and is a good layer of nice-sized brown eggs. The Buff Rock is a free layer, two hens of this variety having produced 216 and 206 eggs respectively in the Utility Poultry Club's twelve months laying competition. White Plymouth Rocks are particularly hardy, and good layers. And there is also a Black Plymouth Rock. All the varieties are very good table birds, and the hens become broody.

POLISH.

SCOTS DUMPY.

LA BRESSE.

REDCAPS.—An old breed, kept mostly in Derbyshire, Nottingham, and Yorkshire. It has a large, double comb. The plumage of the hens resembles that of the Golden Spangled Hamburgh and of the cock that of the Black-red Game. The hens are prolific layers of white eggs. The Redcap is an excellent table fowl, the weight of the male birds being over 7lb. Where there is a large range this fowl is very profitable; but in a confined space it is not to be recommended.

RHODE ISLAND REDS.—American fowls, known for a good many years. Not having been bred with any care the chickens did not come true. Recently a Rhode Island Red Club has been formed, and the breed has been considerably advertised. It somewhat resembles the Red Sussex, which many poultry-keepers consider a superior fowl.

SUSSEX.—A celebrated old breed of table fowl, for a time almost allowed to die out. The varieties are the Red, the Speckled, the Light, and the Brown. The chickens mature quickly, are high-class table birds, with white legs, are very hardy, and the hens are fair layers of white eggs. They are

90

POULTRY—*continued*.

good sitters, and inclined to be frequently broody in warm weather.

WYANDOTTES.—Most excellent fowls, considered by many people to be the most useful of all the breeds of poultry. There are numerous varieties—Silver, Golden, White, Buff, Partridge, Silver Pencilled, Columbian, Blue Laced, and Black. The White Wyandottes have proved their wonderful laying powers by winning the first prize in the competitions promoted by the Utility Poultry Club, not only for a period of twelve months, but for

WYANDOTTE.   HOLLANDAISE.   BLACK SPANISH.

shorter terms. They are very hardy, will thrive anywhere, either in confinement or on a free range, and are very good table fowls. The Silver, the Golden, the Partridge, and the Columbian are handsome birds, and all good for culinary purposes, and free layers of medium-sized, coloured eggs. The hens are good sitters, and easily broken of the desire to incubate.

SOME OTHER BREEDS.—There are other fowls not so often kept as the above. The Lakenfelder is a pretty fowl from Holland, white, with black hackle and tail. The Malines and the La Bresse are two French fowls, for which classes are provided at the Crystal Palace Show. The Courtes Pattes are

PHŒNIX.   YOKOHAMA.

extremely short-legged, black fowls, with single combs. The Black Sumatra Game is supported by a club, as is also the Yokohama, or Long-tailed Phœnix. Scots Dumpies and Scots Greys are hardy and useful fowls. Silkies are small, and of soft and

Span-Roof Poultry House with Run.

No. 121.

This House and Run is intended to be placed against a wall. The house is complete in itself, and the run less one side. The house is constructed of good sound materials, and is complete with nests, perches, and ladder. It has a raised floor, forming a dry run. The run is formed of wood frame hurdles, covered with galvanized wire-netting, including top, and is complete with gate. All outside woodwork painted one coat of good oil-colour. In sections, in readiness for erection, and securely packed on rail.

House, 6ft. from back to front, 4ft. wide, 7ft. high to ridge 5ft. high to eaves; Run, 12ft. by 6ft., 5ft. high £3 10s. Complete if required to be fixed independent of Wall, £4 including other side to Run.

Sprinkle a little of **Cooper's Disinfectas** daily in your Poultry Houses.

Cooper's Egg Producer.

Keep your stock in perfect condition, and have abundance of eggs all the year round. YOUNG CHICKS thrive well on it, and become strong and good layers. LAYING HENS—improves condition, increases number of eggs, and promotes fertility. A WONDERFUL BONE AND SIZE PRODUCER. Keeps the plumage bright; gives protection against climatic changes.

PRICE 1s. 6d., post free. Full directions with each tin.

POULTRY—*continued.*

silky plumage; useful for hatching and rearing Bantams and young Pheasants. And Spanish and Polish are old breeds seldom now seen, but formerly held in great esteem.

SOME USEFUL CROSSES.—Considering the number of hardy and free-laying pure breeds, it seems scarcely necessary to use cross-breeds. However, there is little doubt that a first cross between two pure breeds promotes strength and quick maturing. A favourite cross is that from a short-legged Dorking cock and a Light Brahma hen. The produce lay large eggs of various shades, and are fine table fowls. The Langshan crosses well with the Crèvecœur and the Houdan for table chickens, and with the Andalusian and the Minorca for fine free-laying, all-round birds. The Indian Game is used largely for crossing with the Dorking, the Houdan, the Faverolles, and the Buff Orpington. For laying purposes the Houdan-Leghorn,

SULTAN COCK.   SULTAN HEN.   SILKIE.

the Leghorn-Wyandotte, the Leghorn-Faverolles, and the Red-cap-Minorca are excellent.

Of all the breeds above mentioned, the amateur cannot do wrong if he keeps either White Wyandottes, Minorcas, Faverolles, White Orpingtons, Leghorns, or Columbian Wyandottes.

MOULTING.—Some fowls drop their feathers with little trouble. These generally turn out to be good winter layers. Those that are slow in moulting, and appear weak in health, are not likely to be of any use as layers during the ensuing winter. Non-sitting breeds moult rather more slowly than others. The fowls must have access to shelter, so as not to be exposed to wet when shedding their plumage.

Before they begin to moult it is advisable to let them get slightly below their usual condition. The quantity of food should be reduced and they should have plenty of green vegetables. To bring on the moult the fowls should be placed in a small, warm place, and fed only on a small amount of grain, such as wheat or oats. When the feathers fall freely the quantity may be gradually increased. To keep the hens laying

Span-Roof Poultry House with Large Run.

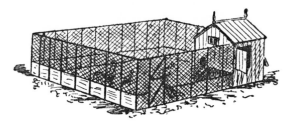

No. 122.

A well-finished Poultry House, constructed of good sound tongued, grooved, and beaded matching on good strong framework; it has a raised floor, forming a dry run underneath the house, and his fitted complete with nests and perches. The roof is formed of feather-edge boards. The run is constructed of strong wooden hurdles, covered with galvanised wire netting, and is complete with gate. All outside woodwork painted one good coat of oil colour; complete in sections in readiness for erection, and securely packed on rail.

Ground space covered by House and Run is 20ft. by 20ft., of which the House is 10ft. by 8ft., 9ft. 6in. to ridge, and 6ft. 6in. to eaves. Cash Price, £8 10s. 0d.

If outside Woodwork painted with our Patent Rot-Proof Composition, 10 per cent. extra.

Egg Transit Boxes.

Very light, but strongly made and well finished.

	s.	d.			s.	d.	
To hold 6 doz.,	7	0	each	To hold 18 doz.,	12	0	each.
„ 9 „	9	0	„	„ 24 „	14	0	„
„ 12 „	10	0	„				

With Brass Padlock, strong, two keys.

These Boxes are specially made for Railway Traffic and Wholesale Merchants for delivering eggs in vans, or otherwise. They will bear a great amount of rough usage, and they are so constructed that it is almost impossible to break the eggs.

POULTRY—*continued.*

as long as possible, the moult may be postponed by keeping the house where they roost cool and feeding as usual without any sudden change of diet. Cocks must be separated from hens when the moult is on, otherwise they will probably illtreat them.

DISEASES.—COLD—The symptoms are running from the eyes and nostrils, sometimes swelling of the face, and loss of appetite. Roup often follows. The cause is exposure to rain, cold winds, or draught. Keep the patient in a fairly warm place, and give eight drops of sweet spirit of nitre in a little milk twice a day. For food, some barley-meal mixed stiffly, and a little raw meat; with whole grain for supper.

COMB, DISEASES OF.—White comb is known by a scurfy appearance like flour, which often spreads over the head, sometimes with loss of feathers. It may be caused by insufficient green food, overcrowding, or dirty condition. Apply carbolised vaseline and give some Epsom salts—a good pinch put dry over the tongue every other day for ten days. Large-combed fowls are occasionally affected by hard frost, the comb first turning pale and then black. A remedy is to rub the comb with compound turpentine liniment.

CRAMP.—A complaint to which young chickens are liable, especially if they do not have access to loose earth in which to scratch. Our Cramp Cure is a sure remedy, particularly when the little birds are allowed some dry earth or sifted ashes to scratch and exercise in.

CROP BINDING is known by a distended crop from which nothing can pass out. The cause is irregular feeding and the fowl gorging itself and drinking a quantity of water; or the collection of food round a stone or a feather that the bird has swallowed. The contents of the crop must be gently worked about by the hand, and a teaspoonful of sweet oil poured down the throat. This should be done three or four times a day. If not successful, the crop must be opened and the contents removed, the crop being afterwards sewn up. The patient must be fed on soft food.

DIARRHŒA. — Induced by stale green food, sour soft food, sudden change of diet, &c. It may be stopped by feeding on rather drily mixed barley-meal, and boiled rice sprinkled with powdered chalk. Green food should be stopped until the fowl is well.

EGG-BOUND.—This is usually caused by an exceptionally large egg which the hen is unable to pass. She will visit the nest and come out without having laid and with drooping wings and tail depressed. The hen must be caught and held so that a teaspoonful of sweet oil can be poured into the vent, then returned to the nest. If the egg does not appear in half an

96

POULTRY—*continued*.

hour, the hen must be held with the vent over a jug of very hot water. This usually results in the passing of the egg.

EGG-EATING HENS.—If only one or two hens are known to have acquired this vice, it is advisable to kill them. If it has spread to all the hens, it may sometimes be stopped by removing the contents of one or two eggs and refilling them with mustard and snuff and placing them in the nest. Repeated daily for a week or so this may be successful.

FEATHER EATING.—The cause of this habit is not certain. It is supposed to be induced by insufficient green food, insect vermin, or want of animal food. When once the vice is thoroughly established it is incurable. The fowls that are being plucked should have the plumage saturated with Jeyes' Fluid, mixed with twice the quantity of water. Some flowers of sulphur should be added to the soft food, and twice a week enough Epsom salts to make the drinking water taste.

GAPES.—A very fatal complaint amongst chickens when between three and eight weeks old. It can be known by the little birds sneezing at first and afterwards by their gasping and "gaping" for breath. The cause is the presence in the windpipe of small red worms. Many preparations for the cure of gapes are advertised. A cure can sometimes be made by putting the affected chickens into a box, puffing smoke from a tobacco pipe into the box, and keeping the chickens in the box until they begin to stagger. Two or three applications of the smoke will be sufficient, on different days. A small piece of camphor—about the size of a tare—pushed down the throat will sometimes cure.

PARASITES.—These can be kept in check by sprinkling our Disinfectas in the house and run and by the free use of our Insect Powder.

ROUP.—When the running at the nostrils and eyes which occurs in an ordinary cold becomes thicker and smells offensively, the bird probably has roup. The sufferer must at once be isolated, as the disease will otherwise quickly spread. The face and nostrils must be bathed three or four times daily, and the mouth washed with a lotion made of a quarter of an ounce of sulphate of copper dissolved in a pint of water. In addition to this our Roup Pills must be given. The food should consist of barley-meal or oatmeal, mixed with milk, to which some minced raw meat is added. When recovering, our Egg Producer will be found valuable in restoring strength and vigour.

SOFT EGGS are caused by overfeeding, insufficient shell-forming material, or too stimulating a diet. Some Epsom salts should be added to the drinking water and the diet corrected.

Improved Range of Span-Roof Fowl Houses and Runs.

No. 124.

The above illustration shows a range of eight Houses and Runs, viz., four on each side; it has a passage-way 3ft. wide down the centre, by which attention to sanitary requirements is facilitated. The Houses are strongly constructed of good sound matching, the roofs being boarded and covered with felt; they have raised floors, thus affording a dry run for the fowls, and each House is fitted complete with nests, perches, and ladder. The Runs are formed of wood framing, covered with galvanised wire netting; each is fitted complete with gate. All outside woodwork painted with our Patent Rot-Proof Composition. Complete in sections, in perfect readiness for erection, and securely packed on rail. Size of each House, 6ft. by 5ft., 11ft. high to top of lantern, 6ft. high to eaves. Size of each Run, 10ft. by 6ft.; 6ft. high.

PRICE for eight Houses and Runs ... ... £30.

Proportionate prices for larger or smaller Ranges, on receipt of full particulars.

Egg Tester.

Invaluable for ascertaining the exact state of freshness of Eggs, which is of such vital importance when setting. The progress made by the germ during incubation is also at once apparent.

INSTRUCTIONS FOR USE.—Put the egg in the Tester, above the oval silvered glass, and look through the small telescopic orifice. The egg is fresh and of prime quality when clear and almost transparent. If it looks opaque, and the contents appear thick or misty, the egg is addled, and therefore useless.

PRICE, 9d., Post Free.

Span-Roof Poultry House.

No. 125.

This is a strongly-built, commodious structure, and is adaptable alike for a large quantity of turkeys, geese, or fowls; it is

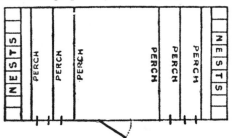

PLAN OF INTERIOR.

constructed of good, sound tongued, grooved, and beaded matching, on good strong framing; the roof is of tongued, grooved boards, covered with felt; all outside woodwork painted with our Patent Rot-Proof Composition and whitewashed inside; complete with nest and perches, but no floor. In sections in perfect readiness for erection and securely packed on rail, at the following respective prices :—

Length.	Width.	Height to Ridge.	Height to Eaves.			
ft.	ft.	ft. in.	ft. in.	£	s.	d.
20	10	9 6	6 6	15	0	0
25	12	11 0	7 0	17	10	0

TO KEEP YOUR STOCK HEALTHY,

Make your Nests with **Cooper's Disinfectas,** and sprinkle some about House daily.

Per Sack (2-bushel), 2s. 6d.; 10 for 22s. 6d.

Range of Hatching Boxes and Runs

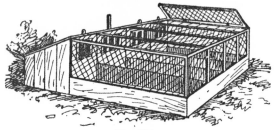

No. 126.

Constructed of good sound tongued and grooved matching roof weather-boards; runs of wire netting, boarded at bottom, tops hinged to open; all woodwork painted outside in good oil colour.

PRICES:

				£	s.	d.
2 Boxes and Runs complete	...	...	0	17	6
4 ,, ,, ,,	...	...	1	5	0
6 ,, ,, ,,	...	...	1	15	0

Curved-Roof Poultry House with Run

This is a neat design, and is constructed of good sound tongued and grooved matching; fitted complete with nests, perches, and ladder; the roof is of galvanised corrugated iron sheets; it has a flap at side for easy access to the eggs; the Run is formed of wood framing covered with galvanised wire-netting, and is complete with gate. All outside woodwork painted one coat good oil-colour. In sections in readiness for erection, securely packed on rail. House, 5ft. by 5ft., 5ft. high to eaves; Run, 6ft. by 5ft.

No. 127.

PRICE
£3 15s.

100

Hatching and Nest Box.

Thousands sold every season.

No. 128.

This is an improved Sitting-box for Hens. The bottom, which is made of fine mesh galvanised netting, is hollowed so as to preserve the shape of the nest, and to keep the eggs from being kicked away from the hen. The bottom is also proof against rats. Thoroughly well made of seasoned match-boards. It is 15in. high, 16in. wide, 13in. deep.

PRICES ... One-Nest Box, 2s. 3d.; 12, 25s.; 100, £9.

Egg Tester.

Invaluable for ascertaining the exact state of the freshness of Eggs which is of such vital importance when setting. The progress made by the germ during incubation is also at once apparent.

INSTRUCTIONS FOR USE.—Put the egg in the Tester, above the oval silvered glass, and look through the small telescopic orifice. The egg is **fresh** and of **prime quality** when **clear and almost transparent.** If it looks **opaque**, and the contents appear **thick** or **misty**, the egg is addled, and therefore useless.

PRICE 9d., post free.

102

The Safety Chicken Coop.

We sell on an average 5,000 of these every season.

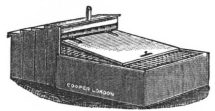

No. 131.

This is a strongly-made and serviceable Coop; matchboard sides and weather-boarded roof. It is fitted with a shutter that can be used either to shade from the sun or to shut off cold winds and beating rain. It is also secure against the attacks of predatory vermin. Complete.

Size: 2ft. wide, 1ft. 10in. deep, 1ft. 10in. high at front, 1ft. high at back, 3s. each, 33s. per doz., £12 10s. per 100.

3ft Movable Wire Run, 2s. each extra, 21s. per doz.

SPRINKLE COOPER'S DISINFECTAS in RUNS DAILY.

"WONDERFUL VALUE."

Linwood, Mossley Hill, Liverpool.

"SIR,—A line to acknowledge receipt of Chicken Coop, with which I am very well satisfied. They are truly wonderful value.

Thanking you for your prompt execution of order.   Yours truly,

(Signed) THOS. WILLIAMS."

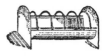

Feeding Troughs.

FOR YOUNG CHICKS.

Strong, well made of zinc.   Last a lifetime.
With removable guard for cleansing.

PRICE ...   ...   1s. 6d.

Drinking Fountains.

FOR YOUNG CHICKS.

Strong, well made of zinc.   Last a lifetime.

Always maintains a fresh supply of clean water, and can be easily filled.

PRICE ...   .   1s. 6d.

Chicken Coop with Sliding Shutter.

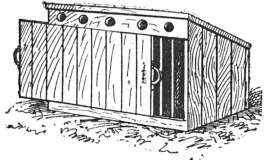

No. 132.

This Coop has an advantage over the ordinary coop with hinged shutter in front, since it is fitted with a sliding shutter; it can be closed to within a quarter of an inch and still admit the rays of the sun the full depth of the aperture; the shutter is fitted with handles, and can be used from either right or left end. The Coop is constructed of good sound tongued and grooved matching; the roof, which is hinged, being of weather boards. Painted outside one coat.

PRICE (complete) ... ... 10s.

"Safety" Chicken Coop.

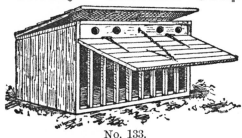

No. 133.

Sides and ends constructed of good tongued and grooved matching, and roof—which is hinged to lift up—of weather boards; the front shutter is also hinged and is fitted with a galvanised chain, thus allowing of shuttering the coop to any degree as may be desired; painted one coat.

PRICE ... ... 6s. each.

104

Pheasant or Chicken Coop and Run.

No. 134.

This Coop and Run is rat and vermin proof, since the chicks cannot stray from the Coop, and have at the same time the

Showing Coop as Closed at night.

advantages of the Run; it is provided with a shutter in front which serves the purposes of a shelter during the day and for closing up the Coop at night. The tops are hinged, thus affording access to both Coop and Run; the Shelter and Run are detachable from the Coop, as shown in illustration. The upper part of Run is formed of galvanised wire netting; all woodwork painted one coat outside.

Coop and Shelter, 3ft. 6in. long, 2ft. wide, 2ft. high; Run, 3ft. long.

PRICE (complete) ... ... 17s. 6d.

Feeding Troughs.

FOR YOUNG CHICKS.

Strong, well made of zinc. Last a lifetime.
With removable guard for cleansing.

PRICE 1s. 6d.

Improved Coop and Run.

Cat, Rat, and Sparrow Proof.

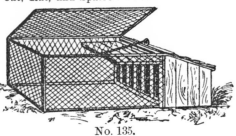

Constructed of good sound timbers, fitted with shutter which serves as a shade during the day and for closing up Coop at night; the shutter being provided with a chain admits of the Coop being shaded to any extent as may be desired; there is also a sliding rod to the Coop to admit of the hen being let into run when desired, and the top hinged, thus affording easy access inside.

No. 135.

The Run is covered with galvanised wire netting, the top being hinged as shown in illustration.

Coop, 2ft. square; Run, 3ft. long, 2ft. high.

PRICE ... ... 15s.

The Safety Chicken Coop and Run.

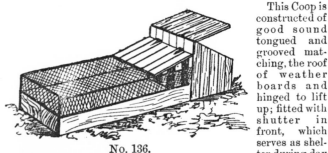

This Coop is constructed of good sound tongued and grooved matching, the roof of weather boards and hinged to lift up; fitted with shutter in front, which serves as shelter during day and for closing the Coop up at night; the Run is formed with boarded base, and is covered with galvanised wire netting; all outside woodwork painted one coat.

No. 136.

Coop, 2ft. by 2ft.; Run, 3ft. long by 1ft. high.

PRICE ... ... 16s.

Chicken Coop with Covered Run.

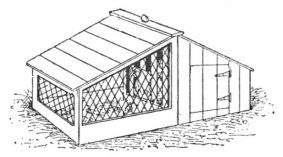

No. 137.

The Coop is soundly constructed of tongued and grooved matching; roof of both Coop and Run of weather-boards; the Run is covered with galvanised wire-netting. All woodwork painted outside one coat of good oil colour, and whitened inside.

4ft. by 2ft., 3ft. high to ridge, 2ft. high to eaves.

PRICE (complete) ... £1 1s.

Chicken Coop with Run.

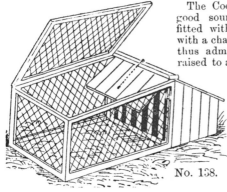

The Coop is constructed of good sound timber, and is fitted with shutter in front with a chain attached to same, thus admitting of its being raised to any degree required. The top is hinged to lift up. The Run is formed of wood framing covered with galvanised wire-netting, the top also being hinged to lift up. All outside woodwork painted one coat.

No. 138.

Coop, 2ft. by 2ft.; Run, 3ft. long and 2ft. high.

PRICE ... ... £1.

Improved Coop and Run.

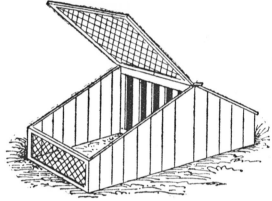

No. 139.

Soundly constructed of good sound timber. Roof of Run covered with galvanised wire-netting instead of weather boards, and hinged to lift up, and the bottom covered with small mesh wire-netting. 5ft. by 2ft. All woodwork painted outside.

PRICE ... ... 12s. 6d.

Feeding Run for Chickens.

No. 140.

By using this Run the difficulty of separating the Chickens from the older birds when being fed is obviated, since only the Chickens have access into it.

Size: 3ft. square, 15in. high.

PRICE ... ... 5s. each.

Span-Roof Poultry Coop with Covered Run.

No. 141.

Constructed of good sound tongued and grooved matchboards, roof of weather-boards, the Coop is provided with sliding shutter at entrance to Run, and is fitted with handles for removal from place to place; the sides and ends of run are covered with galvanised wire netting; all outside woodwork painted one coat. Coop, 2ft. 6in. by 2ft. 6in., 2ft. high; Run, 4ft. long.

PRICE ... ... £1 5s.

Improved Portable Bantam or Chicken House.

The projections at ends form handles, so that the House may be moved with ease to any part of the ground. It is suitable for bantams and chickens. Fitted complete with nest-boxes and perches, and oil-painted outside. 6ft. by 3ft.

PRICE—£1 5s.

No. 142.

Sprinkle Cooper's Disinfectas in House and Run Daily.

Chicken Coop and Run on Wheels.

This is a very neat design, and being fitted on wheels facilitates removal from place to place. The run is complete with floor, and is a safeguard against predatory vermin, sparrows, &c.

No. 143.

6ft. 6in. long by 2ft. 6in. wide.
PRICE ... ... £1 15s.

Bantam or Chicken House and Run.

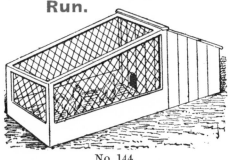

No. 144.

Soundly constructed of tongued and grooved matching, painted, on strong frame. Roof, feather-edge boards. Run covered with galvanised wire-netting 6ft. by 2ft. 6in., 2ft. 6in. high to ridge.

PRICE (complete) £1 1s.

Pent-Roof Poultry Coop with Covered Run.

Very handy for moving about. Strong. Painted one coat.

Coop, 2ft. 6in. high in front, 2ft. 6in. wide; Run, 4ft. long, 2ft. 6in. wide.

PRICE £1 1s.

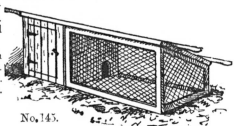

No. 145.

Improved New Coop and Run.

No. 146.

This span-roofed, weather-boarded combination Coop and Run will be found convenient in rearing stock. A hinged door is made at the back of Coop from which the brood may be attended to. The roof of the Run is also flap-hinged, oil-painted outside.

PRICE.

Length 6ft., width 2ft., height at eaves 1ft. 2in., and 2ft. at ridge, £1 2s. 6d.

New Span-Roof Poultry Coop and Run.

No. 147.

This portable Coop can be moved as required for change of ground. It is strongly made and roofed with weather-boards, and fitted with the latest improvements.

The Coop is 2ft. 6in. by 2ft. 6in., and the Run 4ft., measuring in all 6ft. 6in long.

PRICE ... ... £1 2s. 6d.

To Prevent Cramp.

The bottom of every Coop should be covered for about half-an-inch with **Cooper's Disinfectas.** Cheap, Clean, and Healthy. Try it. Per Sack (2-bushel), 2s. 6d., sack included; ten for 22s. 6d.

111

Lean-to Poultry Coop and Run.

This Portable Coop is a requisite in every breeding establishment. It is strongly made of sound material, with weather-board roof, and oil-painted one coat outside. The Coop is 2ft. wide and 2ft. 6in. high in front; the Run 4ft long and 3ft. wide, covered with galvanised wire netting. Fitted with door and handles for moving.

No. 148.

| PRICE | ... | ... | ... | ... | £1 5s. |

Coop and Run for Poultry or Game.

This Coop has a weather-boarded span roof, it is convenient and roomy, and well adapted for young broods. A shelter may be made by using the front door in the daytime to protect the chickens from sun and rain. A small door is fixed in the back at which attention to the requirements of the birds may be performed.

The Run may be detached at night, and the Coop closed up. The Coop is 1ft. 2in. high to eaves, 2ft. high at ridge, and 2ft. wide; together with run it is 7ft. long.

No. 149.

PRICES.

	£	s.	d.
Coop and Run complete	1	5	0
Coop only	0	14	0
Run only	0	12	6

Cooper's Disinfectas.

Cheap, Clean, and Healthy. Nothing to equal it for keeping Poultry in good health. Try it. Per Sack (2-bushel), 2s. 6d

Chicken Coop and Run on Wheels.

No. 150.

Another design of Coop and Run, but being fitted on wheels, with floor, facilitates removal from place to place. Outside painted one coat. Vermin proof.

6ft. 6in. long by 2ft. 6in. wide.

PRICE ...   .   £1 10s.

Improved Bantam or Chicken House and Run.

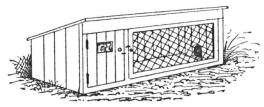

No. 151.

A neat design constructed of good sound match-boards; roof of weather-boards. The House is fitted complete with nests and perches, and has a loose floor. The front of Run is covered with galvanised wire netting, and is hinged to lift up; fitted with handles for easy removal; painted outside one coat good oil colour.

6ft. by 3ft.   2ft. 8in. high in front.

PRICE ...   .   £1 5s.

Be sure and Sprinkle Cooper's Disinfectas in Runs Daily.

Fattening Pen.

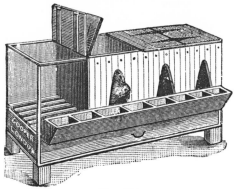

No. 152.

This is the most convenient **Pen** for fattening Fowls, having the advantage of preserving cleanliness in the compartments with a minimum of trouble. The illustration shows an underneath drawer, into which the droppings fall through the floor, which is constructed with bars running lengthways of the Pen. The drawer can be taken out and cleaned as often as necessary and replaced. The birds are put in and taken out at the top, hinged flaps being provided for the covers. The Trough is of zinc for both food and water.

PRICE: For Four Fowls, £1 2s. 6d.; for Six Fowls, £1 10s.

Imperial Black Varnish.

For Iron Fences, Wood Palings, Farm Buildings, Poultry Houses, &c.

18 gal. casks, 20s.; 36 gal. casks, 34s.; Casks included. Carefully packed on rail. Casks not returnable.

1 gal. 1s. 6d. (can 6d.); 5 gal. 5s. (can 2s.).

Poultry Hurdles.

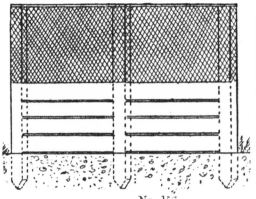

Size: 6ft. long by 5ft. high; boarded 2ft. high; remainder 2in. mesh galvanised wire netting. These Hurdles are strongly made, and if painted occasionally will last for many years.

No. 157.

PRICE ... ... 5s. 6d. each.
Gates 2ft. wide and hinges complete, 4s. each.

Egg Boxes.

No. 158.

Partitions movable. Postal Boxes for Eggs, with separate compartment for each egg.

Boxes to hold any number of Eggs to order. Sample Box to hold twelve eggs, post free 6 stamps. Boxes for Duck and Bantam Eggs made to order.

			Per doz.			Per gross.		
			s.	d.		£	s.	d.
To hold	12	eggs	2	0		0	16	0
,,	15	,,	2	6		0	18	0
,,	18	,,	3	0		1	2	0
,,	24	,,	4	0		1	13	0
,,	25	,,	4	6		1	16	0
,,	36	,,	6	0		2	4	0
,,	48	,,	7	0		2	14	0

115

Portable Duck Houses.

No. 160.

These are handy Duck Houses for placing near to water. A division board is placed inside, forming two compartments in each house, with a separate entrance door hinged at the bottom. A large door is made at the back, and fitted with lock. These

Lean-to.

No. 161.

houses are strongly made with well-seasoned wood, and one coat of oil paint is given to each outside. Dimensions: 5ft. long by 2ft. 6in. wide, 2ft. 6in. high.

PRICE   ...   .   £1 5s.

POULTRY—*continued*.

DUCKS.

When properly fed and treated ducks prove as profitable as ordinary poultry. Many ducks are most prolific, laying every day for weeks together. There is a ready sale for duck eggs, and well-fed young ducks can always be disposed of. Ducks can be kept in health without a pond, provided that a good-sized tub is available—sunk in the ground and filled with water. They will lay freely in a small run, and ducklings can be reared in closer quarters than chickens.

Though a duck is an aquatic bird, the house in which it sleeps must not be damp or sloppy. So the floor must be covered with dry straw or other litter, changed often. Our houses, Nos. 180 and 181, are made for ducks. They are 5ft. long, 2ft. 6in. wide, and 2ft. 6in. high. A division board is inside, forming two compartments, and there are two entrance doors, hinged at the bottom. This enables the ducks to be shut up each evening. Any eggs will then be laid on the bedding, as they usually lay early in the morning. Ducks are not particular where they lay, dropping the eggs about anywhere.

Old ducks are of no more use than old fowls. The stock should, therefore, consist of young birds, if possible, hatched in March, and not more than two years old. Four ducks are enough to run with one drake. If a good number of ducks are kept, our span-roof duck house, No. 183, will be found very suitable. It is 8ft. by 6ft., 8ft. high to the ridge, and 6ft. high to the eaves. Or for an ornamental duck house No. 182 is in much request.

Ducks required for laying must not be overfed. The first meal, especially in the winter months, should be of soft food. Equal parts of middlings and ground oats is a good mixture, mixed stiffly with warm water. At least three times a week some animal food is necessary if the ducks are kept in confinement. Also they require plenty of green vegetables. In the evening they must have a feed of grain—either oats, barley, or wheat thrown into a pan of water. With this some coarse sand or grit to aid digestion. Fat ducks will not lay, so they must not have more food at a time than they can eat greedily.

The usual way to hatch ducklings is under an ordinary hen. Ducks are poor sitters and mothers. The incubating period is twenty-eight days. When the young ducks are hatched give either chopped hard-boiled egg and bread crumbs, with a little fine sand added, or bread and milk and oatmeal. After the first ten days the diet can consist of meal, such as ground oats, barley-meal, maize-meal and middlings, mixed into a crumbly paste, with the addition of some animal food. The latter is necessary for rapid growth. Some grit must be added to the

Ornamental Duck House.

Constructed of weather boards throughout, ornamented with rustic wood additions; all outside woodwork painted two coats.

Size, 6ft. by 4ft.

No. 162.

PRICE £4.

Span-Roof Duck House.

A neat design constructed of matchboards, roof of weather-boards; door in one end in two halves; window in one side; all woodwork painted outside one coat.

Size, 8ft. by 6ft., 8ft. high to ridge, 6ft. high to eaves.

PRICE £3 10s.

No. 163.

Duck House.

Substantially constructed of tongued and grooved matching; roof weather boarded, and has a ledge all round at base; woodwork painted two coats outside.

Size, 4ft. by 4ft.; 4ft. high to top, 2ft. high to eaves.

No. 164.

PRICE £2 5s.

food, as ducklings do not thrive without it. The food should be given in troughs and not thrown on the ground. Our chicken troughs are eminently suited for ducklings, as they are readily cleaned. Water should be allowed the young ducks for drinking.

Cooked rice makes a good change now and then. Chopped green food—such as nettles and lettuce—is necessary if the ducklings are kept in a small space. They ought to be fit to kill, if fed in this way, when from nine to ten weeks old. They should not be kept longer or they will begin to cast their first feathers and lose flesh.

Of recent years some of the old breeds of duck have been improved in size and laying powers, and some useful new breeds have been created by clever crossing. The Aylesbury, one of the oldest breeds, continues to be held in great esteem. It is very large, it grows and matures rapidly, and the flesh is most delicate. Aylesbury ducks are good layers of large eggs. The eggs vary in colour from green to almost white. The pale, flesh-coloured beak of the Aylesbury becomes yellow with exposure to hot sun. This duck is not quite such a free layer as the Pekin, another white duck. The Pekin is more suitable to a small run than the Aylesbury. It is largely kept in America and is particularly hardy. On some of the duck farms in the United States Pekins have averaged over 140 eggs per duck.

The Rouen is a beautiful duck, in plumage the facsimile of the wild mallard. It is not as good a layer as either the Aylesbury or the Pekin, but it attains great size, drakes having scaled 14lb. A fine, large duck is the Cayuga—black in colour, an excellent layer of large green eggs, and of fine flavour for the table.

Where there is a free range the Indian Runner will be found a most prolific layer. It is a non-sitter, lays at about sixteen weeks old, is very hardy, and easily reared. It is small, so not advisable when only ducks for the table are desired. But for a quantity of good-sized eggs, and for a duck that will obtain almost all of its own food by foraging, the Indian Runner is unsurpassed.

A new breed of duck that is gaining many friends is the Campbell Khaki, a buff-coloured duck with bronze neck and tail. It was produced from a cross between the Rouen and the Indian Runner. The Khaki are said to be great layers and good table ducks.

If a cross-bred duck is desired the amateur cannot do better than keep Aylesbury-Pekin, which has the good qualities of both its parents.

GEESE.

A great advantage in geese-breeding is that they can be reared cheaply and that goslings are very easy to bring up. If there

Turkey or Goose House.

This illustration shows a neat design of House for turkeys or geese, and is constructed of good sound tongued and grooved matching; the roof of weatherboards; all outside woodwork painted with our Patent Rot-Proof Composition; complete in sections in readiness for erection, and securely packed on rail.

No. 119.

No.	Length. ft.	Width. ft.	Height at Ridge. ft. in.	Price. £ s. d.
1	8	6	6 0	2 5 0
2	10	7	6 6	3 0 0
3	12	8	7 0	3 15 0

New Poultry House.

No. 120.

This is a new style of House, having two distinct Runs and affording protection in all weathers. A Sliding Shutter keeps the Birds in either part, as may be required. The Dry Run has wire-netting at one end for light and air. The Open Run is 6ft. long, 5ft. wide, and 2ft. 6in. high; wired over the top as well as the sides. The house is well and strongly made, and is fitted with Nest-boxes and Perches. 6ft. long, 5ft. wide.

Carefully packed on rail ... ... £2 15s.

120

POULTRY—*continued.*

ıs an open common or piece of waste land, geese will obtain most of their own food. Unlike ducks and fowls, geese continue profitable for several years. A gander is at his best when five or six years old. Young geese, as a rule, do not lay before they are two years old. Three geese are enough to run with one gander.

Geese generally begin to lay in February if they are comfortably housed. Our house, No. 88, will be found a most convenient one for these birds. As the eggs are laid it is better to remove them and store them out of reach of frost. The gander and geese must have access to a pond or large tub of water, or the eggs will not prove fertile. Most geese are good sitters and mothers, but some pure Toulouse geese do not sit. A goose will cover from eleven to thirteen eggs. A large fowl, such as a Cochin, will hatch from four to six goose eggs. The period of incubation is from twenty-eight to thirty days. The eggs should be sprinkled every few days with water.

When the goslings are hatched out, the mother and her young must be moved to a coop, placed on dry, short turf. A good food for the young birds is chopped-up egg and bread crumbs, mixed with some minced young nettles or onion tops. After a few days of this, barley-meal is a good diet till they can eat grain. Hard food can form the staple diet at a month, and after six weeks no soft food is required. Plenty of fresh water must be given in a shallow dish for drinking. They should not be allowed to swim till most of the feathers have appeared.

The stock geese require very little food. A feed of oats of an evening is usually enough. To fatten young geese for the table they are shut up for a month and fed twice a day—in the morning on a soft food, made of a mixture of barley-meal and middlings; and in the evening on oats or wheat, after the grain has been soaked.

There are two breeds of goose only that are commonly kept in this country, the Toulouse and the Embden. The Toulouse is dark grey, passing into white at the underparts and tail coverts. It is very large and a poor mother, some geese being non-sitters. The Embden is a pure white goose with blue eyes, very hardy and quick maturing. A favourite goose, and the one generally seen, is a cross between these two breeds. The Chinese goose is kept now and then. It is a freer layer than the Embden or Toulouse, and is said to lay upwards of one hundred eggs in the year.

TURKEYS.

Turkey rearing, though it is carried on more than was the case some few years ago, is still considered by many people

Pens Suitable for Pheasants.

No. 153.

The above illustration shows two Pens. They are constructed of wood framing covered with galvanised wire netting, including top; the bottom part is boarded. Each pen is fitted complete with gate; all outside woodwork painted one coat good oil colour. In sections ready for erecting, and securely packed on rail. Size over all of the two pens, 12ft. by 12ft., 4ft. high.

Price ... ... £2 5s.

Pheasant-Breeding Pens.

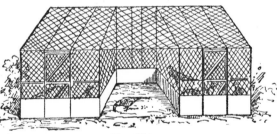

No. 154.

These Pens are constructed of wood framing covered with galvanised wire netting, including tops; the bottom part of sides and ends is boarded up as shown. Each Pen is fitted complete with gate; all outside woodwork painted one coat of good oil colour. In sections ready for erection, and carefully packed on rail at the following respective prices:—

	£	s.	d
Single Pen, 12ft. by 6ft.	1	10	0
Six Pens	7	10	0
Twelve Pens	12	0	0

POULTRY—*continued.*

to be risky and unprofitable; but so much improvement has taken place since these birds have become better understood, that, provided there is a free range, turkeys pay extremely well. Care must be taken to avoid in-breeding by frequent change of blood. And the stock birds must not be allowed to get fat.

The turkeys to produce large offspring must be as large in frame as possible. Hens about 18lbs. in weight do well with a cock of about 30lbs. One mating is sufficient to fertilise all the eggs in one laying of the turkey-hen. But it is none the less better not to run the male with more than twelve hens. If the stock birds are given some warm, soft food, of ground oats and middlings in the morning and of some wheat or other grain at roosting time, the hens should begin to lay in February.

Turkeys are good sitters and mothers. The chicks break the shell from the twenty-sixth to the twenty-ninth day of incubation. They require food when twelve hours old. A most successful mode of feeding is to give milk curds and oatmeal at first every two hours. This is continued for about three days and then replaced with middlings, scalded and dried off with ground oats. Water and grit are supplied. At the expiration of three weeks the young birds need only be fed every three hours, and some chopped-up dandelions or minced onions added to the soft food. The little birds have every evening a feed of groats, or some dry chicken food.

Care must be taken to keep the young turkeys dry and out of the reach of rain until they are from eight to ten weeks old, when they "shoot the red." They can then have ordinary poultry food and are quite hardy. About six weeks before required for the table they should be put in a roomy shed with plenty of ventilation. The food used is ground oats and barley-meal mixed with milk, with a little melted fat added for the last ten days. This is given in the morning. Boiled rice and oatmeal are allowed at noon, and in the evening the morning meal is repeated, varied with boiled grain, such as wheat or barley. This feeding will carry them on until killing time. Clean drinking water and plenty of grit are necessary. The English breeds of turkey, the Norfolk and the Cambridge, have been much improved of recent years in size and hardiness by crossing with the American Bronze turkey.

ROT-PROOF COMPOSITION.

A good preservative for all Woodwork exposed to the weather, and suitable for Farm Buildings, Poultry Houses, Palings, Fences, or any description of outdoor Woodwork.

1 gal. 2s. 6d., 2 gals. 4s. 9d., 5 gals. 10s., 10 gals. 17s. 6d., 20 gals. 30s., 40 gals. 50s.

Put on rail at our Works. Cans and casks included (not returnable).

124

PIGEONS.

HOUSING.—It is not at all necessary that domestic pigeons —with the exception of Flying Homers and Flying Tumblers— should be allowed their full liberty. Very few fancy pigeons ever see the outside of an aviary or loft. We make a variety of cotes and aviaries suitable for all kinds of pigeons. There is the pigeon cote for fixing against a wall, No. 186, and that on the top of a pole, No. 192. Either of these is adapted to the breeding of common pigeons for the table, or as an abode for such birds as Fantails, which are highly ornamental when strutting about a lawn or stable yard. Our pigeon cote, No. 196, to accommodate six pairs of birds, is most compact and useful, especially to the beginner, who can place it near the house, and be able to see at a glance how his pigeons are going on.

For fancy pigeons, and where pigeon-breeding is conducted on regular principles, our houses, Nos. 187, 193, and 201, cannot be surpassed. No. 201 is stocked in three sizes, the largest 20ft. by 10ft., with a 12ft. run. Nest-pans are indispensable to the successful rearing of young pigeons. They can be obtained of glazed earthenware, ordinary red earthenware, or wood. Either of the former are preferable, as less likely to harbour vermin. The nest-pans obviate the risk of the eggs rolling out. Two nest-boxes must be allowed to each pair of birds. The hen lays again before the first pair of young ones can fly, and the second pair of eggs stand a better chance if laid in a nest into which the young birds cannot come.

Flying Homers and Flying Tumblers must have their house constructed so that there is an outlet for the pigeons into the open. This is through a cage, or trap, which is usually fixed outside on a small platform. This trap has a falling door which can be pulled up by a string, so as to shut in the birds and enable them to be caught when desired. In order that the pigeons can get in when the door is closed openings are left at the top of the trap, through which they can pass in from the outside, but up which they cannot fly to make their escape. Openings are also left at the side of the cage called " bolting wires."

APPLIANCES.—The appliances required are a pairing pen, bath, drinking-fountain, a scraper for cleaning, a small hand-broom, a shovel, and a fine sieve through which to pass the grain, to remove dust. Our pairing pen No. 188 is made for mating purposes, and is useful to accustom pigeons to confinement prior to a show. It can also be utilised to hold an occasional invalid. The bath is a most important appliance.

126

PIGEONS—*continued.*

Pigeons are great bathers. The bath should be of galvanised iron, painted or enamelled. The size will depend on the number of birds. In any event it should not have a depth of more than three inches, two inches of water being enough. Young pigeons will often get into the bath when first out of the nest. If they are assaulted by an older bird when they are wet and bedraggled death by drowning is not unusual. The scraper for cleaning should be triangular in shape. The corners and sides of the nest boxes can then be kept clean, the accumulations in the nest being scraped into the shovel; the small hand-broom will help to keep the corners of the aviary free from loose feathers and dust. A sieve is valuable in ridding the grain of dust and dirt.

SELECTING THE STOCK.—The novice should make a start with one breed only, and that of the best pedigree obtainable. The birds should be obtained from a fancier who is known to have bred prize-winners. The catalogue of a show, such as the Crystal Palace, will give names and addresses. If it is intended to begin with two or three pairs they should all be obtained from the same person. There will then probably be the advantage of breeding from one particular strain.

An erroneous idea is that the breeding stock ought not to be related. Yet it is a fact well known to all clever breeders that, to obtain good results, inbreeding to some considerable extent is essential. Inbreeding consists in the mating together of birds that are related to one another, either closely or remotely. If the pigeons with which a beginning is made are healthy, and free from disease, inbreeding may be carried on closely for years, not only without detriment, but with advantage. The more perfect the birds are the better. Any faults should be corrected as far as possible in mating. For instance, if the cock bird has too much colour in the wrong place he should be paired with a hen that has too little. Or if shortness of beak is an important point, a thin-beaked bird should be paired with an extra thick-beaked one. At the end of each season, if the best youngsters are retained and the inferior ones weeded out, with judicious mating and perseverance the character of the stock will greatly improve.

BREEDING.—The mating of most breeds can take place about the middle of February. When a pair of pigeons have been mated for ten days or a fortnight, the first egg may be expected. They will have carried straw into the nest, and the cock will be seen to follow the hen about, and to peck continually at her. This is called "driving to nest." Pigeons lay two eggs, missing a day between laying the first and the second. Some hens begin to sit on the first egg directly it is laid. When this happens one young one will hatch before the other. To avoid

Span-Roof Poultry House, Covered Run, and Pigeon Loft.

No. 116.

This is an ornamental design. The House is complete with nests, perches, and ladder; and has raised floor, thus affording a covered run for the poultry; the Run is composed of wood framed hurdles covered with galvanised wire-netting, and is complete with gate. The structure is complete with pigeon-loft at top. All outside woodwork painted one coat of good oil colour. Complete in sections in readiness for erection, and securely packed on rail.

Size over all.						£	s.	d.
12ft. by 5ft., 7ft. high ..	..	..	..	..	..	5	0	0
14ft. by 6ft., 8ft. high ..	..	..	..	..	..	6	5	0

Cooper's Disinfectas.

Sprinkle a little in House, Run, &c., daily. Cheap, clean, and healthy. Nothing to equal it for keeping poultry in good health. Try it. Per Sack (2-bushel), 2s. 6d., sack included; 10 for 22s. 6d.

Cheshunt Cottage, Cheshunt, Herts.

"GENTLEMEN,—I received the Fowl House in due course on Saturday, and am very pleased with it, and I shall hope to do further business when the opportunity occurs. Thanking you for your prompt attention.—I remain, yours, &c.

(Signed)   W. G. BIRT."

PIGEONS—*continued.*

this artificial eggs made of china or bone are used. The first egg is removed and replaced by an artificial one, care being taken to return the real egg on the appearance of the second egg. The period of incubation is seventeen days from the laying of the second egg.

The young ones are usually cock and hen; occasionally two cocks, and less often two hens. Young pigeons grow at a great pace. At from eight to ten days old they will be covered with sprouting feathers. If they are of good strain it is advisable at this age to take the trouble to ring them with the rings that are issued yearly by the Pigeon Marking Conference. The original object of using these rings was to prevent old birds being exhibited in the classes reserved for young birds only. The rings bear the date of the year and a number. They show the age of a bird throughout its career—not only to the breeder, but to a purchaser—and also enable the bird to be known by the number on the ring, and an easy record to be kept, in the stud book, of its offspring. The operation of "ringing" is performed by holding the young pigeon with one hand, pointing all the toes in the same direction, and drawing them through the ring till the ring is on the leg. It does not matter on which leg the ring is placed. We supply these rings at 2s. 3d. per dozen, post free.

When the young birds are about ten days old their parents will begin to arrange for another nest. While doing this they may not attend to the squabs as much as they ought. This can be ascertained by looking at the squabs in the morning and evening. They should have been fed by ten o'clock in the morning, and before dusk. If on examination the crops of the youngsters are nearly empty some help in the form of hand-feeding is necessary. If the squabs are less than ten days old some bruised dari and wheat should be soaked for twelve hours in cold water, then warmed, and carefully placed, a very little at a time, in the mouth of the bird, over the tongue into the throat. With a little practice this will be found easy, and the youngsters will soon take to it greedily.

Occasionally the parent birds are unable to feed their young when first hatched. The little squabs can be saved by artificial feeding. If a plain biscuit is crushed and mixed with a little oatmeal, to which some warm milk is added, and poured into a small teaspoon, the beak of the small bird dipped in the fluid will generally induce it to suck it up; or a small glass syringe can be used, from which the mixture is dropped into the throat. When artificially feeding young pigeons, the crop should not be more than two-thirds filled. After a young pigeon is a fortnight old the feeding can be done with soaked tares and maple peas.

FEEDING.—During the breeding season the best general

Combination Fowl and Pigeon House.

No. 117.

This House will be found useful in both large and small establishments. Its compactness facilitates the keeping of several kinds of stock under easy management. The main body is constructed for Fowls, under which is a dry run. Above the Fowl House are compartments that may be used for other kinds of stock, such as Rabbits, etc., or they may be used as fattening-pens for Poultry. At the top is a Pigeon Loft, which will accommodate either three or six pairs of birds, according to the position the house is fixed in; if it stands away from a wall, extra chambers can be arranged at the back by inserting a division board—this would allow a depth of 1ft. 9in. for each of six pairs of pigeons. The Fowl house is supplied with ladder to raised floor, nest-boxes, perches, and all necessary fittings. Two doors, with locks, are hinged to the front of the house, and flap at the end for collecting eggs. The whole is strongly built in sections, and painted outside, ready for putting together. Portable for standing out in the open. Carefully packed on rail at the following prices :

	£	s.	d.
8ft. long by 3ft. 6in. back to front. 4ft. 6in. at eaves, and 8ft. 6in. at ridge	4	0	0
Without back, for standing against existing wall	3	0	0

PIGEONS—*continued.*

food is a mixture of equal parts of maple peas, tares, dari, and wheat. When the birds are not rearing young maple peas and tares are sufficient. Tick beans are used by breeders of Homers, Carriers, and some other pigeons, and maize is given by some fanciers. A handful of canary seed now and then is eaten eagerly by pigeons, and is beneficial. There must always be a free supply of coarse gritty sand and plenty of fresh water, renewed at least once a day. Several prepared grits are sold. These are very useful. Some breeders always feed from hoppers; the pigeons can then help themselves at any time. During the long days the pigeons are up and feeding very early, and it is advantageous for them to have access to grain, and not to wait. Moreover, if the birds are fed only at stated times, there are hens, perhaps just hatching, which will not leave the nest, and would not get any food till the second meal in the evening. Both birds assist in incubating, the cock going on the nest in the morning, where he remains till three or four; the hen sitting the remainder of the time. And this practice must be taken into consideration in feeding the pigeons. After the birds have done breeding it is better to feed them twice a day—just enough at each meal for them to eat up with appetite.

In the breeding season it is a good plan to add a few crystals of permanganate of potash to the drinking water. This does not stain the pigeons, helps to prevent the food going sour in the crops of the birds that are feeding young, and obviates canker. A piece of rock salt is wholesome, and affords the pigeons endless pleasure and occupation. Salt-cat is a compound of which the pigeons are very fond, and which is always given by some fanciers. The following is a good recipe for salt-cat: One peck of loam, half a peck each of ground oyster-shell and ground bone-meal, and a quarter of a pound each of aniseed, coriander seed, caraway seed, and cumin seed. Mix well together, and to each half-gallon add a handful of salt and a pint of water. When the salt is dissolved, the liquid is poured over the ingredients, and the whole beaten into a stiff state, and then allowed to dry before using.

SEPARATING THE PAIRS.—Domestic pigeons are usually so well fed that they will continue to breed, if left to themselves, throughout the greater part of the year. This is neither good for them nor their progeny. The constant feeding of young is a great strain on the system of the parents. If they are allowed to continue to breed, the moult will be deferred and irregular. Late-hatched young ones are rarely of any value, even if they survive the winter. Fancy pigeons should be separated by the end of July. Any eggs

Pigeon Cote.

No. 165.

The illustration shows a Cote to accommodate six pairs of birds. It is strongly constructed of good sound matchboards; roof weather-boards. The flights are covered in front with galvanised wire-netting, complete with doors, as per illustration. All outside woodwork, with exception of roof, stained and varnished, roof painted. Complete with back. 5ft. by 2ft., 5ft. high at back, 4ft. high in front.

PRICE ... ... £2 10s.

Dove or Pigeon Cote for Wall.

No. 166.

This cote is thoroughly well constructed of seasoned red deal for fixing against a wall. It is neat in appearance, and is oil-painted with three good coats. Ready fitted.

PRICES:

	£	s.	d.
For Nine Pairs Birds (see illustration) ...	1	10	0
For Seven Pairs Birds	1	7	6
For Six Pairs Birds	1	5	0
For Five Pairs Birds	1	2	6

PIGEONS—*continued*.

laid at that time should be destroyed. It is advisable, if possible, to have the cocks in one part of the aviary, divided away from the hens.

EXHIBITING.—There can be no doubt that the show pen is the objective point of the large majority of pigeon fanciers. The practical proof of the quality of the pigeons can best be shown by sending any that are considered promising to an exhibition. The beginner should attend the show at which his birds are entered, to compare his exhibits with the others. The pigeons must be in the best condition and feather or they will stand slight chance of winning. They must be made as tame as possible by being frequently placed singly in the mating pen, and touched and stroked with a small stick. Many untrained birds crouch in a corner on the approach of the judge and decline to show themselves. While in the pen a few grains of hempseed should be given. Pigeons are naturally so clean, and wash so often, that they rarely require more than their feet and legs, and perhaps the beaks, gone over with a damp sponge. Washing requires a good deal of practice. The experiment should first be tried on a bird that is not to be shown.

Pigeons must be exhibited in their "natural condition." Any operation that is not necessary to the birds' health and comfort constitutes trimming, or otherwise interfering with the natural appearance of the bird, and will, if discovered, cause the exhibit to be disqualified. But such little attentions as removing with scissors the small extra growth which often comes at the tip of the upper mandible of the beak are not objected to.

SOME DISEASES: CANKER is a very troublesome and fatal disease in lofts or aviaries that are overcrowded. It

Portable Outdoor Aviary.

No. 197.

Picturesque design for an outdoor Aviary, substantially constructed. The flight is constructed of fine mesh galvanised wire upon light wood framing. Constructed in sections in readiness for erection.

	Cash Price.
	£ s. d.
6ft. by 6ft., 5ft. high at eaves, 7ft. high to ridge ..	7 10 0
4ft. by 4ft., 4ft. 6in. high at eaves, 6ft. high at ridge	5 10 0

Span-Roof Pigeon House and Flight.

No. 167.

This is an ornamental design, and is substantially constructed of good, sound, tongued and grooved matching. The House is provided with separate compartments for each pair of birds, complete with nests; all doors fitted with locks. The Flight is constructed of wood framing covered with galvanised wire-netting, and fitted complete with gate; the roof of both House and Flight is covered with feather-edge boards, with ornamental ridging and finials. All outside woodwork painted one coat. Constructed in sections ready for erection, and securely packed on rail.

	£	s.	d.
No. 1.—For nine pairs of Birds: 2ft. long, 3ft. 6in. wide, 5ft. 6in. high; flight 6ft. long	3	15	0
No. 2.—For twelve pairs of Birds: 2ft. long, 3ft. 6in. wide, 6ft. 6in. high; flight 6ft. long	4	15	0

There is nothing better to keep your birds healthy and house free from smell than **Cooper's Disinfectas**, 2s. 6d. per Sack.

Dove or Pigeon Cote on Pole.

No. 168.

This picturesque Cote is strongly fixed upon a pole for sinking in the ground. It is well made, and is neat in appearance. It can be had either stained and varnished or oil-painted.

It has nesting accommodation for Eight Pairs of Birds.

PRICE ... ... £1 15s.

PIGEONS—*continued.*

takes various forms. Usually it appears in the throat in the form of cheesy-looking lumps; sometimes in the head under one eye; and again at the beak. A treatment that will often cure is to obtain from a chemist a little creoline, put two or three drops in a teaspoonful of water, and apply to the throat and mouth twice a day with a soft camel's-hair brush. Creoline is also a preventive; a few drops in the drinking water of all the birds will keep them free if canker has attacked one that has been removed. Another mode of treating is to touch the sores in the throat with alum or nitrate of silver. The patient must be isolated, as the disease is contagious. Enough Chemical Food in the drinking water to colour it pinkish should be given.

COLD.—This can be known by a running at the eyes and nostrils, which sometimes turns to roup. If directly this is seen a camel's-hair brush is dipped in paraffin, and the throat mopped out with it twice a day, the trouble will usually cease.

DIARRHŒA can in simple cases be cured by feeding on raw rice, and giving rice water to drink. A drop of chlorodyne made into a pill with a little barley-meal, two or three times a day, is another remedy.

EYE INFLAMED, or one-eyed cold, is a troublesome complaint. One of a bird's eyes becomes swollen and closed, and exudes matter. To bathe with warm water and a little permanganate of potash morning and evening, and keep the bird out of draught, will generally effect a cure.

GOING LIGHT.—When suffering with this complaint the pigeon rapidly loses flesh and strength, accompanied by diarrhœa, the excrement being green. A usual treatment is to give the sufferer a dose of three or four drops of castor oil, and to feed on small grain, such as hempseed, rice, and canary seed. A course of Parrish's Food in the drinking water should be given.

ROUP is very much like canker in general character. It is usually classified as dry, wet, and diphtheritic roup. A cold is the usual forerunner. This must be treated as recommended under "Cold." If after three days there is no improvement, and the secretions thicken, then it is probably roup. The roupy matter must be removed with the end of a feather, and the throat and mouth washed with water and permanganate of potash. For medicine the following is very good: Sulphate of magnesia, 1½ drachms; sulphate of soda, 1½ drachms; common salt, 1 drachm; and water, 1 quart. This mixture should be given in place of the usual drinking water. When the bird begins to improve a tonic should be given, about a teaspoonful to half a pint of drinking water.

Span-Roof Aviary.

This Aviary is artistically constructed for outdoor use. The House is composed of good sound tongued and grooved maching. The roof of House and Flight is of weather boards, and fitted with ornamental ridge, finials, and barge boards. The Flight is formed of galvanised wire work. All outside woodwork stained and varnished.

No. 169.

6ft. by 2ft. 6in.; 5ft. high to eaves.

PRICE ... ... £3 15s.

New Three-Tier Pigeon or Dove Cote.

This Breeding Cote will be found a useful addition to the Fancier's yard. It is in three tiers, each one being divided from the other throughout the flight, and having separate doors back and front. Each tier has a double nesting-place, with a bridge between the nests. Small-mesh galvanised wire-netting encloses each flight. The dimensions are 3ft. 6in. long, 1ft. 9in. wide, 5ft. 6in. high to ridge, and stands well from the ground, as shown in illustration. Oil-painted or stained and varnished.

No. 170.

PRICE ... ... £1 15s.

PIGEONS—*continued.*

Chemical food must be given in china or earthenware, and not in metal.

WING DISEASE.—This is known by a bird flying in a one-sided manner, and, on examination, a swelling on the inside of the wing will be found. The most likely way to cure this is to strip the flight-feathers from the wing. By the time the feathers have grown again the swelling should have disappeared.

THE DIFFERENT BREEDS.

THE ANTWERP.—A large and hardy pigeon bred in three varieties: the Long-Faced, Medium-Faced, and Short-Faced. The head is large, high, and broad, the beak stout, both mandibles of the same thickness, the eye red, the eye cere dark and fine in texture. The colour is silver-dun, red-chequer, and blue and blue-chequer.

THE ARCHANGEL.—Brilliance of plumage is a characteristic feature of this pigeon. Head, neck, chest, and thighs are of a rich bronze; the shoulders, back, and tail a bronze black. The bronze is accompanied by a beautiful lustre. This is an excellent pigeon for the novice to commence with. It is very hardy, a free breeder, and a good feeder.

THE BARB.—The head of this pigeon is short and broad, the skull flat across, the beak short and stout, and the upper mandible curved. The wattle on the beak lies flatly, and round the eye is red in colour, circular in shape, and evenly developed. The eye is white or orange, the beak white. The neck is of medium thickness. Barbs are not very good parents, and the young should be reared under foster-parents, such as Magpies.

THE CARRIER.—This is the most difficult to breed in perfection of any pigeon. The number of points is almost

Pigeon or Dove Aviary.

No. 198.

Soundly made. The Flight is formed of wood framework covered with galvanised wire netting, fitted complete with doors.

4ft. long by 2ft. 6in. wide.

Cash Price, £2.

Pigeon House & Flight combined.

No. 171.

This is a strongly - made structure, fitted complete with door and lock; nests, alighting-boards, and side; shutter covered underneath with galvanised wire-netting along one side. All outside woodwork painted one good coat of oil-colour. Complete in sections at the following respective prices:

No.	Length. ft.	Width. ft.	Height. ft.	Price. £ s. d.	Floor and Joists extra. £ s. d.
1	8	5	7	3 0 0	0 10 0
2	10	6	8	4 5 0	0 15 0
3	12	6	8	5 10 0	1 0 0

Span-Roof Aviary for Outdoor Use.

This is a well-made artistic design. The House is lined inside with tongued and grooved match-boards; roof felted between weatherboards and matching; complete with door, and fitted inside with perches; floor all over base of House and Flight. The Flight also is fitted complete with a rustic perch and two troughs. All outside woodwork painted. In sections for erection, and securely packed on rail. 8ft. 6in. high to ridge; 6ft. high to eaves.

No. 172.

Size, 11ft. by 6ft.; Price £9 10s.

PIGEONS—*continued.*

legion. The Carrier is a large bird—17in. from tip of beak to end of tail. The beak is straight and stout. The wattle on the beak is of the shape of a peg-top or walnut, thickest at the back. The eye wattle forms a complete circle round the eye, and is of even width throughout. The beak and eye wattles should not touch, although this is a common defect in old birds. The skull is flat, narrow, and of even width from back to front. The eye is bright red. Carriers are not good sitters, and feeders should be used for rearing the young. A Carrier is not at its best till three years old.

THE CUMULET is an old breed of pigeon, smart and racy-looking, and a high flyer. It is either white in colour, or marked with a fawny-red chuck somewhat half-moon shaped, or slightly ticked with the same colour on the neck hackle. The head is long, the beak $1\frac{1}{2}$in. in length, and standing straight out from the head. The eye is white. The young birds are usually marked with red, which they lose in the moult.

THE DRAGOON is a very popular pigeon. The head is wedge-shaped, wider at the back than at the front of the skull, the beak straight and about $1\frac{1}{2}$in. long, the wattle large at the back, tapering almost to a point in front; the eye wattle small and hard-looking, the eye cere fine in texture, and in white, red, and yellow dragoons of a white tint; in the other coloured birds of a deep damson. The plumage is close and hard. Dragoons are good nurses and free breeders.

THE FANTAIL.—This very attractive pigeon is fairly hardy, is usually very tame, and can rear its own young. The chief properties are shape, tail feather, carriage, and motion. The latter consists in a constant tremulous movement of the neck. As a rule Fantails with from thirty to thirty-four feathers in the tail have the most circular and best-fitting tails. The tail cannot be carried too erect or be too flat, round and close in its spreading. Very small hens are seldom good breeders.

THE HOMER.—Instead of being only a pigeon used for racing and homing purposes, the Homer has of late years been bred for exhibition, so that there are now Show Homers, Exhibition Flying Homers, and Genuine Flying Homers. The Show Homer has become immensely popular. Several birds of this variety have changed hands at upwards of £100. It is of medium size, the head with an even curve from beak to back of skull, the beak of medium length, both mandibles of equal length and thickness, and black in colour, the face (the portion between beak and eye) broad and full, the eye white in colour, the cere fine and dark, and wattle small and heart-shaped. The Show Homer is of various colours. The black

Portable Outdoor Aviary.

No. 173.

This is a very picturesque design for an outdoor Aviary, and is substantially constructed; being complete with a back can be placed where desired, the services of a wall being unnecessary. The flight is constructed of fine mesh galvanised wire upon light wood framing. Constructed in sections in readiness for erection, and carefully packed on rail, at the following respective prices:

	£	s.	d.
4ft. by 4ft., 4ft. 6in. high at eaves, 6ft. high to ridge	5	10	0
6ft. by 6ft., 5ft. high at eaves, 7ft. high to ridge ...	7	10	0

Portable Span-Roof Pigeon House or Aviary.

This House is stocked in three sizes, but it can be made to any dimensions given. It is a useful and compact Aviary made of best material, painted one coat outside, fitted with nest boxes, &c. It has two doors, one at the back of the House, the other at

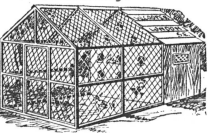

No. 174.

end of run, hinged and locked. A window is fixed in each side, protected by wire netting.

PRICES.		£	s.	d.
12ft. by 6ft. (including 7ft. run) ...		6	10	0
15ft. by 8ft. ,, 9ft. ,, ...		8	10	0
20ft. by 10ft. ,, 12ft. ,, ...		11	10	0

and blue chequers, which are the greatest favourites, are evenly marked. The Exhibition Flying Homer is more prominent in head than the Genuine Flying Homer. Homers are very hardy, strong birds.

THE JACOBIN.—The principal points of this pigeon are the hood, mane, chain, rose, head, shape, carriage, and colour. The hood is formed by the feathers at the back of the skull and upper part of the neck growing forward and arching over the head, fitting closely and evenly. The chain is the continuation of the hood feathers as low down the shoulders as possible. Large birds with good chain and mane should be paired with small hens, narrow in girth, and good in hood.

THE MAGPIE is a very favourite pigeon. The head is long and narrow, the beak long and thin, of a delicate pink colour, and carried in a straight line with the eye. The eye is white, the eye cere and wattle fine and of the same tint as the beak. The flights and tail are long, also the legs, the whole bird small and slender, and tapering gracefully towards the tail. The coloured parts are the head, neck, and breast down to the breast-bone, the back, saddle, tail, and vent. The rest of the body is white. The colours are black, red, yellow, blue, silver, cream, and dun. Young Magpies should not be exposed to the direct rays of the sun or the beaks will become stained. The Magpie is a prolific breeder, rearing its young readily, and often being used as a feeder for other breeds.

Span-Roof Aviary for Outdoor Use.

No. 199.

This is a well-made artistic design. The House is lined inside with tongued and grooved matchboards; roof felted between weather-boards and matching; complete with door, and fitted inside with perches; floor all over base of House and Flight. The Flight also is fitted complete with a rustic perch and two troughs. All outside woodwork painted. In sections for erection, and securely put on rail at Works. Size, 11ft. by 6ft.; 8ft. 6in. high to ridge; 6ft. high to eaves. Cash Price, £9 10s.

141

Double Pigeon House.

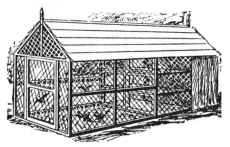

No. 175.

This is a Breeding-house for six pairs of pigeons. Each nest compartment has a door at the back, facilitating the inspection of the nest, and leading from the front of the nesting-chamber is a short flight which opens into the large flight as will be seen by the illustration. The arrangement admits of the birds being parted when desired for pairing off. The entire house is 12ft. long by 4ft. wide, strongly made and roof weather-boarded, stained and varnished, which lends an effective appearance to the construction.

PRICE ...   .   £6.

COOPER'S DISINFECTAS KEEPS BIRDS HEALTHY.

Sprinkle a little in Nesting Chambers and Flights Daily.
Per Sack (2-bushel) 2s. 6d.   10 for 22s. 6d.

Mating Pen for Pigeons.

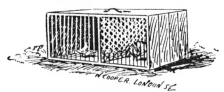

No. 176.

These Pens are useful for mating. Well made of wood and galvanised wire-netting.

PRICE   ...   .   7s. 6d. each.

PIGEONS—*continued*.

THE NORWICH CROPPER.—An old fancy pigeon, formerly known as the Uplopper, this bird has recently found its way into prominence. In colour, markings, inflation of crop, and action the Norwich Cropper resembles the Pouter. It is smaller—not exceeding 15in. in length—and the legs are either clean or very slightly feathered. The tail in blacks and blues is coloured; in reds and yellows it is white. This bird is most tame, companionable, and lively, and, unlike the Pouter, an excellent parent and feeder.

THE NUN.—The body of this bird is white, with coloured head, throat, flight, and tail feathers. The throat marking is called the "bib," which comes as low down the throat as possible. An important point is the shell, or crest, an unbroken crest of white feathers, upright, and spreading from side to side at the back of the head. The eye is pearl white. The Nun is bred in black, red, and yellow, but the blacks are the commonest. This pigeon is hardy and a good breeder and feeder.

ORIENTAL FRILLS is the name given to a number of frilled pigeons that have been brought from the East. The Oriental Turbit has a round, broad skull, short, thick beak, a frill, no peak, clean legs, shoulders and tail coloured, the rest of the bird white. The Turbiteen is marked like the Oriental Turbit, with the addition of three patches of coloured feathers on the forehead and face. There is a peak, and the legs are closely feathered.

Blondinettes, Satinettes, Brunettes, Bluettes, Silverettes are peaked birds of the same character, with the plumage beautifully laced and spangled. None of the Oriental Frills should be mated before April.

THE OWL.—There are three varieties of the Owl, called the English, the African, and the Whiskered. The latter is seldom seen. The English Owl is bred in blue, silver, powdered blue, powdered silver, blue and silver chequer, black, dun, red, and yellow. The head of the Owl is large, massive, and broad, forming a regular arch. The eye is gravel-coloured, and is in the centre of the head, the beak short, thick, and fitting in with the angle of the skull, the wattle slight and smooth, the eye cere fine, the neck short, the chest prominent, gullet full, frill well developed, and flight and tail feathers short. English Owls mature slowly, not attaining their full thickness and size of skull for three or more years. They are hardy and good parents. The African Owl is one of the smallest and prettiest of all our pigeons. It should be a miniature edition of the English Owl, with the eye prominent. It is bred in white, black, black and white, blue, red, yellow, and dun. It is delicate, and should not be paired before the end of April.

PIGEONS—*continued.*

THE POUTER.—Unlike most other pigeons, head properties are not of special importance in the Pouter. The chief points are body structure, shape of the crop, colour, and markings. The Pouter is large, long, and slender, and of very upright carriage; the crop is large and globular, the girth, or waist, narrow, back long and straight, legs and thighs long and clothed with soft feathers. The length of a good specimen is about 20in., and the length of limb from 7in. to 7½in. Pouters are poor sitters and parents.

THE PIGMY POUTER is a lively and bright little pigeon, the original Pouter in miniature, with all the tameness and companionable disposition of the latter. It is a fairly good breeder and nurse.

THE RUNT.—The largest of all our domestic pigeons—not less than 20in. from tip of beak to end of tail, and measuring in girth at least 14in. The head is dove-shaped, the eye pearl, or red, the back broad and long, and the chest wide. Owing to their weight they are clumsy, and apt to break their eggs; so the eggs should be removed and entrusted to common pigeons.

THE SCANDAROON is an old breed of pigeons. It has a long curved beak and an arched and narrow head. The eye is large, encircled by bright red wattle, the wattle on the beak being about the size of that on the Dragoon. The beak is flesh-coloured, and there is a red tinge on the beak wattle and a redness along the line of the mouth.

Span-Roof Aviary.

No. 200.

This aviary is for outdoor use. The House is composed of good, sound, tongued and grooved matching. The Flight is formed of galvanised wirework. All outside woodwork stained and varnished or painted.

6ft. by 2ft. 6in.; 5ft. high to eaves. Cash Price, £3 15s.

PIGEONS—*continued.*

THE SWALLOW.—A conspicuous-looking pigeon. The upper part of the head is coloured—called the cap—the wings and the leg feathers are coloured, and the breast, neck, back, saddle, tail, and thighs are white. There is a crest—a cup-shaped ridge of feathers rising from the neck at the base of the skull. The foot feathering is heavy. The beak is thin and rather long and the eye black. Swallows are good breeders and parents.

THE TRUMPETER.—This is a very peculiar-looking pigeon. The chief points are the rose, the shell, and the foot feathering. The rose is a circle of feathers on the top of the head, radiating evenly, and covering the head, eyes, and greater part of the beak. The shell rises from the back of the head, standing upright, and stretching round below each eye. The legs are short and heavily feathered. The eye is pearl. When pairing Trumpeters the front part of the rose should be cut away and most of the foot feathers cut short, or many of the eggs will be unfertile.

TUMBLERS are a large group of pigeons comprising many varieties. They are separated into two divisions, the Short-faced and the Long-faced. The Short-faced Tumbler is very small, with high and round head, and thin, short, and straight beak. The eye is pearly white, the neck and back short, the flight and tail feathers rather long, and the legs short.

The Almond Tumbler is generally known as the Queen of Pigeons. The ground colour of the plumage is a rich almond. After the first moult black ticks are seen on the neck, breast, shoulders, and back. The bird is at its best when between two and three years old. It is then spangled well, the tail and flight feathers showing "breaks," and divisions of black and white on the ground colour. After the almond is three years old the markings begin to go off.

Among the most charming of the Short-faced Tumblers are the Mottles. These are rich in colour, with an evenly-marked rose of small white feathers on the shoulders and a V-shaped cluster of white feathers in the centre of the back. There are Short-faced Kites, Agates, Self, or Whole-coloured Tumblers, Baldheads, and Beards. Short-faced Tumblers are delicate. They should not be mated before April.

The Long-faced Tumblers are usually classified under two divisions, the Clean-legged and the Muffed-legged. The Clean-legged are subdivided into Self-colours, Mottles, Rosewings, Whitesides, Almonds, Baldheads, and Beards. The head of the Long-faced Tumbler is round, and the beak 1½in. from the tip to the centre of the eye. The eye is pearl. The Rosewings have white feathers on the shoulders like the Mottles, but no markings on the back. The Whitesides are coloured, with the exception of the sides of the wings, which are white.

145

WILLIAM COOPER, Ltd, 751, Old Kent Rd, London, S.E.

PIGEONS—*continued.*

The Muffed-legged varieties are like the other Tumblers in markings, and are heavily feathered on the legs and feet. Tipplers are kept to a great extent in Leicester, Sheffield, and other parts of England. They are wonderful flyers, remaining on the wing for over twelve hours.

THE TURBIT.—With the exception of the shoulders the Turbit is completely white. The shoulders are either black, red, yellow, blue, silver, or dun, according to the variety. The head of the Turbit has been a good deal altered of recent years owing to a strong infusion of Antwerp. The beak is short and stout, the head with an even curve from beak to back of the skull. The eye is full, large, dark, and prominent, the mouth wide, the cheeks full, the gullet filling up the hollow of the throat, the frill long and compact, the mane at the back of the neck ending in a fine peak reaching slightly higher than the crown of the head. High sums are realised for really good specimens. Turbits will rear their own young, but it is advisable when first-class birds are breeding to use foster-parents.

Portable Span-Roof Pigeon House or Aviary.

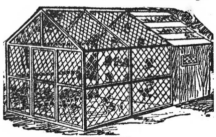

No. 201.

This House is stocked in three sizes, but it can be made to any dimensions given. It is a useful and compact Aviary made of best material, painted one coat outside, fitted with nest-boxes, &c. It has two doors, one at the back of the House, the other at end of run, hinged and locked. A window is fixed in each side, protected by wire netting.

					Cash Price. £ s. d.
12ft. by 6ft. (including 7ft. run)	..	..	..	..	.. 6 10 0
15ft. by 8ft. (including 9ft. run)	..	..	..	..	.. 8 10 0
20ft. by 10ft. (including 12ft. run)	..	..	..	..	.. 11 10 0

146

BIRD-KEEPING IN AVIARIES.

There are so many advantages in keeping birds in aviaries instead of in cages that it is only natural that the former should gradually be becoming more general. A large number of foreign and many British birds will nest and rear their young in aviaries. Cages are, in some instances, too cramped for nesting operations, neither can the habits of the birds be readily studied under such conditions. From experience gained by the use of aviaries it has been ascertained that various foreign birds, formerly considered delicate and only able to live in heated rooms, can exist throughout the entire year if allowed the limited freedom of an aviary out of doors. Brilliantly-coloured parrots, as well as small birds, brought from all parts of the world, can be seen flying about in good health and condition when the temperature is below the freezing point.

The best aspect for an outdoor aviary is south or south-east. We make aviaries of various sizes and descriptions. No. 200 is 6ft. by 2ft. 6in., and 5ft. high to the eaves. There is a house and a flight, the roof of weather-boards is fitted with ornamental ridge, and all outside woodwork stained and varnished. No. 199 is 11ft. by 6ft., and 6ft. high to the eaves; the roof is felted between weather-boards and matching. A very picturesque and useful aviary is No. 197, made in sections in readiness for erection; and No. 201 is most compact, with two doors, one at the back of the house and the other at the end of the run, and a window in each side. This latter aviary is suitable not only for small birds, but also for doves, which are largely kept.

An aviary of British birds is very charming and interesting. Goldfinches, linnets, siskins, bullfinches, and greenfinches make a pleasing mixture, and a few canaries added help still more to brighten the gathering. These finches will thrive on canary seed, rapeseed, hempseed, linseed, and teazel. Always plenty of gritty sand must be provided, and clean fresh water daily for bathing in and drinking.

For beauty there are few birds to equal the Budgerigar or Australian Grass Parrakeet. In an aviary it will breed as freely as the canary, and being naturally gregarious, it does better when there are several pairs together. The male and female are alike in plumage, but they can be distinguished by the membrane surrounding the nostrils. This is blue in the males, light brown or cream colour in the females. They will nest in cocoanut husks or small hollow logs hung up. The hen lays from four to seven white eggs, on which she begins to sit directly the first egg is laid. The food for these birds is very

Pigeon or Dove Aviary.

This is a soundly - made neat design. The flight is formed of wood framework covered with galvanised wire-netting, and is fitted complete with doors. All woodwork stained and varnished, or painted.

4ft. by 2ft., 6ft. high, including legs ... £2.

No. 177.

Span-Roof Pigeon House.

A well-made and neat design. Fitted complete with nests and perches; the flight is formed of wood framing covered with galvanised wire netting; all outside woodwork stained and varnished; complete in sections in readiness for erection, and

No. 178.

securely packed on rail. 12ft. by 6ft.; 9ft. high to ridge; 6ft. high to eaves; suitable for Twelve Pairs of Birds.

PRICE ... ... £10.

148

BIRD-KEEPING IN AVIARIES—*continued.*

simple—canary seed and white millet, in separate vessels, with
a few white oats in addition when there are young. The young
ones will nest and lay when three months old. This should not
be allowed, as the result from such a youthful alliance will be
sickly, and will fledge badly. They should not be permitted to
mate before they are at least six months old. Among the
smaller foreign birds the Parson finch, the Ribbon finch, the
Zebra finch, the Chestnut finch, the Cherry finch, the Java Spar-
row, the Avadavat, the Waxbill, and the Black-headed and the
Bronze Mannikin are all hardy, and do well in an aviary on
canary seed and white millet.

An aviary of Foreign Doves is extremely attractive and
pretty. Many of the Doves are among the most beautiful of
birds. The one most frequently seen in this country is the
Barbary or Collared Dove, pale fawn in colour, with a black
line, in a half circle, at the back of the neck. It is perfectly
hardy, and will breed during the greater part of the year. The
Java Dove is a pure white bird, in size and shape much like
the Barbary Dove. The Diamond Dove is lavender-coloured
in head and breast, the back and wings purplish lilac, with a
number of delicate white spots dotted over. Of the larger
Doves, the Bronze-winged and the Cambayan Turtle Dove are
hardy and desirable aviary birds. The food for the smaller
Doves is canary and millet seed, with now and then some hempseed, and for the larger Doves dari, wheat, tares, and canary
seed.

Range of Span-Roof Pigeon Cotes.

No. 179.

The illustration here shows a very ornamental design for a range of Four Cotes and Flights; the Cotes are constructed of good sound match-boards, roofs of both Cotes and Flights boarded and felted, with ornamental cresting at ridge, the front, ends, and divisions to Flights are formed of strong wooden framework, the bottom part of same being covered with galvanised corrugated iron; each Flight is fitted complete with gate; all outside woodwork stained and varnished; in sections in readiness for erection, securely packed on rail.

Four Houses and Flights, size over all, 16ft. by 10ft.

PRICE ... ... £18 10s.

Lean-to Range of Pigeon Cotes.

No. 180.

Similar in construction to No. 179. Four Houses and Flights, size over all, 16ft. by 10ft.

PRICE ... ... £17 10s.

Make your Nests with **Cooper's Disinfectas.** Better than hay or straw. Per Sack (2-bushel), 2s. 6d.

RABBITS.

There are advantages in rabbit-keeping which cause these animals to take a prominent position in the rank of home pets. They are a source of great interest to the fancier owing to the skill required in breeding them to the requisite standard of points; they are held in esteem as an article of food; and many of the varieties are hardy enough to thrive out of doors in the smallest space.

HOUSING.—One or two breeds, such as the Lop, can only be bred successfully under cover. If one of these breeds is kept, some sort of house or shed is necessary. Special care must be taken to provide proper ventilation. The lower part of the house must have holes, or gratings, and there must be an outlet at the top for the foul air. A blind is necessary for the window when the sun is hot. The coats of some rabbits will turn a rusty brown, instead of black, if exposed to the direct rays of the sun.

We make hutches of various descriptions, suitable both for indoor and outdoor use. There is our cheap rabbit hutch for boys, No. 204; a very useful hutch, No. 203, made either single or double; and our improved outdoor rabbit hutch, No. 202. This hutch is constructed with the breeding chambers above, and run underneath for the young ones when weaned. It is 6ft. long by 2ft. wide, and is fitted with all the latest improvements. The floors of the hutches must be strewn to the depth of an inch with coarse pine sawdust. The sleeping apartment must contain some hay. It is necessary to use feeding troughs, and not to throw the food on the floor.

FEEDING.—Rabbits will eat almost anything in the way of grain, meal, or greenstuff. They benefit by frequent change of diet. If any food is left after a meal it should not be given to the rabbits again. They will seldom touch stale food. They will certainly not thrive on it. With most rabbit-breeders grain is the staple article of food. Of the various grains, oats are the best for all purposes. They can be used in several ways—whole oats, crushed oats (particularly useful for young rabbits which cannot manage whole grain), soaked oats, steeped in cold water for six hours and then drained off, and ground oats, which can be made up in many ways.

Barley is good as a change, but it must not be given daily, or it is liable to cause eruptions and coarseness. The heaviest and best grain should always be procured. It goes further, and is really cheaper. Meal is useful for getting a rabbit into condition or for fattening purposes. Oatmeal, barley-meal, pea-

151

Improved Outdoor Rabbit Hutch.

No. 183.

This hutch is constructed with the Breeding Chambers above, the Run underneath affording plenty of room for the young ones when weaned. It is well made, and fitted with the latest improvements. 4ft. high in front, 3ft. 6in. at back.

6ft. long by 2ft. wide.

PRICE ... ... £2 15s.

Portable Rabbit Hutch and Run.

No. 184.

This hutch is made for placing upon ground, and is constructed with all the latest improvements. It has a galvanised wire-netting bottom, which admits the grass through, and in no way injures the comfort of the Rabbit. The roof is hinged in two parts, affording easy access in attending to the stock. The principles laid down by Major Morant in his treatise upon "Rabbit Rearing to a Profit," are all embodied in this Hutch. It is fitted with Covered Hutch and all necessaries, and the outside is painted.

6ft. long by 3ft. wide.

PRICE ... ... £1 10s.

Any size made to order.

RABBITS—*continued.*

meal, maize-meal, and pollard can all be utilised. They are generally given mixed into a crumbly paste with water, though sometimes in a dry state.

Green food is essential. The following can be given:—Cabbage, lettuce, dandelion, hedge-parsley, sow-thistle, chicory, grass, clover, blackberry leaves, vine leaves, scarlet-runner leaves, nut leaves, mallow, wild tares, and young hawthorn shoots. Cabbage is almost always obtainable, and is useful when little other green food can be had. Lettuce is valuable for does with young. Being of a watery nature, it must not be given too freely. Dandelion is useful and milk-producing. If used in large quantities, or for a lengthy period, it has a powerful effect on the kidneys. Hedge-parsley is a first-rate food in the spring. Chicory is eaten freely by the rabbits, never giving them the scours.

How to give the green food is important. Some breeders give it freshly gathered. Others use it only when it has been cut for some hours and is partially dry. If given fresh, all superficial moisture must first be removed by drying with a cloth. Rabbits are undoubtedly fond of wet green food, and eat it greedily. But the effect is often disastrous. Roots, such as carrots, swedes, mangolds, and parsnips, are useful, especially when green food is not obtainable. Swedes and mangolds should be cut in pieces some hours before required for use.

Bread and milk is a good food, especially when the doe has young or in cases of sickness. Plenty of hay, too, is essential. Soaked peas, a handful of maize slightly bruised, potatoes boiled and mixed with pollard or oatmeal, tea leaves and bran—all of these make a satisfactory change. Clean cold water should be given at least three or four times a week in the summer, and once a week in the winter. It is beneficial to young and growing rabbits, and saves many lives in bad cases

Rabbit Hutch.

No. 203.

Strongly made, sound timber and workmanship, and fitted with divisions for breeding purposes.

SINGLE :
2ft. 6in. long, 4ft. high, 2ft. wide.
Cash Price .. 15s.

DOUBLE :
5ft. long, 4ft. high, 2ft. wide.
Cash Price .. £1 5s.

Rabbit Hutch.

No. 181.

Made of thoroughly seasoned wood, and fitted with divisions for Breeding purposes. Oil-painted outside.

PRICES.

	£	s.	d.
Single, 2ft. 6in. long, 4ft. high, 2ft. wide	0	15	0
Double, 5ft. long, 4ft. high, 2ft. wide	1	5	0

Portable Rabbit Hutch.

No. 182.

This Hutch is also suitable for Ferret Kennel. It is soundly constructed of tongued and grooved matching, roof of weather boards; built on raised legs and fitted with loose floors, thus facilitating cleansing; the front of the Run is covered with galvanised wire-netting, and is fitted complete with door. All outside woodwork painted one coat of good oil colour, and inside whitened.

4ft. by 2ft.; 3ft. 6in. high.

PRICE ... ... £1 7s. 6d.

Cooper's Disinfectas.

For Poultry Houses and Runs, Kennels, Rabbit Hutches, Stables, &c. Clean, cheap, and healthy. Per Sack (2-bushel), 2s. 6d. 10 for 22s. 6d. Sacks included.

RABBITS—*continued*.

of diarrhœa. Three meals a day is a favourite method of feeding: soft food in the morning, greenstuff at noon, and oats or other grain and hay at night. This can be varied often.

BREEDING.—If permitted, rabbits will breed throughout the year. The young ones, however, seldom thrive in the winter. It is better not to allow breeding before the early spring. Both buck and doe must be in good health and condition, with glossy coats and clear, bright eyes, the buck at least a year and the doe not less than nine months old. When in a condition for breeding the doe will be restless, and will stamp her hind feet loudly on the floor. She should be placed in the hutch of the buck for not more than ten minutes, then returned gently to her own quarters. The doe goes with young about thirty days. Young does sometimes have their first litter in twenty-eight days.

A few days before the little ones are expected the doe will generally begin to bite up her bedding, carry it about in her mouth, and pile some of it in a corner. Her appetite will become larger, and her rations should be increased. Some mashes, made of meal, mixed with boiled linseed, will not be amiss at this time. Fresh cold water must not be forgotten. Nearly all does line their nests with fur from their breasts. A good supply of soft hay must be given in the sleeping compartment. With timid does it is as well to darken the hutch. Two days before the young are due the hutch should be cleaned out.

The nest should be examined about three days after the doe has littered. She should be offered some green food or other luxury to attract her attention while this is being done. Any very weakly or dead young can then be removed. Doe rabbits will occasionally destroy their offspring. One reason for this is the practice of handling the litter too soon. Sometimes a doe will desert her young on account of rats or mice. A strange dog or cat appearing near the hutch may cause a doe to rush to her young and trample them to death. Fresh green food must be supplied to the doe liberally when nursing, such as lettuce, sow-thistle, and dandelion. She should also have warm bread and milk, oats, sound sweet hay, and occasionally a mash made of oatmeal and milk, or barley-meal and middlings.

Lops and other rabbits that require to be large should remain with their mother for ten or twelve weeks. The young of other breeds can be taken from the doe at the end of six weeks. Our hutch, No. 202, is most convenient for this purpose. The compartment underneath should be made ready for the young ones by putting in it some fresh straw. They should not all be moved on the same day. The largest and strongest can go first.

RABBITS—*continued.*

The youngsters should be fed three times a day. A good mode of feeding is to give crushed oats and a little lukewarm milk and water to drink in the morning; at noon some sweet hay and a cabbage leaf or two; and at dusk some middlings mixed with milk, or barley-meal scalded with water, then squeezed nearly dry and a little milk added. A good supply of bread and milk helps to bring them on quickly. The young rabbits may be kept together till they are thirteen or fourteen weeks old. After that time the bucks must be placed in separate hutches.

SOME DISEASES: DIARRHŒA OR SCOURS. — A common malady, caused often by stale or wet green food. Give dry food, such as crushed oats and bran, plenty of fresh water to drink, and about 5 grains of carbonate of bismuth daily, put over the tongue at the back.

EAR WAX.—Some rabbits have their ears now and then filled with sores and scabs, which cause discomfort and pain. When this is noticed the wax should be gently loosened and removed with a little piece of wood or with a quill. Then sprinkle into the ear some boracic powder daily three or four times. Or another treatment is to drop a little olive oil into the ear, and, when the scabs are softened, to carefully remove them with a soft rag or sponge.

EYES, INFLAMMATION OF.—When this occurs the eyes will run, and will be inflamed. They should be bathed with a lotion made of boracic acid one scruple, and water 6oz. Young rabbits are subject to ophthalmia. This causes the eye to look swollen and be sometimes closed, and there are red spots round the lids. The eyes should be bathed with a weak solution of alum and water. An hour after bathing apply a ten-grain solution of sulphate of zinc twice daily, dropped into the eye.

SCURF will arise from want of cleanliness, from insufficient

RABBITS—*continued*.

green food, and from contagion. The symptoms are roughness of the skin, which peels off in small white flakes. The sufferer must be isolated, and the affected parts washed with warm water. Half an hour afterwards a solution of strong tobacco water should be applied—an ounce of common shag to half a pint of boiling water, used lukewarm. This must be continued every alternate day for a fortnight.

RED WATER is induced by damp, or by feeding too freely on cabbage or dandelion. The water appears as if tinged with blood. The bed must be dry and clean, no cabbage leaves allowed, but the feeding should be warm pollard mixed with boiled potatoes, hay, a few oats, tea leaves, chicory, and a little garden parsley, and a few drops of sweet spirits of nitre daily.

THE DIFFERENT BREEDS.

THE ANGORA.—One of the most uncommon looking of the numerous breeds, with wool as long as can be obtained, fine in texture, and of equal length all over the body. White Angoras are generally seen, but there are also blue, grey, and fawn specimens. The eye is of a pale ruby colour. The Angora is fairly hardy, and does not require artificial heat. To prevent the long coat becoming damaged the strictest cleanliness must be observed.

THE BELGIAN HARE.—This is a native of Belgium and the Northern parts of France, and derives the name of "hare" from its great resemblance to that animal. Length of limb and freedom from dewlap are important points. It is an excellent rabbit for the table, being of good flavour, and weighing from 7lb. to 10lb. In breeding Belgians dark bucks should be used, otherwise the young ones may be too light.

THE BLACK AND TAN.—A good specimen of this breed is very attractive. The dense black, the rich tan, the short, erect black ears margined with tan, the tan nostrils, and the bright colour on the chest, flanks, and feet all produce a most pleasing effect.

The Blue and Tan is a pretty sub-variety. The points are the same as in the Black and Tan, with the substitution of blue for black.

THE DUTCH is a popular and pretty variety. It is hardy and prolific, and, depending largely on markings, the inferior specimens can be distinguished at an early period. The points of the Dutch lie in the markings, colour, and shape. The ears are neat, erect, and coloured, the eyes matching, and without specks. The colours of this rabbit are black, blue, tortoiseshell, and grey. Dutch mature quickly, and the does can be used for breeding at six months. The young are fit for exhibition when ten weeks old.

THE ENGLISH is bred in the usual rabbit colours. The ears are carried erect, and are coloured. The nose is marked like a butterfly with its wings extended, hence the name of Butterfly Smut sometimes given to this rabbit. There is a spot on each side of the face, clear of the eye circle. A line of colour extends along the spine, the colour being well broken up, continued by the "chains" on either side. The young ones show but little body colour till after the first moult.

THE FLEMISH GIANT.—A very large rabbit, good specimens weighing as much as 15lb. In colour it is grey, with a brown shade ticked with black, after the manner of the Belgian. The Flemish Giant is not so prolific as some other breeds. Size being so important a feature, the doe, though usually a good mother, should not be allowed to bring up more than two or three of the litter.

Portable Rabbit Hutch and Run.

No. 205.

Made for placing upon the ground, with all the latest improvements. It has a galvanised wire netting bottom, which admits the grass through, and in no way injures the comfort of the bottom. The roof is hinged in two parts : affording easy access in attending to the stock. 6ft. long by 3ft. wide. Cash Price, £1 10s. Any Size made to order.

Portable Rabbit or Ferret Hutch.

No. 206.

Soundly constructed of tongued and grooved matching, on raised legs, and fitted with loose floors for cleansing purposes; the front of the Run is covered with galvanised wire netting, and fitted with door.

4ft. by 2ft. ; 3ft. 6in. high.

Cash Price, £1 7s. 6d.

RABBITS—*continued.*

THE HIMALAYAN is one of the prettiest of our domestic rabbits. It has a white body, with the ears, nose, feet, and tail black. The eyes are bright pink, the ears small and neat. As the dark markings are generally inclined to fade and grow lighter, various methods are adopted to prevent this. The Himalayan is a good breeder and fairly hardy. When the young are born they are all white. This continues for two or three weeks, after which the dark extremities will begin to show.

THE LOP-EARED is the oldest of our breeds of fancy rabbits. The most important feature of the Lop is the ear. Lops are reared with the greatest success in a house where the temperature is between 60deg. and 70deg. Not only should the ears be of great length, but they must be as wide as possible throughout the whole extent of the ear. For breeding the buck should have larger ears than the doe. A good Lop should weigh 10lb. or more.

THE PATAGONIAN is another of the large breeds of rabbit not often seen at the present day. It is not very prolific, the litters usually numbering from three to five.

THE POLISH is about the size of the Himalayan, neat and compact in shape. The coat is as fine as possible, short, smooth, and silky in texture. It is a free breeder.

THE SILVER TRIBES are general favourites. The Silver Grey is well known. The silvering and ticking are alike throughout the entire rabbit, the same shade prevailing all over the body and on the extremities, including the head and ears and legs. The Silver Fawn is of a rich fawn, silvered only sufficiently to be discerned. The Silver Brown is of a rich red fawn, finished off by silver tips, with some darker hairs intermingled. These rabbits are hardy, are prolific breeders, and are worthy a place in any rabbitry.

RABBITS FOR THE TABLE.—Rabbit breeding for table purposes only, without regard to fancy points, should, when properly managed, prove lucrative. There is very little outlay required, no special knowledge on the part of the rearer is necessary, and there is a ready sale for plump, well-grown, young rabbits. The system of rearing rabbits in portable hutches, which was originated by Major Morant, is well worth the consideration of anyone thinking of rabbit breeding for profit. Our portable hutch and run, No. 205, is constructed on the principles laid down by Major Morant, having a wire-netting bottom, enabling the rabbits to eat the grass that protudes.

Each doe has a hutch. It is advisable not to allow the does, as a rule, to have more than four litters in a year, and not to breed from them when they are changing their coats in September and October. By not attempting too many litters the

RABBITS—*continued.*

young ones can remain with their mother till they are six or eight weeks old. This hastens their growth. One hundred does and their young will thrive in a ten-acre field. One buck is required for every ten does. The first four weeks the young live entirely on their mother's milk. The last eight weeks—the young ones should be killed at twelve weeks—an average of 1½lb. each of grain and bran, in addition to grass and hay, is all that is necessary. It has been estimated that a full-grown rabbit does not require more than 2oz. of oats, and 2oz. of bran a day, in addition to the grass consumed. Half that quantity is sufficient in fine, dry, warm weather, when the grass or clover is good.

GUINEA PIGS.

The Guinea-pig, or cavy, is a very easily kept pet. Being small it will live comfortably in a space that would not suffice for a rabbit. It is very hardy, it is not expensive to buy, and will allow itself to be handled and carried about without attempting to use its teeth.

With the exception of the Peruvian variety, Guinea-pigs will thrive almost anywhere. We make a most useful house for Guinea-pigs, No. 207. Four sows' hutches comprise the top part, each with breeding chamber. The boars' hutches, three in number, are placed at the bottom. If desired these can be converted into one large hutch by removing the division boards.

There are three varieties of Guinea-pig kept in this country—the English, the Peruvian, and the Abyssinian. The chief

Guinea-Pig House.

No. 207.

This is a pattern supplied to many Breeders. The Boars' Hutches are placed at the bottom, each having a door. This floor can be converted into one large Hutch by removing the division boards. Four Sows' Hutches comprise the top part, each with Breeding Chamber and separate doors.

Size: 3ft. 6in. long, 3ft. high, 1ft. 8in. wide. As illustrated.

Cash Price, £2 10s.

GUINEA PIGS—*continued*.

points of the English, besides colour, are size, shape, shortness and silkiness of coat, large head, neck and shoulders broad and thick, and eyes large and prominent.

The Peruvian is judged chiefly for size, and for the length and quality of the fur. The coat is long, silky, soft, and straight, without the least curl or wave. It is parted down the centre of the back, and hangs on each side of the body, coming also well over the head. The undercoat is dense and long, not thin or open. Compared with the English cavy, the Peruvian is delicate. The coat is brought to perfection by warmth, such as that of a stable. To prevent the long coat becoming soiled the hutch must be cleaned out daily.

The Abyssinian has a harsh coat. This is wiry, rough, and well "rosetted" with circles of stiff, straight hairs radiating from the centre. The number of these rosettes varies in individual cavies. The Abyssinian should be large, with big head, broad shoulders, and large eyes.

Guinea-pigs are fed much as rabbits. They eat more than rabbits in proportion to their size. The food consists of good oats, sweet hay, an occasional mash made of barley-meal and pollard, mixed into a crumbly paste, bread and milk, any kind of green stuff in season, and roots, such as carrots, parsnips, and swedes. Many breeders give their cavies cold water to drink. Peruvians require a somewhat dry diet. They should not have cabbage, lettuce, or watery green stuff.

When breeding Guinea-pigs one boar can run with three or four sows. The sow goes with young about sixty-three days. The little ones are born with their eyes open and clothed with hair. In three days they are able to run about, and will begin to eat bread and milk and nibble the green food. They should be left with their mother till they are about a month old, then they should be removed, the boars being placed in one hutch and the sows in another. At first they should have plenty of bread and milk. After a little while they will be able to eat oats, and manage the same diet as the adults. Cavies will breed when only a few weeks old. This should be prevented. Size is important, so they should not be bred from until they are at least seven months old.

FERRETS.

Originally a native of Africa, the ferret was first introduced into Asia and Southern Europe. It has since been carried into all parts of the habitable globe where its services can be utilised. We make a capital hutch for ferrets, No. 208, divided into two compartments. The hutch must be placed where it is not exposed to wind or rain. A common practice is to stand

FERRETS—*continued.*

it in a dark corner, the idea being that the ferret cannot tolerate bright light; but the animal is healthier and more comfortable when allowed a good amount of light. The floor of the hutch must be covered with clean, coarse sawdust, while the bedding is of wheaten straw. This must often be changed, and the hutch cleaned out.

Two female ferrets can be kept together in the same hutch, but must be separated when young ones are expected. The period of gestation is six weeks. The average litter is from four to six. With regard to diet, bread and milk is largely used. In addition to this, three or four times a week, some flesh, such as a piece of rabbit, or fowl, or other bird. It is not advisable to give them birds or animals that have died of disease, or that are putrid or high. Neither should a quantity of food be given at a time, and allowed to remain until consumed.

If it is wished to bring young ferrets on quickly some beef tea or meat extract added to the food is an excellent thing. They should remain with their mother till they are nine or ten weeks old. This is a good age at which to purchase them. Ferrets must often be handled, so as to make them as tame as possible. If they are only handled when required for use they are liable to bite, and the bite is very severe.

If clean and dry and warm in their houses ferrets are healthy, and give no trouble. If neglected they are liable to many ailments, including foot-rot, mange, and distemper. Foot-rot commonly arises from dirty hutches, and particularly from being put away, after working rabbit and rat holes, while their feet are wet and muddy. The symptoms are great soreness of the feet and tails. These should be washed with warm water, and then anointed with spirits of tar and turpentine in equal parts. Mange can be known by a redness of the skin, especially under the shoulders, and by the animal frequently scratching itself. The simplest remedy is to wash with warm water in which is dissolved a few grains of permanganate of potash. Distemper is practically incurable. It is known by the swollen head and eyes, soreness of the mouth, and loss of appetite. A nutritious diet should be tried, but it is seldom of any use.

Ferret Hutch.

No. 208.

This is a capital Hutch for Ferrets or Guinea Pigs.

3ft. long, 1ft. 6in. wide, 2ft. high.

Cash Price, 15s.

WILLIAM COOPER, Limited,

Horticultural Providers,

751, OLD KENT ROAD, LONDON, S.E.

SECTION III.

Illustrated Catalogue

OF

Dog Kennels,

KENNELS WITH RUNS, PUPPY KENNELS,

PENT=ROOF KENNELS,

STAKES FOR DOG CHAINS,

RANGES OF KENNELS AND RUNS, DOUBLE KENNELS,

&c., &c., &c.

Portable Dog Kennel.
(With Platform.)

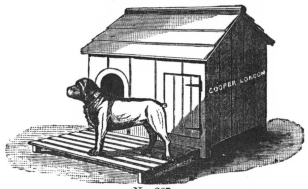

No. 367.

This Kennel is soundly made of red deal, thoroughly seasoned. It has a large door at the side to facilitate attention to sanitary operations, so essential to the well-being of dogs; an open platform is supplied, affording a stand for the dog outside the Kennel free from wet. Oil-painted outside, or stained and varnished.

Packed on Rail at the following Prices :—

No.		£	s.	d.
1.—Suitable for Terriers, 2ft. long, 1ft. 6in. wide, 2ft. high		0	10	6
2.—Suitable for Large Terriers, &c., 2ft. 3in. long, 2ft. wide, 2ft. 6in. high		0	12	6
3.—Suitable for Collies. Retrievers, and Spaniels, 3ft. 6in. long, 2ft. 3in. wide, 3ft. high		0	15	0
4.—Suitable for St. Bernards, Mastiffs, and Newfoundlands. 4ft. 6in. long, 2ft. 6in. wide, 4ft. high		1	5	0

65, Merton Road, Wimbledon, Surrey.

"DEAR SIR,—Kennel to hand all right yesterday, and I wish to say that I am very pleased with same. I like it far better than one I had from another firm about a month ago, and paid 5s. more than I paid you, and both Kennels are the same size (for collie dogs). You were also very quick indeed in delivering (day after order was given), whereas the other firm I refer to kept me waiting nearly a month, so you can guess who will have any future orders from me, and that will be you, and shall be only too pleased to put anything in your way which I can. Such business-like treatment deserves every encouragement.

"You can make what use you like of this, and, in addition, can refer anyone to me, and I'll show them the two kennels, and a blind man could see which was the best. With best wishes.—Yours faithfully, T. H. UPTON."

DOGS.

Naturalists are divided in their opinions regarding the origin of our domestic dogs. Some believe that they have been derived either from the wolf or the jackal, or from some extinct species; others opine that they have originated from several species more or less commingled. But whatever may have been the origin of our present-day dog, there is no doubt that the taste for keeping all kinds of dogs, either for their usefulness, or simply as pets, was never more pronounced than it is now.

FOOD.—If we wish to keep our dogs in health we must not feed them more than twice a day. It is said of many human beings that they dig their graves with their teeth. The same may truthfully be said of numberless house dogs. The greatest enemy to their health, and the cause of much disease and premature death, is over-eating. A dog that is allowed to be present at the family meals almost invariably receives numerous scraps in addition to his ordinary food. It is true that some self-denial is required when we see our pets sitting up on their hindquarters, and eloquently asking for a taste of what we are eating. But most certainly it is mistaken kindness to yield to doggie's appeal.

A valuable article of diet for all kinds of dogs is dog biscuit. For breakfast a biscuit—or a portion, according to the size of the dog—broken up, either dry or soaked. The next and principal meal should be given about five o'clock, or later if more convenient. This can be varied with advantage. Scraps from the table, bread or biscuit mixed with gravy or with the water in which fish has been boiled, or any of the advertised prepared foods for dogs. Two or three times a week some boiled green vegetables must be given, mixed with the other food—no more at a time than the dog will eat eagerly. As soon as he begins to stop feeding and to look about, any remaining must be taken away. A large bone now and then helps to keep the teeth clean, and gives a lot of employment. Fish, game, and fowl bones are bad. Small bones of that description are greedily eaten; but they often lead to perforation of the intestines.

Small toy dogs, such as Poms, do well on biscuit broken up and mixed with gravy, with, three or four times a week, a little minced underdone or raw, lean meat. Big dogs can eat all kinds of things. Paunches, houndmeal, oatmeal, and bullocks' heads can form items in the bill of fare. All dogs should have constant access to clean water for drinking. It is a common practice to put a piece of sulphur in the water provided for dogs. This is quite useless. A pebble might as well be used, as sulphur does not dissolve in water.

Improved Dog Kennel.

No. 368.

The superiority in manufacture of these Kennels has created a great demand for them. The best boards only, grooved and tongued, are employed in construction, and they are rendered thoroughly rain-proof. Painted one coat, or stained and varnished, as may be desired.

Made in Three Sizes.

No. 1. Suitable for Terriers, 10s. 6d.
No. 2.   ,,   Collies, Retrievers, and Spaniels, 15s.
No. 3.   ,,   St. Bernards, Mastiffs, and Newfoundlands, £1 5s.

These Kennels are comfortable, having the gables extended in the front.

Lean-to Kennel with Covered Run.

Constructed of good, sound, tongued and grooved matching, weatherboard roof; iron rods in front, as shown; all outside woodwork painted one coat; all in sections in readiness for erection.

No. 369.

Size, 10ft. long, 4ft. 6in. wide, 7ft. high at back, 5ft. high to eaves.

PRICE ...   .   £4 10s.
Wood Back, 20s. extra.

166

Dogs—*continued.*

HOUSING.—It is not good to coddle dogs, even small toy dogs, in their sleeping quarters. A small pet dog is frequently allowed to sleep on the bed of its owner. Under such conditions the little animal is more susceptible to cold, is more likely to be delicate, and the coat, if a large one, will not be glossy and healthy. We make a great variety of dog-kennels, suitable for all breeds. Our portable kennel, No. 209, is constructed in various sizes, for Terriers, for Collies or Retrievers, and for the largest dogs, such as St. Bernards and Newfoundlands. It has an entrance at the side, a door to enable easy cleaning, and a platform outside, affording a stand free from wet. We make lean-to kennels, with covered runs, of various descriptions, Nos. 210, 213, and 219; a three-quarter span-roof portable kennel and run, No. 211, for dogs of all sizes, and well adapted for breeding purposes, and also for a puppy house; other kennels of different shapes with covered runs, Nos. 217, 221, 223, and 226; and kennels with open runs, Nos. 225, 228, and 229; also different patterns of puppy kennels, notably Nos. 214, 215, 220, and 227.

The kennel must be placed in a dry situation, where damp and wet will be absent. A south or south-east aspect is as good as any. Plenty of sunshine tends to health, provided the dog can obtain shade in hot weather. A good supply of bedding adds much to the comfort of a dog. There is nothing better than clean, well-broken straw often changed. A good supply of disinfectant is a necessity. For this purpose our Disinfectas should be sprinkled frequently in the kennels and runs.

GENERAL MANAGEMENT.—Regular exercise is most important for the health and comfort of the dog. Most dogs suffer from constipation and more serious troubles if they are not allowed at least one good run daily. House dogs should always be put out of doors for a few minutes before going to bed. Exercise should not be given immediately after a good meal. In very hot weather the outing ought to be taken either early in the morning or in the evening—not at the warmest time of day. Certain active breeds of dog require more exercise than heavier dogs, such as the Bulldog; and old dogs will not want as much as younger dogs.

Washing in moderation helps to keep a dog in health, and prevents unpleasant smell. Long-haired dogs must not be washed too often, or the coat will go wrong. The same may be said of wire-haired, hard-coated dogs, the coats of which will become soft with frequent washing. Once a fortnight is often enough to give a bath to most toy dogs, and once a month for dogs such as Fox-terriers, although the time of year must also be taken into consideration, as well as the age of the dog.

To keep a dog's coat in the best condition it is necessary to brush it often. This not only adds to his good looks, but helps

Three-Quarter Span-Roof Portable Kennel and Run.

No. 370.

The above Kennel and Run is suitable for Collies, Retrievers, Terriers, and small dogs, and is well adapted for breeding purposes, and also for a Puppy House; the sleeping compartment is constructed at the back, the top of which forms a day bench; the front is made to lift up for cleaning purposes; both ends are constructed of iron rods 2½in. apart; roof of weather-boards; boarded back, thus doing away with the need of wall or fence. All woodwork painted one coat outside and limewashed inside, and the whole in sections to bolt together and securely packed on rail at the following respective prices:—

No.		£	s.	d.
1.—For Terriers, 3ft. wide, 5ft. deep, 4ft. 6in. high at ridge		2	0	0
2.—For Collies, Retrievers, &c., 3ft. 9in. wide, 6ft. 6in. deep, 5ft. 6in. high at ridge		2	15	0

Wood Batten Floor for Runs, 4s. and 5s. extra respectively.

Dogs—*continued.*

to keep him free from insects, and to remove the old and loose hair. Long-haired toy dogs should be brushed and combed daily. Dogs that carry a short, shiny coat should often be rubbed down with a silk handkerchief to improve the gloss.

A puppy, when intended for the house, must be taught habits of cleanliness when quite young. He is sure to make mistakes occasionally in the house, but this should not entail severe chastisement. A couple of smacks with the hand and a scolding, repeated each time the offence is committed, will in most instances soon stop this, especially if the dog is immediately turned out of doors for a minute or two.

BREEDING.—It is advisable not to allow a bitch to be mated before she is a year old, not even quick maturing, small dogs. Many of the large breeds have not finished growing when eighteen months. These it will be better to keep unmated till two years old. A bitch usually comes in season at intervals of six months, but this cannot always be depended on. The approach of the period can be known by the parts swelling, followed by a discharge that lasts for nine or more days.

The period of gestation is sixty-three days. Before the puppies are expected, a dose of castor-oil is usually given. Small dogs can have some magnesia instead of the oil. The bitch will most likely be restless, and decline to eat for a few hours before the time. She must have water handy for drinking. After the puppies are born the mother should be offered some warm beef tea. The food must be light, and not heating, for the first week—porridge and milk, bread and milk, strong broth, and very little meat. More food will be required as the puppies grow. The supply of meat must be increased.

The different breeds vary considerably in the size of their litters. Fox-terriers, Pugs, and Scotch-terriers seldom have more than seven or eight puppies. The very large breeds have, some of them, from ten to fifteen at a litter. Unless the mother is very strong, it is as well not to allow her to attempt to rear all of a large litter. Small dogs generally find four or five puppies enough; larger breeds, eight or nine. The surplus pups can either be transferred to a foster-parent or drowned. If the latter, the weakest or most unshapely should be got rid of.

When five or six weeks old the puppies can be gradually weaned. They will be able to feed themselves, and can be fed from a plate on finely-broken puppy biscuits, with a little chopped-up underdone meat, or on bread broken up and mixed with gravy, or, for a change, with milk. They should have as much at each meal as they can eat. Four feeds a day for the first three months are not too many.

It is the practice to shorten the tails, or " dock," as it is

Portable Lean-to Kennel and Run.

No. 371.

The accompanying illustration shows a Lean-to Kennel and Covered Run for fixing against a wall or fence, and is constructed in sections to be bolted together; strong framework, boarded with tongued and grooved boards, the end of run also being boarded, thus protecting the run and kennel from draughts; the sleeping compartment is made at one end, the top of which forms a day bench; the front is hung on hinges, by which means the inside can be thoroughly cleaned; the front of run is constructed of iron rods, 2½in. apart, and complete with door; the roof is covered with feather-edge boards; outside woodwork painted one coat. All in perfect readiness for erection, and securely packed on rail, at the following respective prices:

	£	s.	d.
No. 1.—Suitable for Terriers, &c., 6ft. 6in. long, 3ft. wide, 4ft. high at back...	2	10	0
No. 2.—Suitable for Collies, Retrievers, &c., 9ft. long, 3ft. 9in. wide, 5ft. high at back	3	10	0
No. 3.—Suitable for St. Bernards, &c., 11ft. 6in. long, 4ft. 9in. wide, 5ft. 6in. high at back ...	4	10	0

If the back is boarded, making them independent of wall or fence, 10s., 12s., or 20s. extra. Wood batten floors for runs, 6s., 9s., and 12s. extra.

WIRE.

Kemp Town, Brighton.—W. COOPER, 753, Old Kent Road,

"Kennels arrived safe, and give great satisfaction.   ALDERNEY SMITH.

Dogs—*continued.*

called, of certain breeds. This should be done when the puppy is about three days old. There is an idea that the operation is performed by biting off the piece of the tail, but though this was occasionally done in the olden times, the disgusting practice is a thing of the past. Both docking and removing the dew claws are done with a pair of strong scissors. The puppies must be allowed plenty of exercise, and to run in the sunshine and air as much as possible. If it is desired to dispose of any of a litter of puppies, they look prettier when a few weeks old than during the "hobbledehoy." stage, and are more readily and more satisfactorily sold before they have attained three months.

ADMINISTRATION OF MEDICINE.—In many instances medicine can be given in the food without the dog being aware of it. Pills can be inserted in a piece of meat, and powders can often be mixed with the dinner, or in some gravy. When it is necessary to compel the dog to take food as little force as possible must be used, or the animal may be injured. A large dog can best be treated if placed against a wall so that he cannot back. If the operator then stands across the animal, the dog's head can be held between his knees, and the mouth opened by inserting the second finger and thumb of the left hand. If liquids are given, the mouth of the dog can be kept closed, the head raised, the lower lip pulled out so that a funnel-shaped opening is made, and the fluid slowly poured in. A small dog can be held on an assistant's knee.

SOME MALADIES.—If a dog is really ill, it is better to call in skilled aid than to attempt amateur doctoring. A few of the ordinary ailments are here referred to, and some of the remedies given.

BRONCHITIS.—Dogs sometimes suffer from inflammation of the bronchial tubes, caused by exposure to cold and damp. The sufferer must be kept in a warm, moist atmosphere, and hot linseed poultices applied to the chest and sides. The following mixture can be given internally: Liquor morphia, 1 drachm; ipecacuanha wine, ½ drachm; paregoric, 2 drachms; Hoffmann's spirit, 1 drachm; water, 2oz. One teaspoonful to a 20lb. dog twice a day.

BURNS.—The best application to a burn or scald is carron oil, made by mixing equal parts of lime-water and linseed oil. The affected part must be covered with cotton-wool or wadding immediately after the oil is applied. If no oil is obtainable the wound should be freely dusted with flour.

CATARRH, OR COLD IN THE HEAD, sometimes is a prelude to distemper, but when this is the case there is always fever and prostration. A simple cold is denoted by a watery discharge from the nose and eyes, and now and then a cough.

Puppy Kennel and Run.

No. 372.

This Kennel is constructed of good, sound, tongued and grooved matching, weather-boarded roof, which is hinged to lift up. The Run is formed of iron rods in sides and end; with gate in end, the top of Run being of wire-netting and hinged, to open, as shown. All outside woodwork painted one coat, and inside limewashed; the whole complete with floor.

Size, 6ft. by 2ft. 6in.

PRICE ... ... £1 10s.

Dog Kennel with Covered Run.

No. 373.

This is a neat design, and is constructed of good, sound, tongued and grooved matching; roof of weather-boards. The Run is of iron rods in upper part of sides and in end, which is fitted with gate; the whole complete, with floor, in sections in readiness for erection, at the following prices:

No.		£	s.	d.
1. 6ft. by 3ft. by 5ft. 6in., suitable for Terriers...	...	3	0	0
2. 7ft. by 4ft. by 6ft., suitable for Collies, &c. ...	...	3	10	0
3. 10ft. by 5ft. by 7ft., suitable for Mastiffs, &c.	...	5	5	0

172

Dogs—*continued.*

The treatment is to keep the dog in dry quarters, and give twice a day five drops of paregoric and five drops of eucalyptus oil, mixed with a little sugar.

COAT COMING OUT.—Many bitches shed their coats after whelping, and many breeds of dog, owing to improper feeding and other causes, are constantly losing their coats. The coat can be strengthened by freely applying cocoanut oil just warmed. A good stimulant for promoting the growth of hair is a lotion made of ½oz. of tincture of cantharides and 8oz. of water, gently rubbed on the hairless parts twice a day. See also under Eczema.

CONSTIPATION.—Some fluid magnesia—quantity according to the size of the dog—in milk every morning for a time will relieve. Give plenty of exercise, some green vegetables with the food, and let the diet be moist, and not dry.

COUGH.—A cough can in many instances be relieved by giving a dessertspoonful twice a day of the following mixture: Liquor morphia, 1½ drachms; paregoric and Hoffmann's spirit, 2 drachms each; ipecacuanha wine, 1 drachm; syrup of squills, 1oz.; and water to 3oz.

DIARRHŒA.—Ordinary cases can generally be stopped by using the following mixture: Rubini's essence of camphor and chlorodyne, five drops of the former and fifteen drops of the latter twice a day. In chronic diarrhœa, from five to ten grains of bismuth mixed with the food daily will often prove a cure.

DISTEMPER.—The first symptoms of this serious disease are loss of appetite, dulness, a husky cough, and rapid loss of flesh and strength. There is a discharge from the eyes and nose, and purging or vomiting. Distemper takes many forms. If the dog seems very ill skilled advice should be sought. The patient must promptly be put in a warm, dry place. Beef tea, bread and milk, and other light diet are necessary. If the dog is very weak he must be drenched with weak brandy and water or port wine. Puppies are more liable to distemper than older dogs, though the latter are attacked sometimes. It is not a matter of course that a puppy will have distemper. Many dogs are never afflicted with it.

EAR, CANKER OF.—When a dog is constantly holding its head on one side, shaking its ear violently and scratching it, it usually has canker. The ear should be syringed night and morning with a tablespoonful of methylated spirits added to half a tumbler of warm water, then dried with cotton-wool, and some boracic powder dusted into the ear. Or another mode of treatment is to pour in a few drops of the following lotion daily: Glycerine, 2oz.; laudanum, ½oz.; lead acetate, ½ drachm; water, 8oz. Warm before using the lotion.

Puppy Kennel.

No. 374.

This portable Puppy Kennel will be found indispensable to Breeders. It can be moved as often as necessary to maintain cleanliness, and it provides accommodation in any case of emergency. It is strongly made and fitted.

6ft. long, 2ft. 6in. wide, 2ft. 6in. high.

PRICE ... ... £1 7s. 6d.

Larger sizes made to order.

Puppy or Cat Kennel.

No. 375.

The above is a very neat design, and is suitable for indoor use, and is constructed of good, sound, tongued and grooved boards. The Kennel is fitted with zinc pan at bottom, and the top of both Kennel and Run is hinged to lift up; the Run is constructed of iron rods. The whole complete with floor; all outside woodwork stained and varnished.

Size, 5ft. by 2ft. by 2ft. 6in.

PRICE ... ... £2.

Dogs—*continued.*

ECZEMA.—If the dog scratches himself violently, and the coat comes off in patches, and there are sore places. or spots or scales, he probably has some form of eczema. To the irritable places should be applied a lotion made of 1oz. of Wright's solution of coal tar and 8oz. of water, twice a day with a piece of rag; and after food twice a day give four drops of Fowler's solution of arsenic in a dessertspoonful of water. This dose is for a 20lb. dog. The patient should have a fair amount of raw meat.

EYES, WEAK.—Bathe the eyes two or three times daily with a lotion made of 1 grain chinosol and 3oz. water; or bathe with a lotion made of 1 scruple sulphate of zinc, 1 drachm laudanum, and 6oz. water.

FATNESS, EXCESSIVE.—This is common with many house dogs, arising from overfeeding and insufficient exercise. The amount of food should be reduced and the dog should have more exercise. A dose of iodide of potassium—2 grains in water twice daily after meals—will help to reduce the fat.

FITS.—These are of many kinds. The commonest are teething fits in puppies and epileptic fits. For the former it is usually sufficient to give some aperient medicine. For epileptic fits 5 grains of bromide of potassium three times a day is the usual treatment.

MANGE is of two kinds—sarcoptic and follicular. The latter is difficult to treat, and should be dealt with by a veterinary surgeon. In sarcoptic mange the skin becomes dry and rough, the hair comes off in patches, and there are pimples, followed by scabs. It is contagious to human beings, as well as to animals. The sufferer must be dressed all over with a mixture of olive oil 10 parts and sulphur 1 part. This must be well worked into the skin with the fingers, and repeated three times at intervals of four days; then it should be washed off.

PARASITES, EXTERNAL.—There are few dogs that are not troubled with parasites, especially fleas. These can be got rid of by using some of the advertised dog soaps when washing the dog, or by rubbing into the coat a preparation of 1 part paraffin and 2 parts olive oil two or three times at intervals of four days.

Lice can be killed by using a lime and sulphur lotion. This is made thus: Flowers of sulphur, 2lb.; unslaked lime, 1lb.; water, 2 gallons. Slake the lime in some of the water, stir in the sulphur, adding water gradually till it is creamy, then add the remainder of the two gallons, and boil down to one gallon. Let it stand till cold, pour off the clean liquid, and make the quantity to five quarts with cold water. Damp the dog all over with the lotion. Ticks can be destroyed with the above lotion.

Pent-Roof Kennel.

Constructed of good, sound, tongued, grooved, and beaded matching; weather-board roof; complete with floor, and fitted with bench; outside painted, or stained and varnished.

No. 376.

PRICES:

No.	Size.			£	s.	d.	
1.	3ft. by 2ft. 6in.	...	...	2	0	0	Suitable for Terriers.
2.	4ft. by 3ft.	...	...	2	10	0	„ Collies, &c.
3.	5ft. by 4ft.	...	...	3	5	0	„ St. Bernards, &c.

Portable Lean-to Dog Kennel.

No. 377.

This Lean-to House and Kennel is made of the best materials, being strong, yet light in appearance. The Kennel, which is 2ft. 6in. high, is made with movable top, so that its height may easily be increased, if wanted, for a very large Dog. The house is 4ft. wide, and 3ft. 6in. back to front; the run is 6ft. long, 3ft. 6in. deep, and fitted with gate. It is roofed with corrugated galvanised iron, but open iron bars can be had if desired over Run.

PRICE ... ... £5.

Corrugated galvanised iron, 2ft. wide, round bottom of Run or Yard, 7s. 6d. extra.

Dogs—*continued*.

TUMOURS.—Bitches are sometimes troubled with small movable tumours near the teats. These should be rubbed with an ointment made of 1 drachm iodide of potash, 1 drachm mercuria lointment, and 1oz. belladonna ointment. Some old dogs have fatty tumours, smooth and slimy, and not tender when touched. They need not be interfered with unless they become troublesome, then a vet. must be called in to remove them by excision.

WORMS.—One of the most satisfactory remedies for worms is to give santonin in one to three grain doses, according to the size of the dog, after twelve hours' fasting, and one hour afterwards a dose of castor oil. This treatment must be repeated three or four times at weekly intervals.

THE VARIOUS BREEDS.

THE AIREDALE TERRIER, also known as the Waterside, is one of the largest of the terrier family. Some breeders are of opinion that this dog has a good deal of hound blood in its veins. The Airedale is not in the least quarrelsome, he is good-tempered, is an excellent dog for the home, good at killing vermin, and a first-rate water dog.

THE BEDLINGTON TERRIER.—One of the many dogs that have had their origin in the North of Great Britain. Being moderately long on the leg the Bedlington is faster than most terriers, and, having an excellent nose, and being very obedient, he is valuable to the sportsman. He is good-tempered, lively, and intelligent, and most plucky and resolute.

THE BLACK AND TAN TERRIER, called also the Manchester Terrier, is bred in two varieties, but only different in size. The weight of the larger dog is between 10lb. and 20lb. That of the smaller does not exceed 5lb. It is illegal to crop the ears as was formerly done, so the sharp appearance for which these dogs were celebrated has gone.

THE BLOODHOUND, formerly used for hunting and tracking fugitives, became almost extinct when its services were no longer required. But good classes for Bloodhounds appear at the leading dog shows, and attempts are now being made to utilise them for tracing criminals in this country. This splendid hound is most affectionate, rather shy, and very obedient.

THE BORZOI, or Russian Wolfhound, has become very popular in England of recent years. For elegance of conformation there is no member of the canine race to surpass this dog. In shape it is much like the Greyhound, the neck being slightly shorter. The Borzoi is gentle in disposition and reliable in temper, as well as affectionate and companionable.

Dog Kennel with Covered Run.

This is a well-built substantial Kennel and Run, the roof to both Kennel and Run being covered with weather-boarding. The Kennel is provided with day-bench over sleeping compartment. All outside woodwork painted one coat. The Run is constructed of iron rods, and has gate at end.

No. 378.

Constructed in sections, and carefully packed on rail at the following respective prices :

Size 1.   For Terriers ... ...   £5.
Kennel, 3ft. long, 3ft. 6in. wide, 4ft. high; Run, 5ft. long, 3ft. 6in. wide.

Size 2.   For Retrievers and Spaniels ... ...   £6 5s.
Kennel, 3ft. 6in. long, 4ft. wide, 5ft. high ; Run, 6ft. long, 4ft. wide.
If wood spline floor for runs—Size 1, 15s. extra; size 2, £1 extra.

Dog Kennel and Run.

No. 379.

A good, strong Kennel and Run, constructed of good, sound, tongued and grooved matching, weatherboard roof; front of Run formed of iron rods; the whole complete with floor, all outside woodwork painted one coat, in sections in readiness for erection, at the following prices :

No.				£	s.	d.
1. 6ft. by 3ft., suitable for Terriers				2	10	0
2. 7ft. by 4ft., ,, ,, Collies, &c.				3	0	0
3. 10ft. by 5ft. ,, ,, Mastiffs, &c.				5	0	0

Dogs—*continued*.

THE BULLDOG.—After having been rarely seen for some years after bull-baiting was suppressed, the Bulldog has again come into prominence, and is now one of our most fashionable dogs. The courage of the Bulldog is proverbial; and as he is good-tempered, obedient, intelligent, and affectionate, and is formidable-looking, he is naturally in great request both as a pet and a guard. Good specimens realise high prices, so a good female of this breed may prove a satisfactory investment.

THE BULL TERRIER was formerly a coarse-looking dog of various colours. Now he has a long, wedge-shaped head, and the colour is white. He has great pluck, and will fight any dog or tackle any kind of vermin. He is not quarrelsome, and is an excellent companion.

THE CHOW CHOW is an interesting addition to any kennel, and to a man who has only one dog no more pleasant pal can be had. With patience he can be taught all sorts of tricks; he is a very good guard, and very hardy.

THE COLLIE.—It was claimed by the naturalist Buffon that the Collie is the originator of all our domestic dogs; but there is no evidence to bear out this assertion. The general appearance of the Collie is light and graceful, giving evidence of speed, activity, and endurance. The intelligence of the Collie is proverbial.

THE DACHSHUND.—This little dog is probably the most peculiar looking of all our domestic pets. The long, low body, the short legs, bent in at the knees and turned out at the elbows, the large fore feet turned outwards, and the very loose shoulders and long and narrow head make up a regular canine monstrosity. But it is a most affectionate and charming doggie, full of pluck, but rather wilful.

THE DANDIE DINMONT has been immortalised by Sir Walter Scott in his novel "Guy Mannering," though the great novelist did not invent this dog, as is popularly believed. It was one of the hardy terriers kept in North Britain. These terriers accompanied the hounds, and were used to go to earth after vermin. Amongst our many varieties of terrier the Dandie Dinmont continues in favouritism. He is a born sportsman, if in a town he will quickly find his way about, he will fight if called upon, and he will take a thrashing without uttering a sound.

THE DEERHOUND.—If size is no objection it is difficult to name any dog superior to the Deerhound. He is gentle in his manners, he follows well, he is majestic in appearance, and most tractable and faithful.

THE FOX-TERRIER.—The enormous classes of Fox-terriers at dog shows are a proof of their great popularity. They

Dog Kennel with Covered Run.

No. 380.

This is a strongly-built Kennel; sides and back are constructed of good, sound, tongued and grooved matching; roof of both Kennel and Run of weather-boarding. The Kennel is supplied with day-bench over sleeping compartment. All outside woodwork painted one coat. The Run is constructed of iron rods, and is complete with gate at end. The whole in sections in readiness for erection, and carefully packed on rail at the following respective prices:—

Size.	KENNEL. Width.	Length.	Height.	RUN. Width.	Length.		
No.	ft. in.	ft. in.	ft.	ft. in.	ft.	£ s. d.	
1	2 6	2 6	3	2 6	4	3 15 0	
2	3 0	3 0	4	3 0	5	4 10 0	
3	4 0	3 0	5	4 0	6	5 5 0	
4	5 0	3 0	5	5 0	6	6 10 0	

Stakes for Dog Chains.

No. 381.

For driving into the ground, fitted with iron ring to fasten chain to.

PRICE 2s. each.

Dogs—*continued.*

are just the right size, neither too large nor too small, and are clean, quick, active, and intelligent. The Fox-terrier of former times was a different looking animal to our present-day dog, which combines quality with strength, with plenty of galloping power, and is able, when required, to go to earth after a fox. There are two varieties of Fox-terrier, the smooth and the wire-hair. The coat of the former is hard, smooth, straight, and flat; that of the latter hard and wiry.

THE GREAT DANE.—A foreign dog that came to us from Germany, and a useful animal for those who like a very big dog. In no species is there a greater difference between a good and a bad specimen than in the Great Dane. A dog that comes up to the standard of the Great Dane Club is a grand beast. But one that has weak hindquarters, a hollow back, large ears, and a short neck—and there are a good many that answer this description—is a mongrel-looking brute.

THE GREYHOUND is not usually kept as a pet or companion. It is unequalled in speed by any other dog; it has been used for the chase for thousands of years, and is the most elegant member of the canine family.

THE GRIFFON BRUXELLOIS was introduced about twenty years ago from Brussels. A small dog, red in colour, with large dark eyes, black lips and moustache, and a rather human expression, it is a favourite with ladies.

THE IRISH TERRIER has many qualities to recommend him. He is possessed of plenty of character, is easily trained, full of sport and fun, always ready for a fight with another dog, but rarely snappy with human beings. He will usually take freely to the water, and is never happier than when rabbiting or ratting.

THE ITALIAN GREYHOUND.—This beautiful dog came from Italy originally, as the name implies. It is fragile in appearance and delicate in constitution.

THE JAPANESE SPANIEL.—A pretty little dog of black and white or red and white colour, that has become a favourite in this country during recent years. The head resembles that of the King Charles Spaniel, the nose is short, the eyes large, the back and legs short, and the coat long, straight, and silky. The Japanese is not robust.

THE MALTESE DOG.—A small white dog, the most ancient of all the lap dogs. It is most difficult to keep clean and in good condition, owing to the length of coat. It is not often seen.

THE MASTIFF shares with the Bulldog the reputation of having been the indigenous dog of Britain. It is a grand and magnificent animal, with massive head, square muzzle, deep

Range of Three Puppy Kennels.

Substantially constructed of good, sound, tongued and grooved matching, roof of weatherboards; upper part of front fitted with hinged flap to let down, as shown, with iron bars behind, the entire length of front

No. 382.

to open; raised platform in front of the Houses; complete with floor. All woodwork painted one coat.

PRICES:

6ft. by 2ft. ... £2 5s. 0d. | 8ft. by 3ft. ... £3 5s. 0d.

Strong Dog Kennel and Run.

These Kennels are strongly constructed of good sound timbers; sides and ends of tongued and grooved matching; roof of weatherboards, and complete with wood floor; painted three coats of good oil colour outside.

No. 383.

The Run is constructed of iron bars, which are curved inwards at top, thus preventing the dog from jumping over, and is complete with a gate in the end.

PRICES:

No. 1. Suitable for Terriers			... ... £5.		
KENNEL.			RUN.		
Length.	Width.	Height to Eaves.	Length.	Width.	Height to Eaves.
4ft.	4ft.	4ft.	4ft.	4ft.	4ft.

No. 2. Suitable for Retrievers and Collies			... £6.		
KENNEL.			RUN.		
Length.	Width.	Height to Eaves.	Length.	Width.	Height to Eaves.
5ft.	5ft.	5ft.	5ft.	5ft.	5ft.

Dogs—*continued.*

chest, muscular loins, and fawn or brindled coat. It is naturally of a quiet disposition.

THE NEWFOUNDLAND.—Much romance attaches to this dog owing to the high courage and fine swimming powers which enable him to face rough seas and rescue people from drowning. The Newfoundland is a large, heavy dog, weighing between 100lb. and 140lb. The usual colour is black, but there are white and black, bronze, and black and tan dogs. The Newfoundland is highly intelligent, an excellent companion, and as faithful as any dog in existence.

THE PEKINESE SPANIEL is another pretty foreign dog that has attracted much attention and realised large sums. It is fairly hardy, and a most affectionate little creature.

THE POINTER.—A very intelligent dog, though seldom kept as a companion or pet. It is not very sociable.

THE POMERANIAN.—One of the most fashionable of the pet dogs. There are usually many Poms. entered at the various shows, and the classes are surrounded by admirers. Poms. are bred in many shades of colour—black, white, blue, brown, chocolate, sable, red, fawn, and parti-coloured. Fifty pounds is no uncommon price to be given for a toy Pom. It is a bright, active dog, inclined to be noisy and bark a good deal.

THE POODLE.—One of the most intelligent and amusing of dogs; of ancient lineage, as shown by his figuring in paintings so far back as the fifteenth century. The Poodle is gifted with keen scent, will take readily to the water, has plenty of pluck, and will learn almost anything.

THE PUG.—Though of little use as a watch dog or to kill even a mouse, the Pug is such a clean, affectionate little animal that he makes a delightful pet. Few people who have once owned a Pug ever give up their regard for the breed. There are fawn and black Pugs, the latter the newer variety. Pugs, as they become old, are inclined to asthma; and some Pugs are troubled with occasional vomiting. This can usually be cured by sprinkling the principal meal daily for a fortnight or so with a little carbonate of bismuth.

THE RETRIEVER.—There are two varieties of this handsome and clever dog, the Flat-coated and the Curly-coated. And the Labrador, a dog that was formerly classed with the Newfoundlands, has of recent years been called a Retriever by the Kennel Club. The Retrievers are wonderful all-round sporting dogs. The colour is usually black, although liver-coloured Retrievers are to be seen.

THE ST. BERNARD.—Anyone who likes a large dog and has room to keep him cannot fail to admire the St. Bernard. He is naturally good-tempered and easily managed, forming

Lean-to Kennel with Open Run.

No. 384.

A well-built Kennel, constructed of good, sound, tongued and grooved matching, roof of weather-boards, doors in front; fitted inside with storage; the Run is formed of iron rods, and is fitted with gate; wooden platform outside dog's entrance to House, as shown. All outside woodwork painted one coat, and complete in sections in readiness for erection. Size of Kennel, 3ft. wide, 4ft. deep. Run, 5ft. wide, 4ft. deep.

PRICE ... £4 15s. Prices for other sizes on application.

Lean-to Dog Kennel and Covered Run.

No. 385.

Constructed of good, sound, tongued and grooved 1in. matching; roof of both Kennel and Run of weather-boards; the Kennel is complete with bench; the Run is formed of iron rods, fitted with gate; all outside woodwork painted one coat; complete in sections in readiness for erection, securely packed on rail. Size of Kennel and Run, 12ft. by 5ft., 6ft. 6in. high at back, 5ft. high in front.

PRICE ... ... £6 15s.

Dogs—*continued.*

the greatest attachment to his owner. There are two varieties of the St. Bernard, the Rough-coated and the Smooth-coated. The weight of a good specimen is from 170lb. to 210lb.

THE SCHIPPERKE is a quaint little black dog, brought from Belgium. The head is foxy, the ears erect and small, the back rounded off like that of a guinea-pig, and no tail. Some puppies are born tailless. The majority, however, are made so by being docked when a few days old. It is a bright, sharp little dog, and makes a pleasing and useful house dog.

THE SCOTTISH TERRIER is a general favourite. He is always good-tempered and reliable, never treacherous or uncertain; he is endowed with great pluck, yet is not quarrelsome, and he will live anywhere and thrive on anything.

THE SETTER.—There are three varieties of the Setter—the English, the Irish, and the Black and Tan, or Gordon, Setter. In conformation they are much alike, with long and narrow head, and skull slightly domed. The Irish is slightly higher on the leg than the English, and the colour is rich chestnut. The Black and Tan is rather heavier than the others.

THE SHEEPDOG, after being used for years in assisting in driving and herding sheep and cattle, has been made a show dog. In 1888 the Old English Sheepdog Club was formed. The coat quickly mats if not brushed and groomed often. This dog must not be kept chained, and must have a good deal of exercise.

THE SKYE TERRIER.—Whether the present-day Skye Terrier is at all like the hard, vermin-hunting terrier of former times is very questionable. But, at any rate, he has plenty of pluck, and is a most interesting and companionable doggie. There are few dog-lovers who are not fond of the Skye, and who do not consider him one of the handsomest and most desirable of the many terriers.

THE SPORTING SPANIEL.—There are several varieties of this very ancient breed recognised by the Kennel Club, viz., the Clumber, Cocker, Field Spaniel, Irish Water Spaniel, Sussex, and the English and Welsh Springer. The Clumber is a large, heavy, handsome dog, white, with lemon markings. The Cocker is a much smaller dog, that derived its name from having been used largely in woodcock shooting. The Field Spaniel was formerly black only, but is now also bred in tricolour, red-roan, and blue-roan. The Irish Water Spaniel has a top-knot of curly hair, and is of a rich dark liver colour.

The Sussex is one of the oldest of the sporting Spaniels, rich golden liver in colour. This colour is a sign of good breeding.

Curved Roof Kennel with Open Run.

No. 386.

This Kennel is constructed of good, sound matchboards. The front of sleeping compartment is made to open for cleansing purposes; the top of this compartment forms day-bench; roof is covered with curved galvanised corrugated iron sheets; the Run is complete with gate; all outside woodwork painted one coat. Securely packed on rail.

No.	PRICES:	£	s.	d.
1. For Terriers, Collies, and Retrievers, 10ft. by 4ft., 5ft. high to eaves		5	10	0
2. For Mastiffs, St. Bernards, &c., 12ft. by 5ft., 6ft. high to eaves		7	10	0

Dog Kennel and Run.

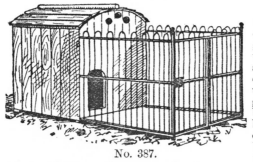

No. 387.

This neat design is constructed of good, sound timbers. Sides and ends are covered with tongued, grooved, and beaded matchboarding; roof of weatherboards. Complete with day-bench and floor. Outside woodwork stained and varnished. Complete with Run as Illustration. Securely packed on rail. Kennel, 5ft. long, 4ft. wide, 6ft. high. Run, 6ft. long, 4ft. wide.

PRICE ... ... £6.

Dogs—*continued.*

The English Springer was formerly called the Norfolk Spaniel. It is not very uniform in type. And the Welsh Springer is white, with red or orange markings.

THE TOY SPANIEL is bred in four varieties—the Blenheim, the King Charles, the Ruby, and the Tricolour, or Prince Charles. The difference is mainly that of colour. The Blenheim is of a white ground, with ruby red or chestnut markings. The King Charles is of a rich black, with tan spots over the eyes and on the cheeks and tan markings on the legs. The Ruby is a rich red, with black nose. The Tricolour has a white body, with black evenly distributed in patches; the ears are lined with tan, and there is tan over the eyes and on the cheeks.

THE WELSH TERRIER is much like a wire-hair Fox-terrier, except in colour, which is black and tan, or black, grizzle, and tan.

THE WEST HIGHLAND WHITE TERRIER.—A dog that has quite recently come to the front, and is making many friends. It strongly resembles the Scottish Terrier, but is white in colour. It is a plucky, hardy little dog, weighing from 14lb. to 18lb.

THE WHIPPET also called the Snap Dog, is like a Greyhound on a small scale. It is used largely for running races and for rabbit coursing.

THE YORKSHIRE TERRIER.—A little dog, under 5lb. in weight, said to have been originally produced from a cross between the Black and Tan and the Scottish Terrier. The coat is very long, straight, and silky, hanging evenly down each side. For its size it is a good watch dog in the house, and is bright, active, and courageous.

Dog Kennel with Covered Run.

Constructed of good sound tongued and grooved matching; upper part of sides, and also end of Run, of iron rods; fitted with gate; the whole complete with floor. All outside woodwork painted one good coat. Despatched in sections, in perfect readiness for erection, at the following sizes and prices:

No. 388.

No.		£	s.	d.
1. 6ft. by 3ft. by 5ft. 6in., suitable for Terriers. ...		3	0	0
2. 7ft. by 4ft. by 6ft., suitable for Collies, &c. ...		3	10	0
3. 10ft. by 5ft. by 7ft., suitable for Mastiffs, &c....		5	10	0

No. 389.

Lean-to Kennel with Covered Run.

This Kennel and Run is similar in construction to No. 378.

Size.	KENNEL.		Height	RUN.	Price.
	Width.	Depth.	to Eaves.	Long.	
No.	ft. in.	ft. in.	ft. in.	ft.	£ s. d.
1	2 0	2 6	2 6	4	3 5 0
2	2 6	3 0	3 0	5	4 10 0
3	3 0	3 6	3 6	6	6 0 0

Nos. 1 and 2 are suitable for Terriers and small dogs, and No. 3 for Collies, Retrievers, &c.

Wood batten floor to Run extra, as follows: No. 1, 5s.; No. 2, 7s. 6d.; No. 3, 10s.

Kennel and Covered Run.

This Kennel is suitable for Mastiffs, St. Bernards, and other large dogs. Complete with day - bench over sleeping compartment, and floor; all outside woodwork painted one coat.

No. 390.

The Run is constructed of iron rods, with gate in end. Securely packed on rail.

Size of Kennel, 4ft. long, 5ft. from back to front, 5ft. high to eaves; Run, 6ft. long and 5ft. wide

PRICE ... ... £7 10s.

Reversible Feeding Trough, 7s. 6d. extra. If with wood spline floor to Run, 25s. extra.

Double Lean-to Kennel with Covered Runs.

This useful design of Kennel is constructed of good, sound, tongued and grooved matching; roof of weatherboards, and is fitted complete with storage, day - benches, and floor. The Runs are constructed of iron rods, with gate in each; all outside woodwork painted one coat. Constructed in sections in perfect readiness for erection.

No. 391.

PRICE £12

Size of Kennels, each 3ft. wide, 5ft. deep, 7ft. high at back. Storage 2ft. 6in. wide, 5ft. deep, 5ft. 6in. high to eaves. Runs, each 4ft. wide and 5ft. deep.

Lean-to Kennels with Runs.

No. 392.

This illustration shows a double House for placing against a wall, and will be found convenient and compact where more than one dog is kept.

The Kennels are constructed of good sound timbers, front and ends being covered with tongued and grooved match-boarding, roof of weather-boards. The Kennels are complete with door, day-bench, and floor; all woodwork painted one coat outside. The Runs are constructed of iron rods with gate in ends, the lower part being covered with galvanised corrugated iron sheets, thus affording protection against draughts. The whole in sections in readiness for erection, and securely packed on rail. Size of each Kennel is 3ft. long, 5ft. from back to front 6ft. high to eaves; each Run is 6ft. long and 5ft. wide.

Price (complete) ... ... £10 10s.

Imperial Black Varnish.

For Iron Fences, Wood Palings, Farm Buildings, Poultry Houses, &c.

18 gal. casks, 20s. ; 36 gal. casks, 34s.; Casks included. Carefully packed on rail. Casks not returnable.

1 gal. 1s. 6d. (can 6d.); 5 gal. 5s. (can 2s.).

Double Lean-to Kennel with Runs.

No. 393.

Well and substantially constructed of good, sound, tongued and grooved 1in. matchboards, with a passage at the back of Kennels; roof of weather-boards, with ventilators in same over passage-way. The Runs are formed of iron rods, and each Run is fitted complete with gate and reversible trough; all woodwork painted outside two coats. Complete in sections, in readiness for erection, and securely packed on rail.

Size of the two Kennels, 10ft. by 5ft.; each Run 6ft. long.

PRICE ... ... £18.

Double Lean-to Kennel and Runs.

Well and substantially constructed of good sound tongued and grooved 1in. matchboards; roof to Kennels and Runs of weather-boards. The runs are formed of iron rods, and are each complete with gate; reversible trough to each

No. 394.

Kennel and Run; all outside woodwork painted one coat. In sections, in readiness for erection, and securely packed on rail Each house, 5ft. by 4ft., 7ft. high at back, 5ft. high in front. Run 5ft. by 5ft.

PRICE ... ... £12 10s.

191

Lean-to Range of Three Kennels and Runs.

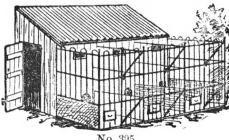

No. 395.

This illustration shows a Range of Three Kennels and Runs, with a passage at the back from which each Kennel is entered, and attention to sanitary requirements thereby facilitated. They are constructed of good, sound, tongued and grooved matchboards; roofs are formed of galvanised corrugated iron sheets. The Runs are constructed of iron rods, and are complete with gate and reversible trough for each; all outside woodwork painted one coat; in sections, in readiness for erection, and securely packed on rail.

Size of the three Kennels, 12ft. by 6ft. 6in. (including the 2ft. 6in. passage-way), 7ft. 6ft. high at back, and 6ft. in front; size of each Run, 6ft. long.

PRICE **£16**

Lean-to Range of Dog Kennels and Runs.

No. 396.

Constructed similar to No. 395, but less the passage-way at back of the Kennels.

Each Kennel, 4ft. by 4ft., 7ft. high at back, 6ft. in front. Run, 6ft. by 4ft.

PRICE—Four Kennels and Runs, £21.

Reversible Troughs, 7s. 6d. each extra.

Span-Roof Range of Dog Kennels and Yards.

No. 397.

The illustration shows a range of six Kennels and Yards, three on either side, passage way in centre 3ft. wide, from which each Kennel is entered, and attention to sanitary requirements thereby facilitated. The Kennels are constructed of good, sound, 1in. tongued and grooved matching, with ventilator in each gable, and are fitted complete with day benches. The Yards are formed of iron rods, and each fitted with gate and reversible trough complete; all outside woodwork painted one coat; constructed in sections in perfect readiness for erection and securely packed on rail.

PRICES:

			£	s.	d.
Range of Four Kennels and Yards	...	27	10	0
„ Six „ „	...	36	0	0
„ Eight „ „	...	45	0	0

Size of each Kennel 5ft. by 4ft.; Yards, each 6ft. by 4ft.
Quotations for ranges of any number of Kennels and Yards on receipt of full particulars.

Interior View of Above.

193

Wrought-iron Kennel Railing.

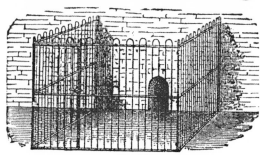

No. 240.

This Railing is specially suitable for a Kennel Run, which permits the dog having his liberty, the use of the chain being obviated. Made in hurdles, 5ft., 6ft., and 7ft. long, usually 6ft. high, but varying to suit the purpose required. Can be put together in a few minutes.

Length.			Width.			Height.			£	s.	d.
5ft.	...	...	5ft.	...	...	5ft.	...	...	3	11	6
5ft.	...	...	6ft.	...	...	6ft.	...	...	4	12	0
7ft.	...	...	7ft.	...	...	6ft.	...	...	5	5	0

Including Gate.

Kennel Railing. (Design as above.)

In 6ft. lengths, Painted. Prices include Bolts and Nuts for fixing.

No. 241.

	Height.	s.	d.	
Five-sixteenths inch rods spaced 2in. apart	3ft.	... 6	9	per yard.
Five-sixteenths ,, ,,	4ft.	... 8	0	,,
Three-eighths ,, spaced 2½in. apart	5ft.	... 10	0	,,
Three-eighths ,, ,, ,,	6ft.	... 11	6	,,
Half ,, spaced 3in. apart	7ft.	... 13	0	,,

Movable Iron Reversible Troughs fitted to Railing, 10s. 6d. each.

Gates for ditto, 2ft. wide, with sliding Bolt and Padlock.

3ft.		4ft.		5ft.		6ft.		7ft. high.	
s.	d.	s.	d.	s.	d.	s.	d.	s.	d.
21	0	... 23	0	... 27	6	... 30	0	... 36	0 each.

Angle Iron Standards, with plate feet, for Corners if required.

3ft.		4ft.		5ft.		6ft.		7ft. above ground.	
s.	d.	s.	d.	s.	d.	s.	d.	s.	d.
1	2	... 1	4	... 1	6	... 1	9	... 2	0 each.

SECTION IV.

Illustrated Catalogue

OF

PORTABLE WOODEN BUILDINGS.

Photographic Studios & Dark Rooms.

CRICKET, FOOTBALL, TENNIS & GOLF PAVILIONS.

Scoring Boxes. Huts. Stores.

STABLE & COACH HOUSES. LOOSE BOXES.

Cow Houses. Shelters. Pigstys.

CYCLE HOUSES.

GRAIN STORES. WORKSHOPS.

&c., &c.

Watchman's Box.

No. 250.

Constructed of good sound 1in. tongued and grooved matchboard walls, on strong frame, the roof of 1in. weather boards (or matchboards if preferred); floor and joists; seat and locker; door in two halves, with bolt, lock and key; unpainted. Size 2ft. 6in. by 3ft., 7ft. high in front, 5ft. 6in. high at back. Cash price £2 17s. 6d.; if less door, £2 7s. 6d.

If Outside Woodwork painted with our Patent Rot-Proof Composition, 10 per cent. extra.

Klosk. (Time-keeper's Box.)

No. 251.

Constructed of good sound 1in. tongued and grooved matchboard and glass sides, on strong frame; roof boarded and covered with zinc; floor of 1in. tongued and grooved boards on strong joists; structure raised from ground on blocks at each corner; door in two halves, upper half glass, and fitted with bolt, lock and key. Made in sections ready to bolt together.

Outside woodwork painted two coats. Desk with cupboard under same included. Zinc gutter, &c. Glass, plain 21oz. Size 4ft. 3in. by 3ft., by 8ft. high to ridge and 7ft. high to eaves.

Cash price £8.

Portable Stable and Coach and Harness House.

No. 64.

These structures are constructed of good strong materials throughout, the sides and ends being covered with tongued, grooved and beaded matching, on 3in. by 2in. selected deal. The roof is covered with stout boards on strong principals and covered with felt, and the buildings are supplied complete with partitions, doors, windows, all necessary ironmongery, and glass. All in sections in perfect readiness for erection, and securely packed on rail at the following respective prices :—

Lot.	Suitable for.	Length.	Width.	Height at Ridge.	Height at Eaves.	£	s.	d.
1	pony and trap	14ft.	10ft.	10ft.	7ft.	9	10	0
1	horse and trap	15ft.	12ft.	12ft.	8ft.	12	0	0
2	horses and trap	20ft.	12ft.	12ft.	8ft.	15	0	0

Above prices do not include floor, which would be best of brick or concrete.

If the whole of Outside Woodwork Painted with our Patent Rot-Proof Composition, 10 per cent. extra.

Cooper's Disinfectas.

Clean, Cheap and Healthy. A little sprinkled about a Stable gives a clean appearance and a pleasant smell. Try it.

Per Sack (2 Bushel) 2s. 6d.   Sack Included.   10 for 22s

Send for Sample Sack.

Cricket, Football, Tennis and Golf Pavilion.

No. 65.

This is a Pavilion thoroughly adapted for cricket, football, tennis, or any other sports. It is soundly constructed of good strong material, with necessary partitions to form two dressing-rooms and open shelter, windows to open as shown. The sides, ends, and partitions are covered with tongued, grooved, and beaded boarding, on strong framing, 2in. by 3in., the roof covered with stout boards, and covered with felt; ¾in. floor-boarding, on 3in. by 2in. joists; all complete in sections, and carefully packed on rail, at the following respective prices :—

Length. ft.	Width. ft.	Height at Ridge. ft.	Height at Eaves. ft. in.	£ s. d.
15	8	8	6 6	13 10 0
17	10	8	6 6	15 10 0
20	12	9	7 0	18 0 0
26	12	9	7 0	22 0 0
32	14	9	8 0	30 0 0

Other sizes at proportionate prices. Estimates for Erecting, free.

If the whole of Outside Woodwork Painted with our Patent Rot-Proof Composition, 10 per cent. extra.

198

Span-Roof Photographic Studio with Dark Room.

No. 66.

This structure is substantially constructed of good sound tongued and grooved matchboards, roof of weather-boards, glass as shown, the dark room is fitted complete with slide, shelf and ruby glass window; floor and joists all over base; complete in sections, in readiness for erection, and securely packed on rail.

	SIZE OF STUDIO.			SIZE OF DARK ROOM.		
Length.	Width.	Height at Ridge.	Height at Eaves.	Length.	Width.	Price.
ft.	ft.	ft. ins.	ft.	ft.	ft.	£ s. d.
12	8	8 6	6	4	4	8 10 0
16	9	8 6	6	5	4	11 0 0
20	10	8 6	6	6	4	12 10 0
24	12	8 6	6	6	4	15 10 0

The dark room can be placed in any position as desired.

If the whole of Outside Woodwork Painted with our Patent Rot-Proof Composition, 10 per cent. extra.

Photographic Studios,

No. 67.

These structures are constructed sides and ends of tongued and grooved matching, on 3in. by 2in. framing ; the roof is constructed partly of glass, the remaining portion being boarded and covered with felt. Floor of ¾in. boards, upon 3in. by 2in. or 4in. by 2in. joists, according to size of building. A sash to open can be had in roof or side, as desired; the structure is complete with panel door, with rim lock and furniture, and has barge boards and finials; constructed in sections in perfect readiness for erection, and packed on rail at the following respective prices :—

Length.	Width.	Height at Eaves.	Complete on rail.
ft.	ft.	ft. ins.	£ s. d.
12	8	7 6	7 15 0
14	10	7 6	9 10 0
16	10	8 0	11 5 0
20	12	8 0	14 0 0
24	12	8 0	15 10 0

If the above be fitted with projecting Dark Room with ruby window, size 6ft. by 3ft., £3 ; 6ft. by 4ft., £3 10s.

If the whole of Outside Woodwork Painted with our Patent Rot-Proof Composition, 10 per cent. extra. Strongly recommended.

Holmbury, St. Mary, Dorking.
" GENTLEMEN,—Span Roof Building arrived safe, which gives every satisfaction. —Yours truly, (Signed) P. P. OVRINGTON."

Pent-Roof Scoring Boxes.

As used at Cricket Matches, &c.

No. 68.

This is a very useful structure for the cricket field, &c. The bottom part is constructed of good sound tongued and grooved matchboards, upper part of glass, with wood flap in centre of front to lift up as shown; roof boarded and covered with felt. The whole structure mounted on legs 1ft. high and complete with floor and two steps up to door; 21oz. glass cut to sizes and packed in box for glazing; constructed in sections in perfect readiness for erection.

8ft. by 7ft.; 8ft. 6in. high in front; 6ft. 6in. high at back, including legs.

PRICE ...　...　...　...　...　...　£5.

If the whole of Outside Woodwork Painted with our Patent Rot-Proof Composition, 10s. extra.

Imperial Black Varnish.

For Iron Fences, Wood Palings, Farm Buildings, Poultry Houses, &c.

18 gal. casks, 20s.; 36 gal. casks, 34s.; Casks included. Carefully packed on rail. Casks not returnable.

1 gal. 1s. 6d. (can 6d.); 5 gal. 5s. (can 2s.).

Span-Roof Photographic Dark Room.

Thoroughly well constructed of good sound tongued and grooved matchboards; roof covered with felt; and fitted complete with floor, ruby glass window and slide; table under window; dark ventilator and door with lock; in sections, in readiness for erection, and securely packed on rail as follows :—

No. 69.

No.	Length. ft.	Width. ft.	Height at Ridge. ft. in.	Height at Eaves. ft. in.	Price. £ s. d.
1	4	4	8 0	6 0	2 5 0
2	5	4	8 0	6 0	2 12 6
3	6	4	8 6	6 6	3 0 0
4	6	6	8 6	6 6	4 0 0

If Outside Painted with our Patent Rot-Proof Composition, 10 per cent. extra.

No. 70.

Pent-Roof Portable W.C.

Constructed of good sound tongued and grooved matchboards. Roof boarded and covered with felt; lattice-wood floor; fitted inside with hinged seat and front complete; door complete; in sections in readiness for erection, and securely packed on rail.

3ft. 6in. by 4ft.; 6ft. high in front; 5ft. high at back.

PRICE ... ... £2 7s. 6d.

If Painted Outside with our Patent Rot-Proof Composition, 5s. extra.

Keeper's Hut and Store.

Substantially constructed of good sound tongued and grooved matching, on strong 2in. by 3in. frame; roof of stout boards, on strong principals covered with felt; window in one side; door in two halves in one end. Complete with floor. Mounted on four strong wheels; the Hut is fitted with stove and chimney; in sections in readiness for erection, and securely packed on rail.

No. 71.

8ft. by 6ft., 8ft. high to ridge, 6ft. high to eaves.

PRICE ... ... £7 5s.

Quotations for other sizes on application.

If Painted Outside with our Patent Rot-Proof Composition, 15s. extra.

Span-Roof Loose Boxes.

No. 72.

The illustration shows a range of three Boxes. They are constructed of good sound tongued and grooved 1in. match-boards, on 3in. by 2in. framing. The roof is formed of stout boards on strong timbers, and covered with felt; doors and window to each box as shown; manger and hay-rack to each. Constructed in sections in readiness for erection, and securely packed on rail. Three Boxes, size over all, 21ft. by 9ft., 9ft. high to ridge, and 6ft. 6in. high to eaves, £17 10s.

Quotation for other sizes, or Single Boxes, on receipt of full particulars.

Span-Roof Cow Houses.

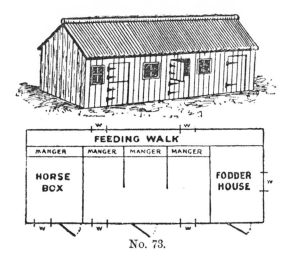

FEEDING WALK

| MANGER | MANGER | MANGER | MANGER |

HORSE BOX

FODDER HOUSE

No. 73.

These Houses are substantially built, the sides and ends being covered with 1in. tongued, grooved, and beaded matchboarding on strong 2in by 3in. frame. The roof is formed of stout boards on strong principals, and covered with felt; the houses are complete with doors and windows, and also partitions as shown, dividing it into loose box, fodder house, set in mangers, and feeder's walk. Constructed in sections in perfect readiness for erection, and securely packed on rail.

Size, 28ft. by 12ft., 11ft. to ridge, and 7ft. to eaves.

PRICE ... ... £25.

Doors and Windows may be had in any position as required.

If Painted Outside with our Patent Rot-Proof Composition, 50s. extra.

Cooper's Disinfectas.

Clean, cheap and healthy; a little sprinkled about the cow-house or stable give a clean appearance and pleasant smell.

TRY IT. Per Sack (2 bushel), 2s. 6d., sack included.

10 for 2s. 6d.

Send for Sample Sack.

Grain Store.

No. 74.

The illustration here shows a most useful building for farmers, it being perfectly rat and vermin proof, and being constructed extra strong throughout will be found to be well suited for the purpose it is intended for; the roof is constructed of strong principals, boarded, and covered with felt, the sides of matchboarding on strong framework; complete in sections in readiness for erection on ground level or piers at the following respective prices:

Length. ft.	Width. ft.	Height to Ridge. ft. in.	Height to Eaves. ft. in.	Packed on Rail. £ s. d.
20	10	11 0	8 0	17 10 0
30	12	12 0	8 6	24 0 0
40	14	13 0	9 0	35 0 0

If painted outside with our Patent Rot-Proof Composition, 10 per cent extra.

Pigsty and Open Yard.

No. 75.

This illustration shows a strongly-made Pigsty and Yard, and is suitable for placing in the open field, &c. The framing is of 2in. by 2in. throughout, covered with strong tongued and grooved boarding. Wood roof covered with felt.

The Pigsty is complete with halved door and ventilator (as shown), and the Yard, with strong door, securely packed on rail in sections to screw together, at the following prices:—

Size of Pigsty.—5ft. long by 5ft. wide by 4ft. 6in. in front by 3ft. 6in. at back.

Size of Yard.—6ft. long by 5ft. wide by 3ft. 6in. high.

Price of Pigsty, £2 15s. | Price of Yard. £1 1s.

Span-Roof Open Shed or Garden Shelter.

No. 76.

This Shed can be adapted for field, farm, poultry yard, or garden use. It is constructed of good, sound, well-seasoned matching; the roof is boarded and covered with felt. In sections, in readiness for erection, and securely packed on rail at the following respective prices:

Length. ft.	Width. ft.	Height to Ridge. ft.	Height to Eaves. ft.	£ s. d.
6	4	7	5	1 10 0
7	5	8	6	2 0 0
10	8	9	6	4 0 0

Span-Roof Garden Shelter.

This is a serviceable Shelter, strongly constructed of tongued, grooved, and beaded matching; roof covered with boards and felted; complete, with floor and seats inside, as shown. Complete, in sections ready for erection, and securely packed on rail.

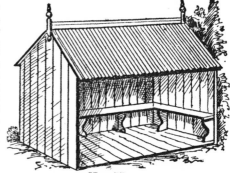

No. 77.

Length. ft.	Width. ft.	Height at Ridge. ft.	Height at Eaves ft.	Price. £ s. d.
6	4	8 0	6 0	3 5 0
8	6	9 0	6 0	4 10 0
10	7	9 0	6 0	5 15 0
12	8	9 6	6 6	7 0 0

Span-Roof Keeper's Hut and Store.

No. 78.

Interior View of above,

No. 79.

A strongly-made structure with raised floor; constructed of good, sound, well-seasoned matching; roof of weather-boards; one window in each side, door in one end; complete with strong floor and bench; in sections in readiness for erection, and securely packed on rail.

If painted outside with our Patent Rot-Proof Composition, 10 per cent. extra.

PRICES.

8ft. by 6ft., 9ft. high to ridge	... ...	£4 10s. 0d.
10ft. by 7ft., 10ft. „ „	... ...	£6 0s. 0d.

Portable Buildings.

(TENANTS' FIXTURES.)

Span-Roof.

These buildings are substantially constructed of good sound tongued and grooved matchboards on strong wood framework; they are complete with door, lock, and fittings, also window and floor; the roof is formed of matchboards covered with felt; in sections in readiness for erection, and securely packed on rail.

No. 80.

Length. ft.	Width. ft.	Height to Ridge. ft. in.	Price. £ s. d.
6	4	6 0	2 10 0
8	8	8 0	5 0 0
14	10	8 6	8 0 0
20	12	9 0	12 0 0

Lean-to.

No. 81.

Length. ft.	Width. ft.	Height at Back. ft. in.	Eaves. ft. in.	Price. £ s. d.	Boarded back extra. £ s. d.
6	4	7 0	5 0	2 10 0	0 7 6
7	5	7 6	5 6	3 10 0	0 12 6
10	6	8 0	6 0	5 0 0	1 0 0

Lean-to Cooking Shed, Workshop, &c.

A very useful structure for gamekeepers; constructed of good, sound, tongued and grooved matching, on strong wood framing, including back; folding doors in front, and glass ventilator in roof; complete with bench and floor; in sections in readiness for erection, securely packed on rail.

No. 82.

Size, 8ft. by 5ft. 6in, 7ft. 6in. at back, 6ft. high to eaves.
PRICE £4 10s.   Suitable stove for above, 30s. extra.

Lean-to Workshop and Cycle House combined.

Similar in construction to No. 87, but with strong bench. 7ft. by 6ft., 8ft. high to ridge, 6ft. high to eaves. Complete, with back.

PRICE
£4 10s.

If painted outside with our Rot-Proof Composition, 10 per cent. extra.

No. 83.

Strong Workshop.

(TENANT'S FIXTURE.)

No. 84.

Fitted with strong bench, bench screw, and back rack. The roof is boarded and covered with felt. The sides and ends are covered with tongued and grooved boarding, on strong framed sections. Complete with door, windows, floor, and joists, &c.

Length. ft.	Width. ft.	Height at Ridge. ft. in.	Height at Eaves. ft. in.	Price. £ s. d.
8	6	7 6	4 6	5 0 0
10	8	7 9	5 0	6 10 0
12	8	8 0	5 3	7 10 0
14	8	8 6	5 6	8 10 0
16	9	9 0	5 9	10 0 0

The floor joists are 3in. by 2in., and 4in. by 2in., according to size of building, and the floor-boarding is ¾in. thick.

If painted outside with our Patent Rot-Proof Composition, 10 per cent. extra.

Span-Roof Portable Hut.

(DESIGN SIMILAR TO ABOVE.)

A well-built structure, constructed of good sound tongued and grooved matching, roof of weather-boards, window in each side to open, folding doors in one end; complete with floor and bench. Constructed in sections in readiness for erection, and securely packed on rail.

Size, 8ft. by 6ft.; 7ft. 6in. high to ridge.

PRICE ... ... £4 10s.

If painted outside with our Patent Rot-Proof Composition, 9s. extra.

Portable Buildings.

Span-Roof.

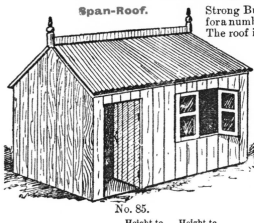

Strong Buildings, useful for a number of purposes. The roof is boarded, and covered with felt. The sides and ends are covered with tongued and grooved boarding on strong framed sections in readiness for erection. Complete with door, windows, floor, and joists, &c.

No. 85.

Length.	Width.	Height to Ridge.	Height to Eaves.	Price.
ft.	ft.	ft. ins.	ft. ins.	£ s. d.
6	4	7 0	4 6	3 0 0
7	5	7 6	5 0	4 0 0
8	7	8 0	5 6	5 10 0

Prices for other sizes on application.

Lean-to.

This structure will be found very useful as an addition to house as kitchen, &c.

No. 86.

Length.	Width.	Height at Back.	Height to Eaves.	Price.
ft.	ft.	ft. ins.	ft. ins.	£ s. d.
10	8	7 6	5 0	5 10 0
10	10	8 0	5 6	6 5 0
12	10	8 6	6 0	7 0 0

If outside painted with our Rot-Proof Composition, 10 per cent. **extra.**

211

Bicycle and Tricycle Houses.

(SPAN ROOF.)

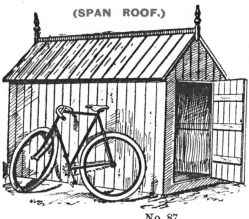

These Houses are substantially constructed of good sound tongued and grooved matching, on strong frame, roof boarded, and covered with felt, and are complete with floor. They are sent in sections in perfect readiness for screwing together.

No. 87.

PRICES.

	£	s.	d.
Bicycle Houses, 6ft. 6in. by 3ft. 6in.	2	0	0
Tricycle Houses, 6ft. 6in. by 5ft.	2	10	0

(LEAN-TO.)

If painted outside with our Rot-Proof Composition, 10 per cent. extra.

No. 88.

	£	s.	d.
Bicycle Houses, 6ft. 6in. by 3ft., with back	1	15	0
Tricycle Houses, 6ft. 6in. by 5ft. „	2	10	0

WILLIAM COOPER, Limited,

Horticultural Providers,

751, OLD KENT ROAD, LONDON, S.E.

SECTION V.

 llustrated ℭatalogue

OF

IRON BUILDINGS:

Churches, Chapels, Mission Rooms, Hospitals, Club Houses, Residences, Dwelling Houses, Cottages, Bungalows, Offices,

Stables, Coach-houses, Workshops, Boat-houses, Schools, Billiard Rooms, Concert and Drill Halls, Ball Rooms, Loose Boxes, Roofing, etc., etc.

The following illustrations show Elevations of a general character, but any deviations from the designs can easily be made as desired, and special Drawings will be forwarded, together with Prices, upon receipt of Specification.

ALL BUILDINGS CONTRACTED FOR ARE PROMPTLY FIXED IN A GIVEN TIME.

Description of Materials used in the Construction of Iron Buildings.

The County Council

demand to be employed in all buildings, materials of a sufficient substance and strength. ALL OUR WORK is in accordance with the necessary requirements.

Brickwork

is only necessary for foundations where buildings are erected within the Metropolitan districts. Outside the boundary we generally employ stone template, placing them under the weight-carrying supports of the building on the level ground. Foundations are not included in our estimates.

Frame-work

is of the following substances: Sleepers and joists, 4in. by 2in.; principal rafters, 5in. by 2in., 6in. by 2in., 7in. by 2in., 3in. by 6in., 2½in. by 7in., 3in. by 8in., and 3in. by 9in., according to width of house; framework 3in. by 2in., 4in. by 2in., and 3in. by 4in.; purlins 4in. by 2in. It is made in sections to faciliate both fixing and removal, which can be easily accomplished at any time at a minimum cost of labour.

Floor Boards

are supplied of thoroughly seasoned deal of ¾in. and 1in. thicknesses.

Lining

is of thoroughly seasoned and selected matchboards of ½in. and ⅝in., tongued and grooved.

Exclusion of Draughts

is effected by a liberal use of felt in the walls and gables. We employ it in all buildings we erect. It has also the advantage of preserving an equable temperature.

Ventilation

is studied in every building, our principle being to thoroughly effect it without causing draught.

Galvanised Corrugated Iron

sheets of standard Birmingham gauge only are used. They are fixed on a principle that admits of their being easily released without damage to the structure.

Ornamental Finish

to gables and pinnacles is studied from the most approved Gothic designs.

Fittings and Glazings,

Locks, Bolts, Bars, Ventilating Gear, Gutters and Downpipes, and all Sundries are of the best make, and are carefully fixed. The Glass used in buildings quoted in this list is heavy 21oz.; but Rolled Plate, or Cathedral, or other qualities may be had at prices accordingly.

All County Council and other fees, if any, to be paid by the purchaser.

Erection Prices

include Delivery and Erection complete, Painting Outside Woodwork two coats best Oil Colour, and Staining and Varnishing Inside, Glazing Windows, &c., by our own men, all Railway Charges, Carriage, Men's Fares, Lodgings, &c., within 150 miles. Beyond this distance extra cost of Carriage, &c., will be charged.

On-Rail or Wharf Prices

include the building complete as above, ready for Erection, carefully marked and packed on Rail or delivered to London Wharf, and a drawing to facilitate erection supplied with each Building.

Deviations from the Designs.

The following Illustrations show Elevations of a general character, but any deviations from the Designs can easily be made as desired, and special drawings will be forwarded, together with Prices, upon receipt of Specification.

Increasing Demand.

Iron Buildings have been in use sufficiently long to put them to the test in every possible way, and from the continually increasing demand for them it may fairly be said that they justify a claim superior to any class of structure, for similar use, that existed prior to their introduction.

Neat in Appearance,

The advantages they possess are at once so apparent it hardly becomes necessary to point them out. On the ground of CLEANLINESS they have no equal. They are NEAT in appearance, The risk from FIRE is minimised, and from an ECONOMICAL POINT OF VIEW they are cheaper, commensurately, than any other form of temporary structures. With ordinary attention to the exterior, they will last a lifetime. All that is necessary for their preservation is to see they are painted, say, every three or four years. Where they are wanted to stand permanently, a four-course brick foundation is advisable. A Special Quotation for all Brickwork is given after a survey of the site, which is necessary, owing to the variation of soils and levels. It will, however, be found more expedient where brick foundation is wanted to entrust this to a local man, once having determined upon the capacity of the building to be placed upon it. Used as a Dwelling-house, there is no necessity for waiting until the walls are dry before entering, inasmuch as no material used in the construction of the

Buildings is even damp, hence the readiness with which medical authorities resort to them for hospitals in cases of emergency. For those who take their pleasures up-river year by year, a portable building affords a means of enjoyment and change upon a scale of economy not found in any other system. We contract for every interior requisite, heating, lighting, cooking apparatus, furniture, &c., &c., whether required for the Church or the Gamekeeper's Cot.

EXPORT TRADE.—Buildings suitable for all Climates—
The Colonies, South Africa, and India.

Great care is necessary, not only in the construction, but in the selection of materials for all Buildings required for use in foreign countries. The experience we have had in this department, combined with assistence rendered to us by old residents abroad, has enabled us to turn out work which has met the full appreciation of those for whom we have contracted.

For Tropical Climes

our Buildings are constructed with a double roof, each end being covered with perforated zinc in order to admit a through current of air. This not only assists to cool the interior, but may be made to act as a thorough ventilator.

Our Buildings are all made in Sections,

and tested as a whole, before leaving our Works. Each part is numbered and lettered to correspond with a diagram which accompanies the Building, so that reference is made easy, and the putting together of the sections is a matter of common intelligence, no technical skill being required.

Packing for Shipment

has the greatest attention, so that the parts may be protected from rough usage, consequent upon a long voyage and transhipments and carriage overland.

Portable and Tenants' Fixtures.

Being portable and tenants' fixtures, these Buildings commend themselves for service in all parts of the world. They can be enlarged or made small with comparative ease in any case of emergency.

If designs in this list do not meet with purchasers' requirements, Special Designs and Estimates will be promptly despatched on receipt of Rough Sketch and Particulars.

Special Designs Free.

Church.

No. 276.

This Church is handsomely designed, and can be constructed to suit any number of people.   Lowest cash estimates given for other sizes on receipt of particulars.   Furniture, Lighting, and Heating Apparatus separately estimated for.   For Specification, see pages 206 and 207.

Delivered nearest Goods Station, and erected complete on purchaser's foundation, or marked for re-erection, and bundled and packed on Rail or Wharf.

PRICES :

60ft. long by 30ft. wide, 9ft. to eaves, 26ft. to ridge,
Erected complete, £300.
On Rail or Wharf, £200.

70ft. long by 40ft. wide, 9ft. to eaves, 30ft. to ridge,
Erected complete, £415.
On Rail or Wharf, £275.

Exclusive of fittings.

Sectional Interior View of No. 276.

Showing construction. This is a much admired and approved design, being in strict accordance with the rules of modern architecture.

Any Building not in stock, or special sizes, can be placed on rail within three days from receipt of order.

Packing for shipment has the greatest attention, so that the parts may be protected from rough usage consequent upon a long voyage and transhipments and carriage over land.

Church.

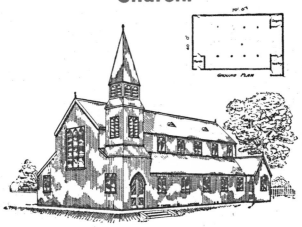

GROUND PLAN

No. 277.

This design is of bold appearance, specially suited for large congregations, seating about 500 adults. Size, 70ft. long by 40ft. wide. Has Two Entrances. These, also Tower, can be placed in any position to suit purchaser. For Specification, see pages 206 and 207.

Delivered to nearest Goods Station, and erected complete on purchaser's foundation, £425; or marked for re-erection and bundled and packed on Rail or Wharf, £285.

Goldsithney.

"NEW MISSION ROOM.—St. James' Mission Room, in connection with the Church of England, and which is in South Road, Goldsithney, is now completed. Considering the time taken (16 days), this structure reflects much credit on the contractors (Messrs. W. Cooper, London). The St. James' Mission Room is called after the ancient Church which formerly stood in Goldsithney, and which was built 502 years ago."—*Vide* DAILY PRESS.

To Messrs. COOPER, LTD.   Chalk House, Green Farm, Elmer Green, Caversham.

"SIRS,—Your man will have finished to day (Wednesday), the Bungalow. Everything is finished perfectly satisfactory, and your Foreman has given me every satisfaction, &c. Should you care to refer anyone to me in the future as regards such a place they might be wanting, I would be glad to give Cooper's, Limited, a good testimonial.—I remain, yours truly,   (Signed)   H. W. BAKER."

Church or Chapel.

No. 278.

This is a very neat design. Substantially constructed, very neat appearance, and well ventilated. Size, 70ft. long by 30ft. wide, 9ft. to eaves, 20ft. to ridge. For Specification, see pages 206 and 207.

Delivered to nearest Goods Station, and erected complete on purchaser's foundation, £265, or marked for re-erection and bundled and packed on Rail or Wharf, £160.

Any size made at proportionate prices.

Messrs. W. COOPER & Co.   101, Wellington Street, Luton.

"DEAR SIRS,—The Trustees of the Wellington Street Baptist Chapel wish me to let you know that the building gives them every satisfaction, both in material and workmanship, and style of erection.—I am, yours, on behalf of the above,

(Signed)   A. E. WITHAM."

113, Plashet Grove, East Ham, E.

"DEAR SIRS,—Received Iron Building to-day; very satisfied with it.—Yours truly,   (Signed)   J. H. CARPENTER & Co.

Church or Chapel.

No. 279.

Another neat design, which is much patronised, well built, and well ventilated. For Specification, see pages 206 and 207.

Delivered to nearest Goods Station, and erected complete on purchaser's foundation or marked for re-erection, and bundled and packed on Rail or Wharf at the following prices :—

Length. ft.	Width. ft.		Height to Eaves. ft.		Ridge. ft.		Erected Complete. £ s. d.		Packed on Rail or Wharf. £ s. d.
30	20	..	8	..	16	..	107 10 0	..	77 10 0
40	20	..	9	..	16	..	132 10 0	..	100 0 0
50	20	..	9	..	16	..	160 0 0	..	115 0 0
60	25	..	10	..	18	..	220 0 0	..	145 0 0

Any size made at proportionate prices.

Tamesa, Kingston Hill, Surrey.

"DEAR SIRS,—I am quite satisfied with the manner in which the iron and woodwork of my Stable and Coach House has been carried out.

To Messrs. COOPER,
    Old Kent Road.

(Signed)   W. E. G. L. FINNY."

Church or Chapel.

No. 280.

This style of Church is suitable either for temporary use or a permanency. Is of economical design, and can be made to any size. For Specifications, see pages 206 and 207.

Delivered to nearest Goods Station and erected complete on purchaser's foundation, or marked for re-erection, and bundled and packed on Rail or Wharf at the following prices :—

Length.		Width.		Eaves.		Ridge.	Erected Complete. £ s. d.	On Rail or Wharf. £ s. d.
30ft.	by	20ft.	by	8ft.	by	16ft.	90 0 0	60 0 0
40ft.	by	20ft.	by	9ft.	by	16ft.	110 0 0	70 0 0
50ft.	by	20ft.	by	9ft.	by	16ft.	130 0 0	80 0 0
60ft.	by	25ft.	by	10ft.	by	18ft.	180 0 0	135 0 0

Any size made at proportionate prices.

High Street, Christchurch, Hants.
" GENTLEMEN,—Shall be pleased to report favourably of Buildings you sent me to War Office enquirers.—Yours truly,   (Signed)   T. H. BARNES "

223

Church or Chapel.

No. 282.

This is a very pretty Design, and has met with approval wherever erected. Is made to seat from 200 people. For Specifications, see pages 206 and 207.

Delivered to nearest Goods Station and erected complete on purchaser's foundation, or marked for re-erection and bundled and packed on Rail or Wharf at the following prices :—

40ft. by 20ft., erected complete, £115 ; on Rail or Wharf, £75.
50ft. by 25ft.,　　,,　　　　,,　　£165 ;　　　,,　　　　,,　£110.

Any size made at proportionate prices.

Design for School Rooms.

No. 282A.

Main Building 60ft. by 30ft., with 12ft. by 12ft. projection.
Erected Complete, £230.　On Rail or Wharf, £145.

Estimates for other sizes, also for Partitions to form separate rooms, free on application.

Mission Room   (Interior View).

No. 283.

Delivered and erected upon purchaser's foundation. Platform not included. For Specification, see pages 206 and 207.

Delivered to nearest Goods Station, and erected complete on purchaser's foundation, or marked for re-erection, and bundled and packed on Rail or Wharf at the following prices:—

Length.	Width.			Erected Complete. £ s. d.			On Rail or Wharf. £ s. d.
10ft. by	8ft.	..	..	12 0 0	..	..	9 10 0
14ft. by	10ft.	..	..	20 0 0	..	..	14 15 0
18ft. by	12ft.	..	..	30 0 0	..	..	22 0 0
22ft. by	14ft.	..	..	45 0 0	..	..	35 0 0
26ft. by	16ft.	..	..	60 0 0	..	..	40 0 0
30ft. by	18ft.	..	..	65 0 0	..	..	45 0 0
40ft. by	20ft.	..	..	90 0 0	..	..	60 0 0
50ft. by	24ft.	..	..	125 0 0	..	..	80 0 0
60ft. by	30ft.	..	..	175 0 0	..	..	110 0 0

This Building has plain front, with door in centre and window each side. Porch can be added at a small extra charge on above prices. Any size made at proportionate prices.

225

Swimming Baths.

No. 285.

This Design has been well considered, and can be made to accommodate any number. Delivered and erected upon Purchaser's foundation and bath. Size of Building, 65ft. by 30ft. With 24 compartments, Hall, Office, and Caretaker's Room. For full specification, see pages 206 and 207.

Delivered to nearest Goods Station, and erected complete, £300; or marked for re-erection and bundled and packed on Rail or Wharf, £205.

Any size made at proportionate prices. Plans Free.

Brickwork

is only necessary for foundations where buildings are erected within the Metropolitan districts. Outside the boundary we generally employ stone template, placing them under the weight-carrying supports of the building on the level ground. Foundations are not included in our estimates.

Village School.

No. 206.

This is a very Convenient Building for a Mixed School, which has had careful consideration. Is divided into two Rooms, one 20ft. by 20ft., the other 20ft. by 30ft., with Entrance Hall, 10ft. by 8ft. Delivered to nearest Goods Station, and erected complete upon purchaser's foundations, or marked for re-erection, and bundled and packed on Rail or Wharf.

Size 40ft. by 30ft.

Erected Complete, £155 ; on Rail or Wharf, £110.

Ground Plan Free on Application.

Erection Prices

include Delivery and Erection complete, Painting Outside Wood-work two coats best oil colour, and Staining and Varnishing Inside, Glazing Windows, &c., by our own men, all Railway Charges, Carriage, Men's Fares, Lodgings, &c., within 150 miles. Beyond this distance extra cost of Carriage, &c., will be charged.

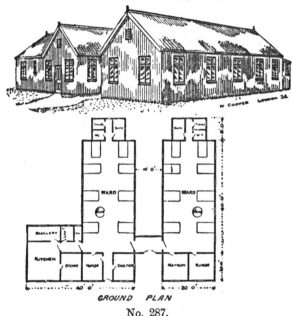
229

230

Hospital (Isolated).

No. 289.

Is specially adapted for infectious diseases. Is built to accommodate from Sixteen to Thirty-two Patients, and contains both Male and Female Wards, Doctor's Room, Waiting Room, Nurse's Rooms, and Kitchen, well ventilated. For Specification, see pages 206 and 207.

Delivered to nearest Goods Station and erected complete upon purchaser's foundation, or marked for re-rection and bundled and packed on Rail or Wharf.

For 16 Beds, Erected Complete, £400;   on Rail or Wharf, £280
  „ 24   „   „   £525;   „   „   £350
  „ 32   „   „   £600;   „   „   £375
Ground Plans Free on application.

Hospitals despatched within 24 hours after receipt of Order, and erected complete, ready for occupation, within 14 days.

Galvanised Corrugated Iron.

Sheets of standard Birmingham gauge only are used. They are fixed on a principle that admits of being easily released without damage to the structure.

Iron Portable Hospital.

No. 290.

Constructed for the isolation of infectious diseases on the most approved sanitary principles. Well ventilated, both by windows, which are made to open, and through the roof. Contains Male and Female Wards, Doctor's and Nurse's Rooms, Kitchen, Scullery, Bath Room, and Lavatories. For Specification, see pages 206 and 207.

Delivered to nearest Goods Station, erected complete upon purchaser's foundation, or marked for re-erection, and bundled and packed on Rail or Wharf.

For 8 Beds, Erected, £225; on Rail or Wharf, £175
   ,, 12   ,,   ,,   £285;   ,,   ,,   £210
   ,, 16   ,,   ,,   £350;   ,,   ,,   £250

Special Estimates for Foundations, which are not included in these prices.

Can be despatched at 24 hours' notice, and erected complete ready for occupation within 14 days.

On-Rail or Wharf Prices

include the building complete as above, ready for erection, carefully marked and packed on Rail or delivered to London Wharf, and a drawing to facilitate erection supplied with each building.

232

Cottage Hospital.

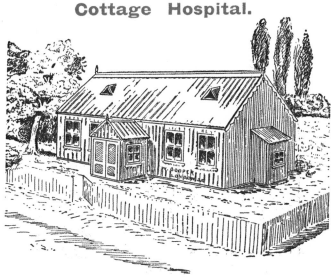

No. 291.

This Design has been thoroughly considered, and is especially adapted for the purpose for which it is intended. Contains both Male and Female Wards, two Lavatories, Nurses' Room, Bedroom, and Kitchen. For Specification, see pages 206 and 207.

Delivered to nearest Goods Station and erected complete upon purchaser's foundation, or marked for re-erection and bundled and packed on Rail or Wharf.

For 8 Beds, erected Complete, £200; on Rail, £150.
For 12   ,,   ,,   £260;   ,,   £185.
For 16   ,,   ,,   £320;   ,,   £220.
For 20   ,,   ,,   £380;   ,,   £250.

Plans and full Specification on application.

Exclusion of Draughts

is effected by a liberal use of Felt in the walls and gables. We employ it in all buildings we erect. It has also the advantage of preserving an equable temperature.

School, Mission, Living Rooms, Offices, Workshops, &c., &c.

No. 292.

Can be divided to make separate rooms, &c., at small extra charge. For Specification, see pages 206 and 207.

Delivered to nearest Goods Station and erected complete on purchaser's foundation, or marked for re-erection, bundled and packed on Rail or Wharf, with or without lining, &c., at the following respective prices:—

Length. Width.		Erected Complete.		Complete on Rail or Wharf.		Building only on Rail. No Flooring, Matching, Gutters, or Felt. Otherwise Complete as Specification.
8ft. by 6ft.	..	£10 0 0	..	£8 0 0	..	£5 0 0
10ft. by 8ft.	..	12 0 0	..	9 10 0	..	7 10 0
14ft. by 10ft.	..	20 0 0	..	14 15 0	..	9 15 0
18ft. by 12ft.	..	30 0 0	..	22 0 0	..	15 0 0
22ft. by 14ft.	..	45 0 0	..	35 0 0	..	25 0 0
26ft. by 16ft.	..	60 0 0	..	45 0 0	..	28 0 0
30ft. by 18ft.	..	65 0 0	..	47 10 0	..	31 0 0
40ft. by 20ft.	..	90 0 0	..	60 0 0	..	40 0 0
50ft. by 24ft.	..	125 0 0	..	80 0 0	..	66 0 0
60ft. by 30ft.	..	175 0 0	..	110 0 0	..	70 0 0

Door and Windows can be placed in any position to suit purchaser.

234

235

School, Mission, Living Rooms, Offices, Workshops, &c., &c.

No. 294.

Can be divided to make separate rooms, &c., at small extra charge.   For Specification, see pages 206 and 207.

Delivered to nearest Goods Station and erected complete on purchaser's foundation, or marked for re-erection, bundled and packed on Rail or Wharf, with or without lining, &c., at the following respective prices :—

Length. Width.		Erected Complete.		Complete on Rail or Wharf.		Building only on Rail. No Flooring, Matching, Gutters, or Felt. Otherwise Complete as Specification.
		£ s. d.		£ s. d.		£ s. d.
8ft. by 6ft.	..	10 0 0	..	8 0 0	..	5 0 0
10ft. by 8ft.	..	12 0 0	..	9 10 0	..	7 10 0
14ft. by 10ft.	..	20 0 0	..	14 15 0	..	9 15 0
18ft. by 12ft.	..	30 0 0	..	22 0 0	..	15 0 0
22ft. by 14ft.	..	45 0 0	..	35 0 0	..	25 0 0
26ft. by 16ft.	..	60 0 0	..	45 0 0	..	28 0 0
30ft. by 18ft.	..	65 0 0	..	47 10 0	..	31 0 0
40ft. by 20ft.	..	90 0 0	..	60 0 0	..	40 0 0
50ft. by 24ft.	..	125 0 0	..	80 0 0	..	65 0 0
60ft. by 30ft.	..	175 0 0	..	110 0 0	..	70 0 0

Door and Windows can be placed in any position to suit purchaser.

School, Mission, Living Rooms, Offices, Workshops, &c., &c.

No. 295.

Can be divided to make separate rooms, &c., at small extra charge.   For Specification, see pages 206 and 207.

Delivered to nearest Goods Station, and erected complete on purchaser's foundation, or marked for re-erection, bundled and packed on Rail or Wharf, with or without lining, &c., at the following respective prices :—

Length. Width.	Erected Complete. £ s. d.	Complete on Rail or Wharf. £ s. d.	Building only on Rail. No Flooring, Matching, Gutters, or Felt. Otherwise Complete as Specification. £ s. d.
8ft. by 6ft.	10 0 0	8 0 0	5 0 0
10ft. by 8ft.	12 0 0	9 10 0	7 10 0
14ft. by 10ft.	20 0 0	14 15 0	9 15 0
18ft. by 12ft.	30 0 0	22 0 0	15 0 0
22ft. by 14ft.	45 0 0	35 0 0	25 0 0
26ft. by 16ft.	60 0 0	45 0 0	28 0 0
30ft. by 18ft.	65 0 0	47 10 0	31 0 0
40ft. by 20ft.	90 0 0	60 0 0	40 0 0
50ft. by 24ft.	125 0 0	80 0 0	66 0 0
60ft. by 30ft.	175 0 0	110 0 0	70 0 0

Door and Windows can be placed in any position to suit purchaser.

School, Mission, Living Rooms, Offices, Workshops, &c., &c.

No. 296.

Can be divided to make separate rooms, &c., at small extra charge. For Specification, see pages 206 and 207.

Delivered to nearest Goods Station and erected complete on purchaser's foundation, or marked for re-erection, bundled and packed on Rail or Wharf, with or without lining, etc., at the following respective prices :—

Length. Width.		Erected Complete. £ s. d.		Complete on Rail or Wharf. £ s. d.		Building only on Rail. No Flooring, Matching, Gutters, or Felt. Otherwise Complete as Specification. £ s. d.
8ft. by 6ft.	..	10 0 0	..	8 0 0	..	5 0 0
10ft. by 8ft.	..	12 0 0	..	9 10 0	..	7 10 0
14ft. by 10ft.	..	20 0 0	..	14 15 0	..	9 15 0
18ft. by 12ft.	..	30 0 0	..	22 0 0	..	15 0 0
22ft. by 14ft.	..	45 0 0	..	35 0 0	..	25 0 0
26ft. by 16ft.	..	60 0 0	..	45 0 0	..	28 0 0
30ft. by 18ft.	..	65 0 0	..	47 10 0	..	31 0 0
40ft. by 20ft.	..	90 0 0	..	60 0 0	..	40 0 0
50ft. by 24ft.	..	125 0 0	..	80 0 0	..	66 0 0
60ft. by 30ft.	..	175 0 0	..	110 0 0	..	70 0 0

Door and Windows can be placed in any position to suit purchaser.

School, Mission, Living Rooms, Offices, Workshops, &c., &c.

No. 297.

Can be divided to make separate rooms, &c., at small extra charge. For Specification, see pages 206 and 207.

Delivered to nearest Goods Station and erected complete on purchaser's foundation, or marked for re-erection, bundled and packed on Rail or Wharf, with or without lining, &c., at the following respective prices :—

Length. Width.		Erected Complete.				Complete on Rail or Wharf.				Building only on Rail. No Flooring, Matching, Gutters, or Felt. Otherwise Complete as Specification.		
		£	s.	d.		£	s.	d.		£	s.	d.
8ft. by 6ft.	..	10	0	0	..	8	0	0	..	5	0	0
10ft. by 8ft.	..	12	0	0	..	9	10	0	..	7	10	0
14ft. by 10ft.	..	20	0	0	..	14	15	0	..	9	15	0
18ft. by 12ft.	..	30	0	0	..	22	0	0	..	15	0	0
22ft. by 14ft.	..	45	0	0	..	35	0	0	..	25	0	0
26ft. by 16ft.	..	60	0	0	..	45	0	0	..	28	0	0
30ft. by 18ft.	..	65	0	0	..	47	10	0	..	31	0	0
40ft. by 20ft.	..	90	0	0	..	60	0	0	..	40	0	0
50ft. by 24ft.	..	125	0	0	..	80	0	0	..	66	0	0
60ft. by 30ft.	..	175	0	0	..	110	0	0	..	70	0	0

Door and Windows can be placed in any position to suit purchaser.

Mission, School, Billiard, or Entertainment Room.

No. 298.

A cheap, well-made structure. Can be partitioned off into two rooms. Floored and match-lined. For Specification, see pages 206 and 207.

Delivered to nearest Goods Station and erected complete on purchaser's foundation, or marked for re-erection, bundled and packed on Rail or Wharf, with or without lining, &c., at the following respective prices :—

Length.	Width.	Erected Complete.	On Rail or Wharf.	Building only on Rail. No Flooring, Matching, Gutters, or Felt. Otherwise Complete as Specification.
8ft. by	6ft.	£10 0 0	£8 0 0	£5 0 0
10ft. by	8ft.	12 10 0	9 10 0	7 10 0
14ft. by	10ft.	20 0 0	14 15 0	9 15 0
18ft. by	12ft.	30 0 0	22 0 0	15 0 0
22ft. by	14ft.	45 0 0	35 0 0	25 0 0
26ft. by	16ft.	60 0 0	40 0 0	28 0 0
30ft. by	18ft.	80 0 0	45 0 0	31 0 0
40ft. by	20ft.	90 0 0	60 0 0	40 0 0
50ft. by	24ft.	125 0 0	80 0 0	66 0 0
60ft. by	30ft.	175 0 0	110 0 0	70 0 0

Door and Windows can be placed in any position to suit purchaser.

Workmen's or Gardeners' Cottages.

No. 299.

Three-room Cottages, containing Two Bedrooms, each 9ft. by 7ft.; Kitchen, 14ft. by 13ft.; and Scullery, 6ft. by 6ft.; specially suitable for estates, large works, &c. For Specification, see pages 206 and 207.

Delivered to nearest Station, and erected complete on purchaser's foundation, in Blocks of two, as illustration, £60 each, or £120 per Block; six Blocks, £110 each; twelve Blocks, £100 each; or marked for re-erection and bundled and packed on Rail or Wharf, one Block, £85; six Blocks, £82 10s. each; twelve Blocks, £80 each, if ordered at one time. Brick chimneys not included.

Ground plan free on application.

Special quotation given for large numbers.

Fittings and Glazing,

Locks, Bolts, Bars, Ventilating Gears, Gutters, and Down-pipes, and all sundries are of the best make, and are carefully fixed. The Glass used in buildings quoted in this List is heavy 21oz.; but Rolled Plate, or Cathedral, or other qualities may be had at prices accordingly.

Cottage, School, Storeroom, or Workshop.

No. 300.

A Serviceable and Inexpensive Structure.

This building is suitable for a number of purposes. The door and windows can be placed in any position, also any number of partitions may be added, forming separate rooms, to suit purchaser's requirements, at a small extra cost.

Delivered to nearest Goods Station and erected complete on purchaser's foundation, as per Specification, pages 206 and 207, or marked for re-erection and bundled and packed on Rail at the following prices :—

			Erected Complete.			On Rail or Wharf.
8ft. by 6ft.	..	..	£10 0 0	..	..	£8 0 0
10ft. by 8ft.	..	..	12 10 0	..	..	9 10 0
14ft. by 10ft.	..	..	20 0 0	..	..	14 15 0
18ft. by 12ft.	..	..	30 0 0	..	..	22 0 0
22ft. by 14ft.	..	..	45 0 0	..	..	35 0 0
26ft. by 16ft.	..	..	60 0 0	..	..	40 0 0
30ft. by 18ft.	..	..	65 0 0	..	..	45 0 0
40ft. by 20ft.	..	..	90 0 0	..	..	60 0 0
50ft. by 24ft.	..	..	125 0 0	..	..	80 0 0
60ft. by 30ft.	..	..	175 0 0	..	..	110 0 0

Portable Gardener's Cottage.

No. 301.

Four Rooms containing Two Bedrooms, 9ft. by 7ft.; Sitting Room, 13ft. by 14ft.; and Kitchen, 13ft. by 7ft.

This is a cheap and serviceable structure, and will be found admirably adapted for use by a Gardener, Groom, or Gamekeeper. For Specification, see pages 206 and 207.

Delivered to nearest Goods Station, and erected upon purchaser's foundation, £65, or marked for re-erection, and bundled and packed on Rail or Wharf, £45.

If three or more are ordered at one time, £60 each erected, or £42 10s. each on Rail.

Ground Plan free on application. Brickwork not included.

Our Buildings are all made in sections. Each part is numbered and lettered, so that the putting together of the sections requires no technical skill.

Dwelling House, Cricket, Tennis, or Golf Pavilion.

No. 302.

This handsome design contains five rooms, consisting of two Bedrooms, 13ft. by 8ft., Dining Room, 13ft. by 12ft., Drawing Room, 13ft. by 12ft., and Kitchen, 10ft. by 7ft.; or Saloon, Refreshment Room, two Dressing Rooms, and Lavatory. Main Building 30ft. by 24ft., with 5ft. Verandah and 7ft. Back addition. For Specification, see pages 206 and 207.

Delivered to nearest Goods Station, and erected complete on purchaser's foundation, £125, or marked for re-erection and bundled and packed on Rail or Wharf, £90.

Ground Plan free on application.

Frame-work

is of the following substances : Sleepers and joists, 4in. by 2in.; principal rafters, 5in. by 2in., 6in. by 2in., 7in. by 2in., 3in. by 6in., 2½in. by 7in., 3in. by 8in., and 3in. by 9in., according to width of house; framework, 3in. by 2in., 4in. by 2in., and 3in. by 4in.; purlins, 4in. by 2in. It is made in sections to facilitate both fixing and removal, which can be easily accomplished at any time at a minimum cost of labour.

Floor Boards

are supplied of thoroughly seasoned deal of ¾in. and 1in thicknesses.

Lining

is of thoroughly seasoned and selected matchboards of ½in. and ⅝in., tongued and grooved.

Bungalow.

No. 303.

Design for Ten-Roomed Bungalow, comprising Dining Room, Sitting Rooms, Five Bed Rooms, Kitchen, Scullery, Bath Room, and w.c. The main building measures 48ft. by 25ft., with small additions at back ends and front, as shown on ground plan. The position and sizes of rooms may be altered to suit purchaser's requirements. For full Specification, see pages 206 and 207.

Delivered to nearest Goods Station, and erected complete on purchaser's foundation, £230, or marked for re-erection and bundled and packed on Rail or Wharf, £190.

Erection Prices

include delivery and erection complete, painting outside wood-work two coats best oil colour, and staining and varnishing inside, glazing windows, &c., by our own men, all railway charges, carriage, men's fares, lodgings, &c., within 150 miles. Beyond this distance extra cost of carriage, &c., will be charged.

On-Rail or Wharf Prices

include the building complete as above, ready for erection, care-fully marked and packed on rail or delivered to London wharf, and a drawing to facilitate erection supplied with each building.

Dwelling House.

No 304.

A well-planned design, constructed upon the most approved principles, containing two Bedrooms, Drawing Room, Dining Room, and Kitchen. It has a Verandah in front. For Specification, see pages 206 and 207.

Inside arrangement can be altered to suit purchaser's requirements.

Delivered to nearest Goods Station and erected complete upon purchaser's foundation, or marked for re-erection and bundled and packed on Rail or Wharf.

30ft. by 20ft.   Erected Complete, £120; on Rail, £80.

Ground Plan on application.

Frame Work

is of the following substances : Sleepers and joists, 4in. by 2in. ; principal rafters, 5in. by 2in., 6in. by 2in., 7in. by 2in., 3in. by 6in., 2½in. by 7in., 3in. by 8in., and 3in. by 9in., according to width of house ; framework, 3in. by 2in., 4in. by 2in., and 3in. by 4in. ; purlins, 4in. by 2in. It is made in sections to facilitate both fixing and removal, which can be easily accomplished at any time at a minimum cost of labour.

Bungalow Style of Residence.

No. 305.

This is an exceedingly neat and pretty design, with 3ft. Verandah all round, and is greatly in demand. It comprises Six Rooms and usual Domestic Offices; Two Bedrooms, 12ft. by 10ft.; One Bedroom, 9ft. by 12ft.; Dining Room, 15ft. by 12ft.; Sitting-room, 15ft. by 12ft.; Kitchen, 9ft. by 12ft; Scullery, Bath Room, and w.c.   For Specification, see pages 206 and 207.

Delivered to nearest Goods Station and erected complete on purchaser's foundation, £175; or marked for re-erection and bundled and packed on Rail or Wharf, £110.

Ground Plan free on application.   Main Building 35ft. by 28ft.

Buildings for Foreign Countries.

Great care is necessary, not only in the construction, but in the selection of materials for all buildings required for use in foreign countries.   The experience we have had in this department, combined with assistance rendered to us by old residents abroad, has enabled us to turn out work which has met the full appreciation of those for whom we have contracted.

Dwelling House.

No. 306.

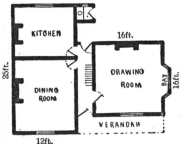

PLAN OF GROUND FLOOR.

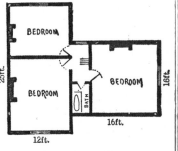

PLAN OF FIRST FLOOR.

This is a Residence of a well-planned Design. It contains Drawing Room, Dining Room, Kitchen, three Bedrooms, Bath Room, and w.c. Having a verandah, gives it a handsome appearance. For Specification, see pages 206 and 207.

Delivered to nearest Goods Station and erected complete on purchaser's foundation, £250; or marked for re-erection and bundled and packed on Rail or Wharf, £160.

Brick Chimneys, w.c. Fittings, and Stoves not included. Portable Stoves supplied, prices on application.

Residence.

No. 308.
45ft.

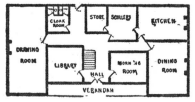

GROUND PLAN.

Handsomely designed Residence. For Specification, see pages 206 and 207.

Delivered to nearest Goods Station and erected complete on purchaser's foundation, £425; or marked for re-erection and bundled and packed on Rail or Wharf, £300.

Could be altered to suit purchaser's requirements.

Brick Chimneys, w.c. Fittings, and Stoves not included. Complete Estimate on application.

Residence for Hot Climate.

No. 309.

Specially Designed for Tropical Countries.

Every attention is given to suit the climate, and special requirements of purchasers. For full Specification, see pages 206 and 207.

Everything complete, packed, marked, and bundled ready for re-erection. Delivered London Docks, £375.

Full working Drawings, Plans, &c., sent with every Building.

Being Portable and Tenant's Fixtures,

these Buildings commend themselves for service in all parts of the world. They can be enlarged or made small with comparative ease in any case of emergency.

Ventilation

is studied in every building, our principle being to thoroughly effect it without causing draught.

African Merchant's Station.

No. 310.

SPECIALLY CONSTRUCTED FOR TROPICAL COUNTRIES.

Warehouse, Shop, and Residence combined. Everything complete, packed, marked, and bundled ready for re-erection. Delivered London Docks, £400. Every attention is given to suit the climate and special requirements of purchasers. For full Specification, see pages 206 and 207.

Full working Drawings, Plans, &c., sent with every Building.

For Tropical Climate.

For tropical climes our Buildings are constructed with a double roof, each end being covered with perforated zinc in order to admit a through current of air. This not only assists to cool the interior, but may be made to act as a thorough ventilator.

Workshop.

Lean-to.

No. 311.

Constructed of strong Wooden Framework, and covered with Galvanised Corrugated Iron Sheets. Not lined. Made in sections, and fitted ready for erection. Glass cut to sizes. Carefully packed on Rail or Wharf.

10ft. by 8ft., £7. 18ft. by 12ft., £14. 30ft. by 18ft., £30.
60ft. by 30ft., £60.

Doors and Windows can be placed in any position to suit purchaser's requirements.

Galvanised Corrugated Iron

sheets of standard Birmingham gauge only are used. They are fixed on a principle that admits of their being easily released without damage to the structure.

Iron Buildings

have been in use sufficiently long to put them to the test in every possible way, and from the continually increasing demand for them it may fairly be said that they justify a claim superior to any class of structure, for similar use, that existed prior to their introduction.

Workshop.

Span Roof.

No. 312.

Constructed of Galvanised Corrugated Iron Sheets upon strong Wooden Framework with floor. Complete, with Door, Glass, &c., and is made in sections and fitted ready for erection. Windows and Doors can be had in any position required. Carefully packed on rail.

	£ s. d.			£ s. d.
8ft. by 6ft.	5 0 0		26ft. by 16ft.	28 0 0
10ft. by 8ft.	7 10 0		30ft. by 18ft.	31 0 0
14ft. by 10ft.	9 15 0		40ft. by 20ft.	40 0 0
18ft. by 12ft.	15 0 0		50ft. by 24ft.	66 0 0
22ft. by 14ft.	25 0 0		60ft. by 30ft.	70 0 0

These prices do not include any Lining or Felt.

The County Council

demand that materials of a sufficient substance and strength be employed in all buildings. All our work is in accordance with the necessary requirements.

Portable Iron Stable, Coach-House, and Harness Room Combined.

No. 313.

Stable match-boarded, Harness-room floored and match-lined.

Very substantially constructed. Neat design. For Specification, see pages 206 and 207.

Delivered to nearest Goods Station and erected on purchaser's foundation, or marked and bundled ready for re-erection and packed on Rail or Wharf at the following prices :—

Length. Width.				Erected Complete.		On Rail or Wharf.
8ft. by 6ft.	..	..	..	£10 10 0	..	£8 0 0
10ft. by 8ft.	..	..	..	12 10 0	..	9 10 0
14ft. by 10ft.	..	..	..	20 0 0	..	14 15 0
18ft. by 12ft.	..	..	..	30 0 0	..	22 0 0
22ft. by 14ft.	..	..	..	50 0 0	..	35 0 0
26ft. by 16ft.	..	..	..	60 0 0	..	40 0 0
30ft. by 18ft.	..	..	..	65 0 0	..	45 0 0
40ft. by 20ft.	..	..	..	90 0 0	..	60 0 0
50ft. by 24ft.	..	..	..	125 0 0	..	80 0 0
60ft. by 30ft.	..	..	..	175 0 0	..	110 0 0

Ground plans for foundations free.

Brickwork

is only necessary for foundations where buildings are erected within the Metropolitan district. Outside the boundary we generally employ stone template, placing them under the weight-carrying supports of the building on the level ground. Foundations are not included in our estimates.

WILLIAM COOPER, Ltd, 751, Old Kent Rd, London, S.E.

Cricket, Lawn Tennis, or Golf Pavilion, with Verandah.

No. 314.

This is a very neat and useful design. Can be divided to make Dressing Rooms, Refreshment Bar, Saloon, Lavatory. &c., to purchaser's requirements. For Specification, see pages 206 and 207.

Delivered to nearest Goods Station and erected complete on purchaser's foundation, or marked for re-erection and bundled and packed on Rail or Wharf at the following prices :—

Main Building. Length. Width.				Erected Complete.		Complete on Rail or Wharf.
8ft. by 6ft.	..	..	..	£11 10 0	..	£9 10 0
10ft. by 8ft.	..	..	..	13 5 0	..	10 10 0
14ft. by 10ft.	..	..	..	22 0 0	..	15 10 0
18ft. by 12ft.	..	..	..	33 0 0	..	23 0 0
22ft. by 14ft.	..	..	..	50 0 0	..	37 0 0
26ft. by 16ft.	..	..	..	67 10 0	..	42 0 0
30ft. by 18ft.	..	..	..	72 0 0	..	47 10 0
40ft. by 20ft.	..	..	..	100 0 0	..	63 0 0
50ft. by 24ft.	..	..	..	132 0 0	..	84 0 0
60ft. by 30ft.	..	..	..	195 0 0	..	117 10 0

Above sizes are without Verandah.

Exclusion of Draughts

is effected by a liberal use of Felt in the walls and gables. We employ it in all buildings we erect. It has also the advantage of preserving an equable temperature.

256

Billiard Room.

No. 315

Is very neat in design, is well ventilated, and well adapted for a variety of purposes. For Specification, see pages 206 and 207.

Delivered to nearest Goods Station, and erected complete on purchaser's foundation; or marked for re-erection, bundled and packed on Rail or Docks, at the following prices:—

Length.	Width.		Erected Complete.		On Rail or Wharf.
22ft.	by 14ft.	..	£50 0 0	..	£35 0 0
26ft.	by 16ft.	..	67 10 0	..	45 0 0
30ft.	by 18ft.	..	85 0 0	..	50 0 0
40ft.	by 20ft.	..	100 0 0	..	62 10 0

Any size made at proportionate prices.

Windows and doors can be placed in any position, also can be divided to suit purchaser's wishes.

Ornamental Finish

to gables and pinnacles is studied from the most approved Gothic designs.

Fittings and Glazing,

Locks, Bolts, Bars, Ventilating Gear, Gutters, and Down-pipes, and all Sundries are of the best make, and are carefully fixed. The Glass used in buildings quoted in this list is heavy 21oz.; but rolled Plate, or Cathedral, or other qualities may be had at prices accordingly.

Billiard Room, Club House, or Studio.

No. 316.

This is a very pretty design; having a bay window gives it a handsome appearance. Size of building, 25ft. long, 19ft. wide. For full Specification, see pages 206 and 207.

Delivered to nearest Goods Station, and erected complete on purchaser's foundation, £87 10s.; or marked for re-erection and bundled and packed on Rail or Wharf, £62 10s.

Buildings Suitable for all Climates.

Great care is necessary, not only in the construction, but in the selection of materials for all Buildings required for use in foreign countries. The experience we have had in this department, combined with assistance rendered to us by old residents abroad, has enabled us to turn out work which has met the full appreciation of those for whom we have contracted.

For tropical climes our buildings are constructed with a double roof, each end being covered with perforated zinc in order to admit a through current of air. This not only assists to cool the interior, but may be made to act as a thorough ventilator.

258

Boathouse, Workshop, &c.

No. 317.

This design has been supplied by us to many boat owners, and has answered their purpose in every way. It is constructed of Galvanised Corrugated Iron Sheets upon Wooden Framework, no Lining or Floor. Carefully marked for re-erection, and bundled and packed on Rail or Wharf at the following prices :—

10ft. by 8ft.	..	..	£7 10 0	30ft. by 18ft.	..	..	£31 0 0
14ft. by 10ft.	..	...	9 15 0	40ft. by 20ft.	..	..	40 0 0
18ft. by 12ft.	..	..	15 0 0	50ft. by 24ft.	..	..	66 0 0
22ft. by 14ft.	..	..	25 0 0	60ft. by 30ft.	..	..	70 0 0
26ft. by 16ft.	..	..	28 0 0				

Doors and windows can be placed in any position.

Estimates for erecting on purchaser's foundation on application.

On-Rail or Wharf Prices

include the Building Complete as above, ready for erection, carefully marked and packed on Rail or delivered to London Wharf, and a drawing to facilitate erection supplied with each Building.

Portable Loose Boxes.

No. 318.

These Boxes are a useful acquisition for stabling Hunters, &c. Can either be partitioned off or have loose boxes, according to purchaser's option. Complete with Partitions, Hay-rack, and Mangers. Made in Sections, marked for re-erection, and bundled ready for purchaser to erect. For full Specification, see pages 206 and 207.

Packed on Rail or Wharf.

		£	s.	d.			£	s.	d.
1 Box,	10ft. by 10ft. ..	11	5	0	1 Box, 10ft. by 12ft. ..	..	14	10	0
2 ,,	20ft. by 10ft. ..	20	5	0	2 ,, 20ft. by 12ft. ..	..	27	10	0
3 ,,	30ft. by 10ft. ..	28	10	0	3 ,, 30ft. by 12ft. ..	..	38	0	0
4 ,,	40ft. by 10ft. ..	40	10	0	4 ,, 40ft. by 12ft. ..	..	49	0	0

		£	s.	d.
1 Box,	12ft. by 12ft. ..	15	10	0
2 ,,	24ft. by 12ft. ..	28	10	0
3 ,,	36ft. by 12ft. ..	40	10	0
4 ,,	48ft. by 12ft. ..	53	10	0

Ground Plans and Estimates for Erecting Free.

Superior to any Class of Structure.

Iron Buildings have been in use sufficiently long to put them to the test in every possible way, and from the continually increasing demand for them it may fairly be said that they justify a claim superior to any class of structure, for similar use, that existed prior to their introduction.

Portable Game Larder.

No. 319.

These Larders are invaluable to Sportsmen for storing game after killed; perfectly ventilated, and are necessary acquisitions for keeping game fresh. Complete on Wheels.

12ft. by 8ft. £15. Marked for re-erection, bundled, and packed on Rail or Wharf.

Refreshment Bar.

No. 320.

This is a very neat and useful Design, being constructed of Galvanised Corrugated Iron on strong Wooden Framework. The roof of the verandah is made to let down, and can be bolted inside, thus making it perfectly secure when left. No Floor or Lining included.

Made in Sections, marked for re-erection and bundled and packed on Rail or Wharf.

10ft. by 8ft., £7 10s.   14ft. by 10ft., £11.   18ft. by 12ft., £16. 22ft. by 14ft., £22.

Ball Room, Drill, or Lecture Hall.

No. 321.

This is a very handsome design, and is suitable for a variety of purposes. For Specification, see pages 206 and 207.

Main Building 60ft. by 35ft., with 5ft. Verandah Front and Sides.

Delivered to nearest Goods Station and erected complete, £275; or marked for re-erection and bundled and packed on Rail or Wharf, £185. These prices do not include any Band Stand, Counter, or Lavatory Fittings.

Any size made at proportionate prices.

This building can be divided to suit customer's requirements, making a handsome dwelling.

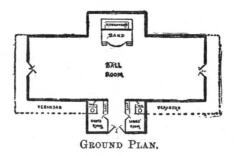

GROUND PLAN.

Club House or School Room.

No. 322.

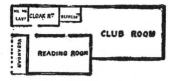

GROUND PLAN.

This design is very neat in appearance, and contains Club Room, Reading Room, Refreshment Room, Cloak Room, and Lavatory. For Specification, see pages 206 and 207.

Delivered to nearest Goods Station and erected complete upon purchaser's foundation, or marked for re-erection, bundled and packed on Rail or Wharf. 48ft. by 21ft. Erected Complete, £200; on Rail or Wharf, £140.

Position or number of rooms may be altered to suit purchaser's requirements.

Ornamental Finish

to gables and pinnacles is studied from the most approved Gothic designs.

Club House.

No. 323.

This handsome design is the result of careful consideration. It contains two Lavatories, Steward's Rooms, Billiard Room, Reading Room, Hall, and has a Stand on Roof. But the inside can be fitted or divided to suit any requirements. Plan on application. For Specification, see pages 206 and 207.

Delivered to nearest Goods Station and erected complete, or marked for re-erection, and bundled and packed on Rail or Wharf. 50ft. by 28ft. Erected Complete, £325 ; on Rail or Wharf, £210.

Ground plan free on application.

Floor Boards

are supplied of thoroughly seasoned deal of ¾in. and 1in. thicknesses.

Lining

is of thoroughly seasoned and selected matchboards of ½in. and ⅝in., tongued and grooved.

Ventilation

is studied in every building, our principle being to thoroughly effect it without causing draught.

Club House.

No. 324.

GROUND PLAN.

This neat design contains two Lavatories, Gentlemen's Room, Ladies' Room, Bed Room, Kitchen, and Club Room. For Specifications, see pages 206 and 207.

Delivered to nearest Goods Station and erected complete upon purchaser's foundation; or marked for re-erection and bundled and packed on Rail or Wharf.

40ft. by 36ft. Erected complete, £225; on rail, £160.

Concert, Drill Hall, Ball Room, or Entertainment Hall.

No. 325.

Handsome Design, light and well ventilated. Upper portion of windows made to open, and every part substantially constructed from good sound materials only. For full Specification, see pages 206 and 207.

Delivered to nearest Goods Station, and erected complete on purchaser's foundation. 100ft. long by 60ft. wide, £650; or marked for erection, and bundled and packed on Rail or Wharf, £400.

Plans free. Any size made at proportionate prices.

Exclusion of Draughts

is effected by a liberal use of Felt in the walls and gables. We employ it in all buildings we erect. It has also the advantage of preserving an equable temperature.

Ventilation

is studied in every building, our principle being to thoroughly effect it without causing draught.

Promenade Shelter.

No. 326.

This new and handsome design seems to have met with great favour, as several have already been erected. It is constructed with Galvanised Corrugated Iron Roof upon Wooden Framework. The inside being Match-lined, Stained, and Varnished, and very strongly floored.

Delivered to nearest Goods Station, and erected complete upon purchaser's foundation, 30ft. by 16ft., £120; or marked and bundled ready for re-erection and packed on Rail or Wharf, £80

Frame-Work

is of the following substances: Sleepers and joists, 4in. by 2in.; principal rafters, 5in. by 2in., 6in. by 2in., 7in. by 2in., 3in. by 6in., 2½in. by 7in., 3in. by 8in., and 3in. by 9in., according to width of house; framework, 3in. by 2in., 4in. by 2in., and 3in. by 4in.; purlins, 4in. by 2in. It is made in sections to facilitate both fixing and removal, which can be easily accomplished at any time at a minimum cost of labour.

Floor Boards

are supplied of thoroughly seasoned deal of ¾in. and 1in. thicknesses.

Lining

is of thoroughly seasoned and selected matchboards of ½in. and ⅝in., tongued and grooved.

267

Range of Sheds.

No. 328.

Specially adapted for Agriculturists, &c. Is very useful for stacking straw, grain, or hay. Centre house can be used as a Cattle Shed. Is constructed of galvanised corrugated iron, upon very strongly made wooden framework.

Delivered to nearest Goods Station, and erected complete upon purchaser's foundation, or marked for re-erection and bundled and packed on Rail or Wharf.

60ft. by 35ft., Erected Complete, £166; on Rail or Wharf, £110.
100ft. by 50ft,   ,,   ,,   £350 ;   ,,   ,,   £225.

These prices do not include any floor or lining.

Another Design of Covering.

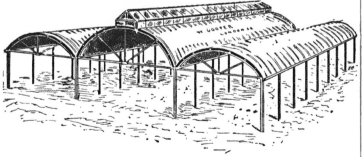

No. 329.

Constructed of Galvanised Corrugated Iron, with Lantern Top on Centre Span. Estimates on application.

Bungalow.

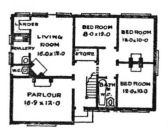

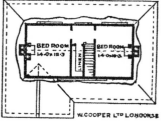

No. 643.

This very handsome and convenient Bungalow is constructed
of timber framework, the outside walls are rough cast, with Tile
Roof, and the walls internally can be lined with Fire Resisting
Material or Matchboarding.

Made to any size.   Prices upon application.

Outside walls and roof can be of Corrugated Iron if preferred.

Club House or Bungalow.

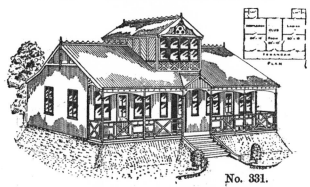

No. 331.

    This artistic building is suitable for either bungalow or club house, and if raised as shown in illustration gives a particularly striking effect. The main building is 40ft. long by 20ft. wide, and a verandah 4ft. wide runs the entire length of front. There are five rooms on ground floor with usual offices, and one large room over, 20ft. by 10ft.

    Delivered to nearest Goods Station and erected complete on purchaser's foundation, £300; or marked for re-erection and bundled and packed on Rail or Wharf, £225.

    The inside can be divided to form larger or smaller rooms as required. Any size made at proportionate prices.

Illustration,

showing the principle of fixing our Galvanised Corrugated Iron on to Timber-framed roof.

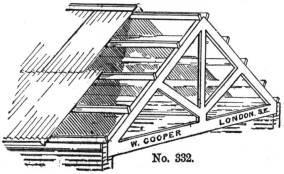

No. 332.

Section VI.

llustrated Catalogue

OF

LATEST DESIGNS

IN

RUSTIC WORK.

Repairs of all kinds executed by thoroughly experienced workmen, who are sent to all parts of the country if required.

Rustic Bridges and Other Rustic Work to Order.

All Rustic Work is Manufactured at our Works, under our own supervision.

ESTIMATES FREE.

Folding Trellis Arbour,

Hundreds sold every season.

No. 271.

This neat and well-made Arbour is made to fold together so as to pack away in a small space when not in use. The sides, front, roof, &c., being hinged together, the whole may be taken down or erected in two minutes.

Complete with Seat each side, also Table.

6ft. long, 2ft. wide, 6ft. high,　　　PRICE, £1 15s.

If a creeper is trained over Arbour it adds to the appearance.

Of Rustic Work the most extensive display is made by Messrs. W. Cooper, 751, Old Kent Road, S.E., who have a considerable variety of houses of various kinds, ranging from the good-sized thatched house to the small lean-to rustic arbour.—*Vide* Daily Press.

Summer Houses.

No. 188.

5ft. wide by 3ft. 6in. deep.

Price, £4.

No. 189.

6ft. wide by 5ft. 6in. deep.

Price, £7.

No. 190.

5ft. wide by 3ft. 6in. deep.

£4 15s., with Table.

Nothing lends a more picturesque appearance to a garden than a rustic-built Summer House, while its utility as a retreat in open air is a convenience at all times. Houses made in sections; can be put together in a short time by the purchaser, no skilled aid being required. All Houses are carefully packed on rail.

Rustic Lawn Tennis House.

This House is made roomy and suitable for a large party. Being made in sections, it can be fixed and re-fixed at will, with very little trouble.

No. 191.

Strongly made, stained and varnished.

10ft. long, 5ft. deep.

Complete for £10, on rail.

Rustic Summer Houses.

No. 192.

No. 193.

A handy little House, made in sections, stained and varnished, and fitted with seat at back, well made, and neat in appearance.

5ft. long, 3ft. 6in. deep.

Packed on rail, complete, Price £3 10s.

Open front, and side window opening, with ledge, handsome gable roof overhanging in front, thoroughly well made, in sections for easy fixing, stained and varnished.

6ft. long, 5ft. 6in. deep.

Packed on rail, complete, Price £9.

Special Cheap House.

ANY

SIZE

MADE

AT

PROPORTIONATE

PRICES.

No. 194.

PRICE £5. Carefully packed on rail.

The demand for this house being great, owing to its general appearance and compactness for fixing where space is limited, we make a leading feature of it. It is thoroughly well constructed in sections, and can be removed as easily as it is put together. It is a useful and ornamental house wherever fixed. A climbing plant trained round and over the window-opening lends a charm to its appearance. Size 5ft. by 3ft. 6in.

Special Portable Oblong Summer House.

No. 195.

HUNDREDS OF THESE SOLD EVERY SEASON.

This is a squarely-built house, suitable for placing against a wall. It is convenient for a small garden, is thoroughly well made in sections, stained and varnished. Anyone can fix it. Size—5ft. long, 3ft. deep. Packed on rail, complete.

PRICE £3 10s.

Portable Hexagon Summer House.

This is a roomy, six-sided house, and will be found convenient for placing in a shrubbery. It is 5ft. 6in. deep, and 6ft. from angle to angle. It is fitted with seats, and is stained and varnished.

Being made in sections, with each part lettered, it is easily fixed by the purchaser. It is of a design that commands general admiration, and the price at which it is offered finds for it a ready sale.

No. 196.

PRICE £6 10s.   Carefully packed on rail.

Special Garden Seat.

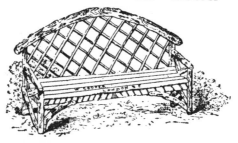

No. 197.

A comfortable Seat, slightly hollowed. It is well made, with rustic oak arms and cross-pieces, and the seat of yellow deal slats. Stained and varnished, and put on rail at following prices :—

4ft., £1 ; 5ft., £1 4s. ; 6ft. £1 7s. 6d.

Portable Hexagon-shape Summer House.

This is a very ornamental House. It is made in sections, and is easily fixed. It is fitted with seats, and strongly made throughout with the best materials, stained and varnished.

It is a pretty rustic structure, and convenient for embellishing with drooping plants from the window boxes, and climbers up the sides; for the latter the clematis tribe give a charming effect.

No. 198.

PRICE £7.

Packed on rail.

From Angle to Angle. ft. in.	DIMENSIONS OUTSIDE. From Back to Front. ft. in.	Height under Eaves. ft. in.	Price. £ s. d.
6 0	5 6	6 0	7 0 0
6 6	6 0	6 0	9 0 0
7 0	6 6	6 6	10 0 0
7 6	7 0	6 6	11 10 0
8 0	7 6	6 6	14 0 0

Roofing Felt.

Patent Asphaltic Rolls, 25yd. long by 32in. wide, 3s. 6d. per roll; better quality, 4s. 6d.
Nails for fixing Felt, in Boxes of 250, 6d. ; 500, 1s.

Roslin, Middleton Cheney, Banbury.
"DEAR SIR,—I beg to acknowledge the safe arrival of Summer House. We are greatly pleased with the goods, and although the various parts have not yet been fitted owing to lack of time, yet I do not see how we can fail to be satisfied. Faithfully yours, (Signed) M. THOMSON."

Hexagon Rustic Summer House with Porch.

This hexagonal house is made of the best materials thoroughly seasoned. It is constructed with a handsome porch, and is of a very ornamental character.

Made in sections it is easily fixed and removed. It is fitted with seats stained and varnished. It is an effective and useful addition to any garden or grounds.

No. 199.

PRICE £9.

Carefully packed on rail.

From Angle to Angle. ft. in.	Dimensions Outside. From Back to Front. ft. in.	Height under Eaves. ft. in.	Price. £ s. d.
6 0	5 6	6 0	9 0 0
6 6	6 0	6 0	11 0 0
7 0	6 6	6 6	12 0 0
7 6	7 0	6 6	13 10 0
8 0	7 6	6 6	15 15 0

30, Wheeley's Road, Birmingham.

"I am glad to say the Rustic Arches are to hand to-day, and give every satisfaction. (Signed) F. E. H. LLOYD."

Doverhay Cottage, Porlock, Somerset.

"Mrs. Sydney J. Rogers writes to inform Mr. W. Cooper that the Rustic House came to hand on Monday evening, and is very satisfactory."

Parksquare, Bondgate, Ripon.

MR. COOPER,
"DEAR SIR,—I am pleased to say that the House is completed, and we are highly satisfied.—I remain, yours obediently, (Signed) J. T. KIRBY."

Portable Hexagon-shape Summer House.

This is a very pretty design, highly rustic in character and shape, and forms a charming place of retreat in the garden.

No. 200.

The outside is thatched with heath, and lined with straw inside; all woodwork thoroughly seasoned, stained, and varnished.

PRICE £12. Carefully packed on rail.

Easily fixed in two hours.

From Angle to Angle.	Dimensions Outside. From Back to Front.	Height under Eaves.	Price.
ft. in.	ft. in.	ft. in.	£ s. d.
6 0	5 6	6 0	12 0 0
6 6	6 0	6 0	14 10 0
7 0	6 6	6 6	16 10 0
7 6	7 0	6 6	18 10 0
8 0	7 6	6 6	20 10 0

This Thatched House is strongly recommended, being thoroughly well made and guaranteed waterproof.

Can be had Octagon shape if required at slightly increased cost; also fitted with windows and doors.

Sexangular Thatched-Roof Summer House.

This is a cheaper kind of thatched house, strongly made and sound in every part; all boards tongued and grooved, stained and varnished.

This pattern has a large sale. For quality of workmanship the price is very low. It is unsurpassed by any in the trade.

No. 201.

PRICE £10 10s. Packed on rail.

Dimensions Outside.

From Angle to Angle.	From Back to Front.	Height under Eaves.	Price. £ s. d.
6ft. 0in.	5ft. 6in.	6ft. 0in.	10 10 0
6ft. 6in.	6ft. 0in.	6ft. 0in.	13 10 0
7ft. 0in.	6ft. 0in.	6ft. 6ft.	15 10 0
7ft. 6in.	7ft. 0in.	6ft. 6ft.	17 10 0
8ft. 0in.	7ft. 6in.	6ft. 6ft.	19 10 0

Portable Summer House.

No. 202.

This is a commodious structure of handsome elevation, double-boarded roof, interlined with felt. A substantial erection, suitable for large parties. 12ft. long by 5ft. wide by 7ft.

PRICE £21. Carefully packed on rail.

Pent Roof.

No. 203.

Size, 5ft. by 6ft. by 3ft. 6in., outside measure.

PRICE £4. Carefully packed on rail.

Well built in sections, easily put together; a useful house.

Portable Rustic Summer House.

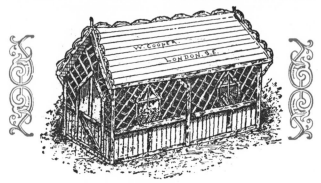

No 204.

This is a roomy house, fitted with door, and windows each side. It makes a convenient summer-house in summer, and a useful store-room for a gardener in winter, at the same time a handsome ornament to any garden. Thoroughly well constructed, stained, and varnished. 12ft. by 5ft.

PRICE £17 10s. Packed on rail.

Sports Rustic House.

No. 205.

Open front, span-roof house, suitable for grounds where amusements and sports are held. Soundly built of well-seasoned materials. Stained and varnished. Easily fixed and removed. Fitted with seat complete. 12ft. by 4ft.

PRICE £9. Carefully packed on rail.

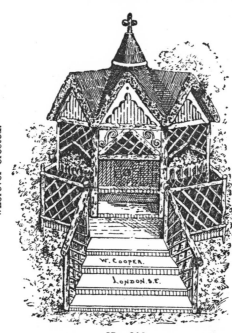
285

Portable 3-Gabled Thatched-Roof Rustic Summer House.

This is after the style of No. 206 without steps and balcony. It is enclosed with door and windows of cathedral glass, handsomely fitted throughout, and is of imposing elevation.

No. 207.

Made in any size to order, with or without windows and door. All work of the best character and finish. Size 8ft. by 8ft. Carefully packed on rail.

Thatched Roof, £32; if Boarded Roof, £22.

Rustic Summer House.

A handsome design, and finished throughout with care and skill, door and windows of cathedral glass Swiss lined within and ornamented without. Soundly thatched, and put together in the very best manner.

Size 10ft. by 10ft. Carefully packed on rail, £50.

Other sizes at proportionate prices.

No. 208.

Swiss Rustic House.

A beautiful structure of the most elegant design, Swiss in style, and replete with finish in every detail. Its lines afford scope of an exceptional character for the purpose of illumination at night, which, effectively carried out, displays it a gem of unequalled beauty.

Size 10ft. by 10ft., 12ft. by 12ft., 20ft. high.

Carefully packed on rail, £55.

Other sizes at proportionate prices.

No. 209.

Portable Rustic Summer House.

No. 210.

Roof double-boarded and interlined with felt. A handsome structure, well finished. Size 12ft. by 10ft.

Price £22, complete. Packed on rail.

Lawn Tennis House.

No. 211.

Can be put together easily in two or three hours.

Special Lawn Tennis House, double-boarded roof, felted between boards, thoroughly water-proof.

Size, 12ft. by 7ft.

For the cricket field or tennis ground this House will be found extremely useful; thoroughly well built in sections, roof double-boarded and inter-lined with felt, easily fixed and removed when necessary.

Price £17 10s. complete. **Packed on rail.**

Rustic Arch with Ornamental Edges.

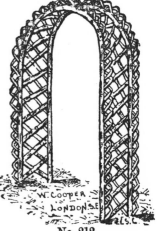

No. 212.

4ft. across path, 12in. deep, and 8ft. high.

£1 5s. each.

Larger Sizes—for every additional 3in. across path, 1s. 6d., and for every additional 3in. in depth, 4s. extra.

Stained with best oil stain, and varnished two coats.

288

Rustic Arch with Plain Edges.

No. 213.

4ft. across path, 12in. deep, 8ft. high, 20s. each.

Larger Sizes—for every additional 3in. across path, 1s. 3d., and for every additional 3in. in depth, 3s. extra.

Stained with best oil stain, and varnished two coats.

Rustic Porch for Doorway.

6ft. wide, 3ft. deep.

With window opening each side; ornamental boarded roof. Stained best oil stain, and varnished two coats.

Price £5.   Carefully packed on rail.

Of RUSTIC WORK the most extensive display is made by Messrs. W. Cooper, 751, Old Kent Road, S.E., who have a considerable variety of Houses of various kinds, ranging from the good-sized Thatched House to the small Lean-to Rustic Arbour.—*Vide* Daily Press.

289

Rustic Arches.

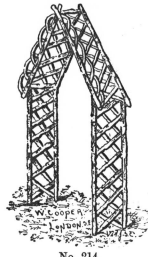

No. 214.   No 215.

Either pattern, 4ft. across path, 12in. deep, 8ft. high.
PRICE 17s. 6d. each.

Rustic Bridge.

No. 216.

4ft. wide, 16ft. across. Complete with steps each side.
Stained best oil stain, and varnished two coats. Carefully
packed on rail.   PRICE £15 15s.
Any other sizes at proportionate prices.

Rustic Garden Seats.

No. 217.

A good design, strongly made with comfortable hollowed seats.
Prices: 4ft., £1; 5ft., £1 4s.; 6ft., £1 7s. 6d.

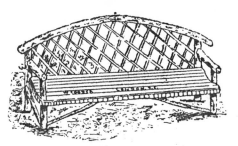

No. 218.

Very comfortable hollowed seats of yellow deal slats, oak
rustic arms and back, strongly made. Stained and varnished.
Prices: 4ft., £1; 5ft., £1 4s.; 6ft., £1 7s. 6d.

Double Rustic Arch.

Design similar to No. 212. 6ft. wide, 3ft. deep, and 8ft. high.
Stained best oil stain, and varnished two coats.
Price £5 5s.

Garden Shelter.

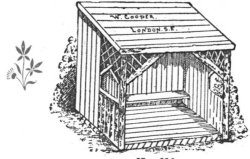

No. 219.

Size, 5ft. by 3ft. Portable and easily fixed. Stained and varnished. Very suitable for School Playgrounds, &c.

PRICE £3.

Rustic Flower Stand.

(3ft. long, three steps.)

No. 220.

This is a very useful article, strongly made, well finished, and varnished.

PRICE 10s. each.

Rustic Garden Chairs.

This Arm Chair is very strongly made and well finished.

PRICE 15s.

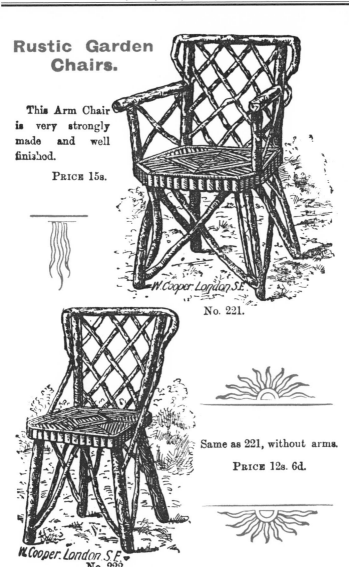

No. 221.

Same as 221, without arms.

PRICE 12s. 6d.

No. 222.

Rustic Garden Chairs.

W. Cooper London S.E.

No 223.

Strongly made, stained, and varnished; a comfortable chair.

PRICE 12s. 6d.

Same as above, without arms.

PRICE 10s. 6d.

No. 224.

Rustic Garden Seats.

No. 225.

A Gothic-backed seat, the rustic part substantially constructed of oak, the seat hollowed and made of best yellow deal slats. The whole stained and varnished.

PRICES : 4ft., 22s. 6d.; 5ft., £1 7s.; 6ft., £1 10s.

No. 226.

A slight variation in design of the preceding number. The quality of the material is the same.

PRICES : 4ft., £1 2s. 6d.; 5ft., £1 7s.; 6ft., £1 10s.

Rustic Garden Seats.

No. 227.

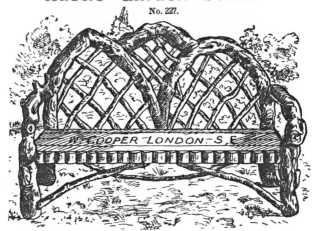

Triple Gothic pointed back seat, hollowed and made of best of deal, soundly put together throughout. Stained and varnished.

PRICES .. 4ft., 22s. 6d. .. 5ft., £1 7s. .. 6ft., £1 10s.

No. 228.

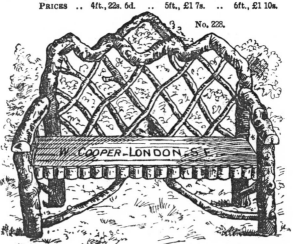

This is a pretty design, same in quality as above, with deal laths.

PRICES .. 4ft., 22s. 6d. .. 5ft., £1 7s. .. 6ft., £1 10s.

Rustic Garden Seat.

No. 229.

A good design, strongly made, and comfortable hollowed seat of yellow deal laths, stained and varnished.

PRICES: 4ft., 22s. 6d.; 5ft., £1 7s.; 6ft., £1 10s.

Rustic Arm Chairs.

No. 230.

A good Chair, strongly made, stained and varnished. Extra selected wood, 12s. 6d.

No. 231.

Strongly made, roomy, and comfortable, 15s.

Hexagon Rustic Tub.

No. 232.
For large ferns or shrubs, 18in. in diameter. Price 15s. Other designs and sizes to order.

Rustic Vase.

10in. in diameter
Price
10s.

15in.,
15s.

20in.,
£1.

25in.,
£1 5s.

No. 233.

Elm Bottom Conversation Seat.

So constructed that persons face each other when seated. A delightful piece of Garden Furniture.

Price,
27s. 6d. each.

No. 234.

Rustic Stools.

Either Pattern,
Price 3s. 6d. each.

No. 235.

No. 236.

Rustic Tree Seat.

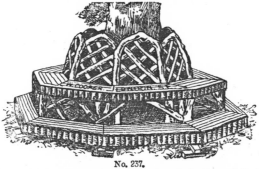

No. 237.

These are very useful seats for parties, and can be built round the trunk of a tree, affording shade from the sun, 5s. per foot run, from front edge of seat; footboard to match, 1s. per foot. Stained and varnished.

Hexagon Shape Rustic Vases.

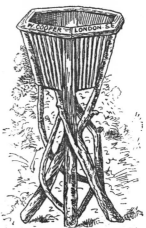

No. 239.

Diameter inside.

	s.	d.		s.	d.
10in.	..	10 0	18in.	..	18 0
12in.	..	12 0	20in.	..	20 0
14in.	..	14 0	22in.	..	22 0
16in.	..	16 0	24in.	..	24 0

No. 238.

Either pattern, stained and varnished.

Rustic Table

Swiss Top Rustic Table.

No. 240.

2ft. diameter.　　Price 17s. 6d.

No. 241.

2ft. diameter.　Price 21s.

Double Rustic Vase.

Rustic Cork Vase.

Rustic Table.

No. 242.

10in. diameter.
Price 7s. 6d.

No. 243.

Lower vase, 30in. diameter, top ditto,
12in.　　Price £2 5s.

No. 244.

15in. diameter.
Price 10s. 6d.

300

Rustic Vase.

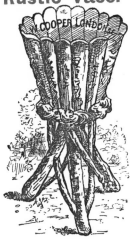

No. 245.
9in. in diameter.
PRICE 7s. 6d.

Rustic Pot Bracket.

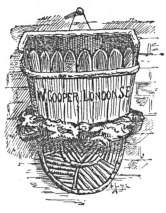

No. 246.

PRICE 3s. 6d.

Imperial Black Varnish.

For Iron Fences, Wood Palings, Farm Buildings, Poultry Houses, &c.

18 gal. casks, 20s. ; 36 gal. casks, 34s.; Casks included. Carefully packed on rail. Casks not returnable.

1 gal. 1s. 6d. (can 6d.); 5 gal. 5s. (can 2s.).

Cooper's Disinfectas.

For Poultry Houses and Runs, Kennels, Rabbit Hutches, Stables, &c. Clean, Cheap, and Healthy.

Per Sack (2-bushel), 2s. 6d. ; 10 for 22s. 6d., sacks included.

Rustic Garden Furniture.

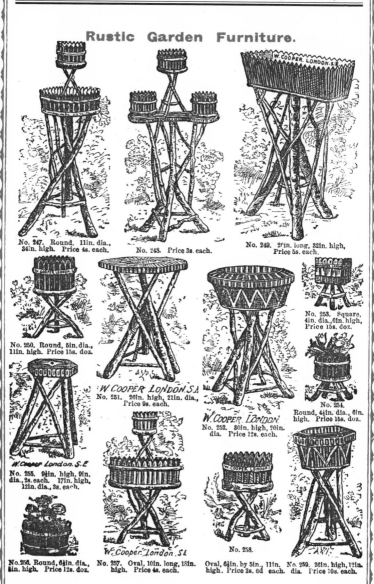

No. 247. Round. 11in. dia., 34in. high. Price 4s. each.

No. 248. Price 3s. each.

No. 249. 2ft. long, 32in. high, Price 5s. each.

No. 250. Round, 5in. dia., 11in. high. Price 15s. doz.

No. 251. 26in. high, 21in. dia., Price 9s. each.

No. 252. 30in. high, 20in. dia. Price 12s. each.

No. 253. Square, 4in. dia., 6in. high, Price 15s. doz.

No. 254. Round, 4½in. dia., 6in. high. Price 15s. doz.

No. 255. 9½in. high, 9in. dia., 2s. each. 17in. high, 12in. dia., 3s. each.

No. 256. Round, 6½in. dia., 5in. high. Price 12s. doz.

No. 257. Oval, 10in. long, 18in. high. Price 4s. each.

No. 258. Oval, 6½in. by 5in., 11in. high. Price 2s. 6d each.

No. 259. 26in. high, 12in. dia. Price 10s. each.

Rustic Window Box.

No. 260.
Made any length.
Price, 3s. per foot.

Rustic Window Box.

No. 261.

From 3s. per foot run.

Rustic and Tiled Window Box.

No. 262.

From 4s. per foot run.

Raised Pattern Tile Window Box.

No. 263. From 5s. per foot run. Very handsome. Tiles in front.

Flat Pattern Tile Window Box.

No. 264. From 6s. per foot run. Very neat. Tiles front and ends.

Both Rustic and Tile Window Boxes can be made in a variety of Patterns and Designs.

Strong Garden Barrows.

These have an immense sale. Nothing to beat them in the Market.

Strongly made from well-seasoned timbers, and are light to handle. With **wooden wheels**, painted.

12in. sides. Price 21s.

No. 265.

The above, with shifting top, 6s. extra, as illustrated.

No. 266.

Stable and Garden Barrow.

12in. sides.

Price 17s. 6d.

Including **shifting handle** boards.

Shifting top, 7s. 6d. extra.

No. 267.

Garden Swing.

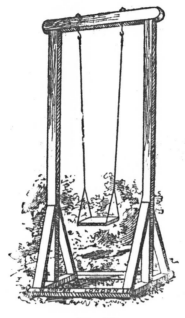

No. 268.

A capital Swing, rigidly built and bolted at top, so that it can be easily taken to pieces when necessary. Fitted with strong wrought-iron hooks securely held by nuts. Best hempen rope and solid seasoned wood seat. Oil-painted two coats. Packed on rail at following prices:—

Height.	Width.	Cash Price.
10ft.	4ft.	£1 10 0
12ft.	5ft.	1 15 0

Strong Garden Seats.

No. 272.

Painted Ironwork
and Varnished
Legs.

Wrought-Iron
Standards and
Arm Rests.

As Supplied to the Principal Parks, Gardens, &c., throughout the Kingdom.

PRICES : 3ft., 10s. 6d. ; 4ft., 14s. ; 5ft., (3 Standards), 17s. 6d. ; 6ft. 21s. ; 7ft. (3 Standards), 24s. 6d.

Special quotations for large quantities. Any design made to order.

Folding Chairs.

Strong Iron Frame. Wooden Lath
Seat. Nicely varnished.

No. 273.

PRICE ... ... 3s. each.

Open.

Folded.

Portable Folding Flower Stands.

Trellis Garden Arches.

No. 274.

4ft. long, 2ft. 6in. high.
PRICE 4s. each.
Suitable for Greenhouse, Garden,
Dwelling House, &c.

No. 275.
Strong, Portable, Painted,
PRICE 6s. 6d. each.